THE RATIONALITY OF RELIGIOUS BELIEF

Professor Basil Mitchell, M.A.

THE RATIONALITY
OF
RELIGIOUS BELIEF

Essays in honour of
BASIL MITCHELL

Edited by
WILLIAM J. ABRAHAM
and
STEVEN W. HOLTZER

CLARENDON PRESS · OXFORD
1987

Oxford University Press, Walton Street, Oxford OX2 6DP

Oxford New York Toronto
Delhi Bombay Calcutta Madras Karachi
Petaling Jaya Singapore Hong Kong Tokyo
Nairobi Dar es Salaam Cape Town
Melbourne Auckland

and associated companies in
Beirut Berlin Ibadan Nicosia

Oxford is a trade mark of Oxford University Press

Published in the United States
by Oxford University Press, New York

British Library Cataloguing in Publication Data
The Rationality of religious belief: essays
in honour of Basil Mitchell.
1. Faith and reason
I. Abraham, William J. II. Holtzer,
Steven W. III. Mitchell, Basil
201 BT50
ISBN 0–19–826675–8

Library of Congress Cataloging in Publication Data
The Rationality of religious belief.
"Basil Mitchell's principal writings": p.
Includes index.
1. Philosophical theology. 2. Faith and reason.
3. Mitchell, Basil. I. Mitchell, Basil. II. Abraham,
William J. (William James), 1947– . III. Holtzer,
Steven W.
BT40.R37 1987 230'.01 86–18281
ISBN 0–19–826675–8

Set by Litho Link Limited
Printed in Great Britain
at the Alden Press, Oxford

Preface

The production of this volume was inspired by the stature of the philosopher to whom it is dedicated. Its nature was determined by the desire to offer a volume of essays which would be sufficiently focused to stand as a worthwhile contribution to philosophy of religion. Given Basil Mitchell's exceptionally diverse gifts and graces in philosophy and theology it is quite impossible to do justice to all of them in their entirety. Breadth was therefore subordinated to depth when the decision was made to concentrate on the rationality of religious belief. The editors believe that this represents a crucial element in Mitchell's work which deserves extended attention in its own right and in the contemporary debate about natural theology. We deeply regret that we cannot here explore and examine Mitchell's fascinating contribution to ethics, political philosophy, theology, and education.

The debts of gratitude are manifold. We wish to thank Oxford University Press and its staff for their generosity and help in preparing the manuscript. Thanks are due to the many colleagues who have assisted us in the enterprise, especially those who would gladly have presented a paper but for whom no room could be found. Thanks are also due to Theresa Smith and Ann Johnson of Perkins School of Theology for their splendid work in the typing of this volume.

Contents

1

The Reasonable Man: An Appreciation

OLIVER O'DONOVAN

Basil Mitchell is fond of alluding to Aristotle's apparently circular definition of virtue as a disposition to choose in accord with the mean 'as determined by reason—that is to say, in the way that the reasonable man would determine it'.[1] The appearance of circularity, he reminds us, points to something of undisputable importance in the formation of moral judgement: 'the reasonable man' commands the moral authority to serve as a model for how reasonable judgements are to be made. His capacity for discerning and well-judged action sets the standard by which others learn to conduct themselves. It is a favourite Mitchell theme; and it will do very well as an account of the respect in which Basil Mitchell himself is generally held. For fifteen years as Oxford's Nolloth Professor of the Philosophy of the Christian Religion he has consistently represented to the theological and philosophical communities, both in his own university and more widely, that combination of intellectual and moral authority which is typical of the Aristotelian *phronimos*, rendered in English (all too weakly) as 'the reasonable man'.

To announce an 'appreciation' seems to promise something alarmingly unphilosophical. 'And now', we may be taken to be saying, 'let us tell you something about Basil Mitchell *the man*!' And, of course, there are philosophers about whom one could tell just that. Of Plotinus, to name one of the greatest, Porphyry was able to recount with some satisfaction that he attended with diligence and financial acumen to the estates of the orphaned children entrusted to his care, looking closely to the accuracy of the accounts. 'And yet all this labour . . . never interrupted, during waking hours, his intention towards the Supreme.'[2] A fascinating glimpse, that, of Plotinus 'the man',

---

[1] *Nicomachean Ethics* 1107a, 1.
[2] *Life of Plotinus* 9, tr. S. Mackenna.

poring over the accounts! But we get the point at once of Porphyry's 'and yet': Plotinus the philosopher was busy somewhere else, attending to the Supreme. This disjunction is unthinkable with the reasonable man. He is what he is by virtue of the philosophical bearing of his practical life and the practical bearing of his philosophy. He is concerned with making particular and immediate judgements (with 'ulti- mates', *eschata*, in Aristotle's sense), and he makes them in relation to the meaning of human life seen as a whole (*eschata* in the Bible's sense). And so it is that Basil Mitchell the man can hardly be described except in terms suggested by Basil Mitchell the philosopher. A defender of the importance of social institutions, he has not only served existing institutions of learning and worship tirelessly, but has contributed to the development of new ones. A champion of the place of religious belief in public debate, he has shown himself master of a courteous, articulate, and committed style of debating— reinforced, it may be said, by an enviably fluent but never rhetorical command of the spoken English language. The only feature of his character for which it is difficult to find explicit philosophical warrant is his kindly and urbane wit. But the silence, no doubt, is itself philosophically eloquent: laughter is too mercurial a subject to bear the ponderous weight of theory; it should break into serious discourse welcome but unannounced.

Basil Mitchell conceives of himself as a professional philosopher who is a Christian. Not as a 'Christian philosopher' in the sense that the phrase sometimes bears, suggesting the self-conscious programme of formulating 'Christian philosophy'. He has been content to abide within the constraints of the philosophical tradition that has pre- vailed in his university throughout his working life—debating with his colleagues, sustaining a Christian apologetic within the terms of the discussions that concern them, and ensuring that the 'great rolling themes of philosophy' should not be forgotten. In the course of his career, he often remarks, the attitude of philosophers to Christian belief has softened dramatically. It did not in the end fall to Basil Mitchell to occupy the place of an *Athanasius solus contra mundum* which at one point he might have thought himself doomed to fill. He does not conceive of himself as a theologian. He cherishes the right of the simple believer—especially when the simple believer happens to be a philosopher—to shake his head quizzically at the ways of professional theologians, especially the more sceptical ones; but his theological colleagues have never been tempted to doubt his sympathy with their most important concerns. He seems himself as a *professional* philosopher, in the sense that he does not regard what he does, and does well, as the most important business of human life. That business is conducted in his family circle, together with his wife Margaret and their children; and in his parish church, where he may be found Sunday by Sunday reading the lesson, preferably, and in defiance of both scholarship and fashion, from the Authorized Version, 'because', as he declares, 'I want to defend the purple passages!' As a simple believer he doubts the theologians' assertions that Saint Paul, had he written in English, would have so lacked the Spirit's guidance as to begin one of his greatest utterances with the words 'What I mean is . . .' (2 Cor. 5: 19 NEB).

To suggest the scope of his practical endeavours we may mention two Oxford institutions with which he is closely associated. Neither was his own idea originally, but each could properly claim him as its founder, since in each case it owes its existence to his affectionate labours and creative imagination. From the early seventies there dates the Joint Honour School of Philosophy and Theology. Someone unacquainted with Basil Mitchell's university might find it hard to understand why the creation of a new undergraduate course in an obviously suitable combination of subjects should be a labour worthy of especial notice and congratulation. The explanation lies, in part, with Oxford's traditional conception of educational discipline: never enthusiastic about the principle of student choice, it has preferred to march its undergraduates in columns up and down the well-built military roads of the established faculties. The late sixties were, however, a period of cautious experiment, and the times were propitious for attempting new combinations. Yet even in such times collaboration between the philosophy subfaculty and the faculty of theology might have struck some observers as too improbable a goal to be worth pursuing. There is, of course, much important literature from every period of Western civilization in which philosophical and theological concerns are deeply intertwined, and a rewarding educational specialization could be quarried (as in other places it has been) out of this great intellectual deposit. But it was clear that if the two Oxford faculties were to agree on anything, it would be that this deposit should be largely ignored, and a joint course fused together out of the existing elements of theological and philosophical education. This meant, on the one side, a strong component of modern philosophical logic, and on the other an extensive induction into Biblical criticism. To the scornful it looked as though the unhappy children of this marriage of incompatibles would be nourished, as it were, on a diet of vitamin pills and emetics.

That something emerged which was not merely tolerable to both sides but had distinct educational virtues was due to the capacity of the Nolloth Professor, who, as the sole figure with official membership in both academic bodies, was cast in the role of honest broker, to inspire everybody's trust. His success was a fruit not only of his enthusiasm for the new course but of his regard for the distinctive strengths represented by the two apparently incompatible intellectual traditions. In *Law, Morality, and Religion in a Secular Society*,[3] written at about this time, he expressed his view, *vis-à-vis* the Franks Report on the structure of Oxford University, that there were 'characteristic excellences', peculiar to particular places and particular ways of doing things, which deserved protection in their own right. If his theological and philosophical colleagues trusted him enough to permit him to lead them into an unfamiliar working relationship with each other, it was because they knew that he understood and respected the characteristic excellences which were cherished on either side. His own account of how his efforts came to fruit is more modest and more entertaining. He discovered, he likes to claim, an important new scientific law about University business: the proposal that is recommended with the weakest argument capable of sustaining the case is sure to succeed. 'If your arguments are too weak, your colleagues will not take your proposal seriously. If they are too

---

[3] *Law, Morality, and Religion in a Secular Society* (Oxford University Press, London, 1967).

strong, they will amuse themselves by thinking up a refutation. To win the vote you must make them say, "I could have put up a *much* better argument than that!"'

More recently his efforts have given us the Ian Ramsey Centre for the study of ethical problems arising from scientific and medical research and practice, which was opened at St Cross College early in 1985. For the background to this undertaking we must pay attention to a feature of Basil Mitchell's work over two decades which, though a sideline in itself, has proved to be a formative and important one. He was a member of a series of Church of England working parties, the majority of them under the aegis of the Board for Social Responsibility, studying the moral questions that were thrust suddenly upon the church for the first time in the sixties by a combination of escalating technical advances in medicine and the sudden collapse of the conventional Christian moral consensus in the West. Basil Mitchell's name is to be found attached to BSR reports on sterilization (1962), the limits of medical care for the dying (1965), abortion (1965), euthanasia (1972), and homosexual relationships (1979), as well as to the Board of Education report on religious education in schools (1970) and the Doctrine Commission's *Believing in the Church* (1981). It is no coincidence that this series includes some of the best work produced by church-based working parties in recent years. The working-party formula works well when there are the right people to make it work. A little experience of such labour is enough to make anyone appreciate the achievement of these reports in drawing the opinions of a mixed interdisciplinary group not merely to an agreed set of conclusions but to a lucid argument to commend them. It also inspires respect for the patience of anyone who is prepared to incur the attendant frustrations of the exercise time and time again. One of the striking features of these early BSR working parties is the persistence of a core membership which moved on from report to report and came to function as a team. The name of R. M. Hare, long-time friend, colleague, and philosophical sparring-partner, is associated with a number of them. So is that of the philosophical theologian Ian Ramsey, Bishop of Durham at the time of his death in 1972 and Basil Mitchell's predecessor as Nolloth Professor, whose enthusiasm for interdisciplinary moral discussion contributed importantly to shaping the style and success of these reports.

Basil Mitchell's attitude to the work of his predecessor is not without its ambiguities. Far more than Ramsey, he is a part of the mainstream of English philosophical discourse, and he has kept his intellectual distance from Ramsey's illuminist type of epistemology, finding that the famous Ramseyan moment when 'the penny drops' has proved stubbornly unilluminating. But Ramsey's influence was wider than the influence of his philosophical idiosyncrasies. He was a church leader capable of drawing intellectuals together and getting their best work out of them; and it was in the context of interdisciplinary enquiry as Ramsey perfected it that Basil Mitchell found a way in which he could function effectively as a philosopher who was a Christian, and make a serious contribution to the moral deliberations of church and society. It was a context that suited his conception of what ethical discussion ought to be—a search for the convergences between the empirical, the moral, and the religious perceptions of reality, something answering to Ramsey's call for a 'rehabilitation of Natural Law'. (Basil Mitchell, though, treats that difficult notion with more subtlety and awareness of the tensions between the different perspectives. He has sometimes remarked that Ramsey's weakness was his great facility at discovering agreements!) It was also a context that suited his individual gifts: for lucid and forceful debate and for evoking the confidence of those who disagreed with him, so that they would entrust to his pen the written expression not only of his own views but of theirs. Whether the working-party method can produce effective results without being able to call upon individual participants so exceptionally suited to its demands as were Ramsey and Mitchell, I do not know. However, Ian Ramsey dared to speculate that there might be an institution committed to supporting such work on a permanent basis, and that it might have its home in a university. It is one of those highly satisfying turns of events that his successor in the Nolloth chair has been the chief agent in giving Ramsey's speculation practical effect.

Of Basil Mitchell's writing there is too much that could be said. It is, as all who have had occasion to read it will acknowledge gratefully, approachable. This very virtue may conceal its more profound strengths. It is unwise, at any rate, to trust the unpretentious air with which the characteristic Mitchell discussion gets on its way, presuming no more than to clarify the extent of some vexatious or interesting disagreement. It follows an unhurried, dialectical course (using the latter epithet in its Socratic sense), devoting immense care to the examination and exposition of its collocutors' views, postponing the elaboration of the author's own, and treating all participants with quite exceptional courtesy. At some point the threads of the argument are drawn together in a carefully crafted parable, an illustrative technique of which Basil Mitchell is a master. (We do not forget those parables. Recall, for example, the delectable parlour game designed to illustrate the debate about situation ethics: one team chooses an adverb —say 'lovingly'—and the other team has to guess it by challenging members of the first team to perform a series of actions in the manner of the adverb—say, 'putting on a kettle or strangling your wife'.) It may have appeared to some critics that no one who so commits himself to retracing the perambulations of others' arguments can have any very interesting goal of his own in view. But it is not so; Basil Mitchell's arguments move discreetly forward. Like a walker who follows a route that keeps to field paths and farm tracks, they reach their destination, not directly but with a comprehensive coverage of the countryside. Only when they have arrived does the reader appreciate how carefully the whole journey has been planned from the beginning, and how much intellectual ground has actually been covered. *Law, Morality, and Religion in a Secular Society* affords one of the most striking examples. Starting from the celebrated debate between Professor H. L. A. Hart and Lord Devlin about the enforcement of morals, it succeeds, by what appear at the time to be no more than a series of clarifications, in revising the terms of the debate so thoroughly that by the end the issue has imperceptibly become the structure of morality itself. Not only is this what the author has intended to teach us about all along, but he has gently suggested to us that Hart and Devlin really needed to talk about it too, and failed only by the merest oversight to see that this was their proper theme.

Mention of this, Basil Mitchell's first full-length book (1967), reminds us that his continued involvement with inter-disciplinary moral enquiry had results that were as important for his own thinking as for his purely practical endeavours. His pen continually returns to the right and obligation of Christians to make a confessional contribution to the moral debates of a secular society, and he has been a penetrating critic of that conception of public morality (based on an undernourished shadow of the old concept of Natural law) which has led Christians and unbelievers alike to suppose that religion has no place in the secular forum. He writes:

Our legislators may listen to Lady Wootton; they may also listen to the Archbishop of Canterbury, and to the views of Christian laymen as well as to the views of non-Christians. The proposal that we are considering is, put crudely, that they should be permitted to listen to Lady Wootton, but not to the Archbishop of Canterbury (unless, perhaps, he forgets his theology).[4]

A glance at the Mitchell bibliography shows how important this cluster of questions has been for him. Two of his three major books have had as their theme the insufficiency of a purely humanist ethic, insulated from religious and metaphysical concerns, to sustain the humane social morality that satisfies the demands of 'the traditional conscience'. I hope I may be forgiven the opinion, which may seem out of place in a collection largely devoted to celebrating Basil Mitchell's influence on those whose concerns are the central themes of the philosophy of religion, that his contribution to Christian moral and social theory may prove to be of more lasting significance. If this opinion is dismissed as partial (which may be no more than it deserves), I will at least be permitted, in making some remarks about his intellectual achievement, to concentrate on this side of his thought.

There are two distinctive arguments that recur in varying forms in Basil Mitchell's discussions of morality, which are capable, if we will learn their lessons well, of changing the terms in which the questions will be raised in the next genera-tion. One is his critique of what in *Law, Morality, and Religion in a Secular Society* he calls 'the new liberalism', which reappears

[4] *Law, Morality, and Religion in a Secular Society*, p. 129.

in *Morality: Religious and Secular* (1980) as 'liberal humanism'. These are his names for the pervasive idea (which belongs not only in humanist philosophy self-consciously developed but more widely throughout the culture of the English-speaking world, not least in the church) that morality is a two-storey structure. The lower storey comprises the universal and unarguable principles which are essential to the life of any conceivable society and protect its members' fundamental interests, while the upper storey may be any one of a range of alternative 'ideals', influenced by religious or metaphysical belief, in respect of which an individual must be free to choose and a society should retain strict neutrality. The attractiveness of this idea is that it seems to afford a justification for the pluralist inclinations of Western democracy on a purely analytic foundation, involving no loss of face for religious or moral ideals. It promises to exclude theocracy while maintaining a benevolent neutrality in respect of religion, and this, no doubt, is why Christians have championed it as enthusiastically as non-Christians. The idea has, of course, confronted a variety of critics. Many have doubted the sincerity of its benevolent neutrality, and some have pointed out the dangerously privatizing implications for religious belief and practice. But Basil Mitchell's objections are distinctive, in that they have aimed to demonstrate the practical incoherence of the idea; and to my judgement at least they appear to be quite decisive.

As often, the Mitchell argument is compelling because it does not attempt too much. There are certain elements of the liberal humanist idea which our author is, on the whole, ready to concede. Morality can indeed be analysed into 'platitudes' and 'ideals': on the one hand, commonplace universal moral ideals which we cannot imagine any society doing without and which owe nothing significant to religious belief—not, at any rate, to the belief of any particular religion; and on the other hand, beliefs and practices which vary from society to society and which derive in a strong way from religious and metaphysical traditions. Having made this concession, however, he is ready to raise his principal objection: the relation between these two aspects of morality has been misunderstood by the liberal humanist programme. The proposal to restrict the concern of society to the enforcement of the platitudes, while leaving the sphere of ideals to the preference of the individual, is shown to be incoherent by an argument in two steps: (*a*) the platitudes are empty of content until they are given some definite interpretation in terms of social institutions; (*b*) social institutions themselves are not platitudinous and universal, but differ from society to society and are shaped by alternative competing ideals. The example Basil Mitchell usually treats most fully is that of marriage; so let us take a different one to show how his case works there too. Suppose we agree (a platitudinous agreement) that any conceivable society must require that people should pay what they owe. Why should any society not confine itself to the merely regulative task of exacting positive debts, and take no position whatsoever on the *morality* of indebtedness? Because there is no universally valid definition of what constitutes a positive debt. The rule that people should pay what they owe is an abstraction. In order to enforce it, any concrete society must specify its meaning by a set of formal or informal financial and legal institutions which determine such things as how a valid debt may be contracted and by whom, what levels of interest may legitimately be charged, how debts may be liquidated, what recourses are legitimate in the case of default, and so on. But in framing such institutions a society will be guided very considerably by its view of the morality of indebtedness; its decisions will depend upon the store it sets by different and competing values, such as self-determination, economic independence, social compassion, freedom of contract, and so on. The history of the development of the Limited Liability Company is a pre-eminent illustration of this. These differing moral priorities will in turn be shaped by religious or metaphysical ideals.

It is therefore vacuous to counsel society to observe neutrality in relation to these ideals, for society cannot perform its most unarguable function, that of preserving the interests of its members, without presuming upon institutions which are shaped by definite ideals and which determine how the interests of its members are to be commonly understood. But if this is the case, then society must have a further function, over and above the unarguable one of preserving its members' interests. It must have the function of protecting the institutions themselves, not against reasoned and deliberate amendment, but against wholesale subversion. To take another example: if someone, in order to secure rental accommodation in a situation of great scarcity, signs an agreement with a landlord renouncing the protections which society customarily extends to tenants, it will be the duty of the courts to declare this agreement void. It could even conceivably be the duty of the legislators, if such agreements became the fashion, to invoke criminal sanctions against them, as against black-market trading. In so doing they would not merely be protecting the interests of tenants *simpliciter*; they would be protecting a certain *conception* of what the real interests of tenants actually were, a conception which could be intelligently challenged—and might well be challenged by many tenants as well as by landlords—but which, being in possession of the public conscience, and embodied in public institutions, should not be overthrown by main force in a period of panic.

With this argument, which is a major feature of his social thought, Basil Mitchell assumes a significant place among contemporary critics of modern liberalism. He would wish to insist, quite rightly, that his is an exercise in liberal *self*-criticism. The term 'liberal', he thinks, should not be deprived of its proper width of reference, which embraces all who set a high store by individual liberty. There are liberals, among whom he counts himself, who value individual liberty for distinctively Christian reasons, and he is not prepared to surrender the term to certain modern-day followers of J. S. Mill, who have, moreover, taken Mill's thought in a new direction by superimposing upon it the voluntarist or 'romantic' notion that ideals are a matter of choice rather than intellectual conviction. But it would be equally correct to think of Basil Mitchell's argument as a moderately conservative one, giving the term 'conservative' its proper sense of sustaining a prejudice in favour of existing social institutions. It could count only as *moderately* conservative, for Basil Mitchell believes far too strongly in the ultimate critical control of metaphysical truth to allow existing institutions anything more than an initial and rebuttable prejudice. (On this point he parts company with the more thoroughgoing, and therefore more relativist, conservatism of Lord Devlin.) But he does advance a version of that objection to modern liberalism, common to its conservative and Marxist critics alike, which complains that it systematically ignores the significance of structures and institutions for human welfare.

Mention of his hostility to a voluntarist interpretation of moral and religious ideals brings us to the second argument which I would think to be of enduring importance. This is his argument against a radical interpretation of the autonomy of ethical judgements. Commonly he introduces it with a reference to the famous—and 'preposterous'—statement from Kant's *Grundlegung*: 'Even the Holy One of the Gospels must first be compared with our ideal of moral perfection before we can recognize him as such.' The radical conception of autonomy which modern humanism consistently adopts from Kant pretends to spear us on a false dilemma, which is meant to demonstrate the irrelevance of authority (all authority, but especially theological) to moral judgement. Either one has already reached a judgement about right and wrong on one's own, so that recognition of 'the Holy One' is not, in the strong sense, acknowledgment of an *authority* at all, or one has not reached it, so that in accepting his authority one acts on non-moral grounds.

It is in response to this that Basil Mitchell likes to remind us of the Aristotelian 'reasonable man'. By watching and imitating the reasonable man we learn to be reasonable. He deals with the dilemma about autonomy, then, by drawing our attention, patiently and repeatedly, to this entirely familiar feature of our moral experience. (Is it impertinent to wonder whether there lies behind this argument the memory of a model who was of especial importance to Basil Mitchell at a time when he was discovering what it meant to be a Christian thinker—that of Austin Farrer?) If the dilemma were a genuine one, if it were in fact the case that we had to make all the reasonable judgements on our own account before we could recognize the reasonable man, then we could never learn by example. The very idea, indeed, of learning by example would be inherently nonsensical. *Quod est absurdum*. Whatever we are to say about the autonomy of moral judgements must at least allow that we can do what we know that we actually do: recognize the authority of a suitable example and learn from our observation and imitation. By this response Basil Mitchell invites us, in Johnsonian fashion, to try striking our foot against a stone.

It is the sign of a good argument not only that, like the deliveries of moral authority itself, it appears self-evident once one has grasped it, but that it repays extensive further reflection. This argument certainly does, though we can only hint at how such reflection might proceed. It invites comparison with the leading argument of Plato's *Meno*, where Socrates undertakes to prove, from the fact that the slave-boy actually *learns* geometry under his instruction (not merely repeating what he is told, but drawing conclusions for himself), that knowledge proceeds from within. Only an interior source of knowledge, Socrates argues, can account for the phenomenon of recognition and discovery. At first sight Basil Mitchell simply turns this argument on its head. From the fact that the disciple learns *by example*, he undertakes to show that moral knowledge proceeds from without. But the matter is more complicated than that. Although he does directly contradict what looks like a Socratic premise—'it does not, fortunately, take a saint to recognize a saint'—the implications of this contradiction are not such as to disrupt what is important in the notion of autonomy. It is rather that moral knowledge does not come *whole and entire* from within. Its realization depends upon the occurrence of instruction and example from without. Central to his understanding of the paradigm of learning is that it is progressive: we move from the immediate and vestigial insight to the clearer perceptions of rational comprehension. At every point the subject's moral understanding is 'autonomous' in the sense that it is his own moral understanding, but the development of his understanding takes him outside of himself, and that is why learning requires a loyal adherence to authority—not as a substitute for autonomous judgement but as a means to enlarging its range and insight. The argument has, of course, a wider extension than its concern with the knowledge of the good. It is recognizably the same argument that underlies the defence of commitment in academic pursuits which was the theme of Basil Mitchell's Inaugural Lecture, 'Neutrality and Commitment'.

Implicitly this is far more than an argument against the 'subjectivism' of contemporary moral theory. It is an invitation to rethink in its entirety the voluntarist metaphysic which has sustained the range of subjective moral theories in the modern period, to give an account of the good which will succeed, where the prevalent voluntarism has so eminently failed, in making sense of the commonest of our moral experiences, learning. Basil Mitchell does not himself embark upon any such metaphysical reconstruction, for this would take him too far from the characteristic dialectical and apologetic style of his writing. But he offers some hints. It is clear that for him knowledge of the good is a form of knowledge of the *world*: it is tied in with the 'world-view' which plays so large a part in the argument of *The Justification of Religious Belief*, and is theologically associated with the doctrine of creation. And the way in which moral authority presents itself, he suggests, is more like a challenge from without than a choice from within:

It is, indeed, often misleading to talk . . . about choosing a model for imitation; what more often happens is that the model, by its sheer impressiveness, demands our imitation and in so doing not merely develops, but radically revises, our previous notions about what is worth imitating.[5]

Yet this encounter with reality-as-the-good, embodied in a particular example of active goodness, is not the same as the religious encounter with God, nor are moral convictions simply a function of religious belief. And neither moral nor religious beliefs are identical with that other form in which we know reality, the kind of factual discovery which scientific research may put in our way. Rather these three forms of knowledge of reality, religious, empirical, and moral, are distinct, yet mutually correcting and so ultimately convergent. That is why moral discussion must proceed in the interdisciplinary way to which Basil Mitchell has continually committed himself, and that is why it is fatally flawed if it cannot call upon a strong contribution from a religious faith which understands its own authority in terms of revelation.

Here, then, is an agenda for the 'new realism' to take up: how are we to give an account of reality which does justice to

---

[5] *Morality: Religious and Secular* (Clarendon Press, Oxford, 1980), p. 153.

the distinct forms of our knowledge of the world, and which allows for the objective authority with which moral reality commands our subjective conviction? And there is an agenda of a broader kind set us by Basil Mitchell's own authority as a Christian thinker; for it is the mark of the truly authoritative that it evokes the free response of grateful and creative imitation in those who have learned from it.

2

Cumulative Case Arguments for Christian Theism

WILLIAM J. ABRAHAM

This essay has three aims. First, it seeks to draw attention to the existence of a form of natural theology which utilizes cumulative case arguments to defend the rationality of religious belief. It thus plans to highlight a very important though much neglected account of the relation between faith and reason which has been overshadowed by classical forms of both natural theology and fideism. Secondly, it seeks to display the distinctiveness of Basil Mitchell's contribution to this tradition of natural theology. Thirdly, it focuses on one particular problem in Mitchell's position which has not as yet been resolved. Hence the aspiration is that this paper will stimulate further discussion on the merits of Mitchell's contribution to natural theology.

I

The revival of cumulative case arguments in modern philosophical theology is a remarkable development. The list of participants is impressive by any standards. Any thorough historical survey would have to include figures as diverse as Charles Hartshorne, Richard Swinburne, Elton Trueblood, Basil Mitchell, J. R. Lucas, Austin Farrer, and Gary Gutting. All of these have in one way or another deployed cumulative case arguments to support the rationality of religious belief. In doing so they have highlighted and retrieved an approach to natural theology that can be traced right back through F. R. Tennant and John Henry Newman to Joseph Butler.

This way of developing natural theology was almost totally ignored by the last generation of philosophers of religion. It is not difficult to see why. For one thing, philosophers were so preoccupied with the nature of religious language that any time left over for the rationality of religious belief was devoted almost exclusively to classical natural theology and to side-glances at fideism. Few stopped to ask whether there could be a genuine alternative to these which was worthy of sustained attention. This posture was aided and abetted by the absence of a good historical analysis of cumulative case arguments. Butler and Newman, for example, are scarcely mentioned in the standard texts, and as yet no one has provided a fully criti-cal account of the tradition they represent. Moreover, cumula-tive case arguments tended to be championed and deployed by popular apologists like C. S. Lewis and G. K. Chesterton. It is difficult to take their work seriously within philosophical theology for they made no pretensions to be philosophers. Their primary interests lay elsewhere and they unashamedly wrote as polemicists and apologists. Add to this the fact that *prima-facie* cumulative case arguments seem dreadfully sus-pect. They resemble pale reflections of the more standard arguments in philosophy; they look like last-ditch efforts to salvage an appearance of rationality once the rigour and elegance of proof have been abandoned. Flew captured this nicely as he dismissed them with an aphorism: 'If one leaky bucket will not hold water that is no reason to think ten can.'[1] Alasdair MacIntyre was equally curt in his dismissal:

One occasionally hears teachers of theology aver that although the proofs do not provide conclusive grounds for belief in God, they are at least pointers, indicators. But a fallacious argument points nowhere (except to the lack of logical acumen on the part of those who accept it). And three fallacious arguments are no better than one.[2]

It is one of the lasting merits of *The Justification of Religious Belief* that it challenges at its foundations the prevailing attitude to cumulative case arguments. It shows at the very least that the latter constitutes a fascinating alternative to the prevailing options in philosophy on the rationality of religious belief. Thus in a characteristically Anglican fashion it seems to chart a *via media* between the classical proofs of the natural

---

[1] Antony Flew, *God and Philosophy* (Hutchinson, London, 1966), p. 62.
[2] Alasdair MacIntyre, *Difficulties in Christian Belief* (Philosophical Library, New York, 1959), p. 63.

theologians and the voluntarism of the fideists. In a way it should have been obvious that a cumulative case argument for theism should have been explored, for, ironically, both classical natural theology and fideism often share the common assumption that unless an argument is strictly formal in character then we do not really have an argument at all. This is surely an extremely odd assumption to make given the extent to which our arguments even on non-metaphysical issues fail to reach that goal. Hence the attempt to read the enduring debate about the rationality of theism as the embodiment of a cumulative case argument was thoroughly natural and long overdue.

It is important to bear this in mind if there is to be a thorough assessment of this position. The fundamental issue at stake is the nature of rationality and how it is to be attained. Thus the concept of a cumulative case is not some new weapon to be lodged in the apologetics for theism. The basic idea is that a rational or reasonable case can be made out for a position by the patient accumulation of various pieces of evidence. This is not a device which can be used only by theists. On the contrary, it is a respectable operation which can be deployed by the astute atheist and agnostic, as the work of J. L. Mackie[3] and Stewart R. Sutherland[4] amply testifies. Moreover, it is insufficiently recognized that the basic idea of a cumulative case argument can be interpreted in radically different ways. Perceptive readers will have noticed this already in the list of representative figures identified at the beginning of this paper, for it is obvious that figures as far apart as Charles Hartshorne and Richard Swinburne are not playing the same tune when they speak of cumulative case arguments. Nor is Basil Mitchell for that matter.

II

We can express this concisely by noting that the concept of a cumulative case argument is a thoroughly contested one. There are persistent and radical disagreements on how a cumulative case is to be conceived and executed. A brief

---

[3] J. L. Mackie, *The Miracle of Theism* (Clarendon Press, Oxford, 1982).

[4] Stewart R. Sutherland, *God, Jesus and Belief* (Basil Blackwell, Oxford, 1984).

survey of the nature of argument as illustrated by the work of Hartshorne and Swinburne will establish this clearly. It will also furnish a valuable set of contrasts for highlighting the pecularity of Mitchell's position.

Looked at schematically, any argument for or against religious belief can be placed on a grid which has at least three dimensions. It will have certain premisses, a certain structure, and a certain conclusion. Each of these can differ in crucial respects. Thus the premisses may differ in their form and their precise content. They may, in regard to form, be either logically necessary or they may be logically contingent, while their content may differ from one proponent to the next. Likewise with the structure of the argument. The argument may be empirical or non-empirical, it may be deductive or inductive, it may be formal and quantifiable, or it may be informal and non-quantifiable. Finally the conclusions may differ. They may differ in their modality, with one argument leading to a logically contingent proposition and another leading to a logically necessary proposition. They may also differ in their scope, with one argument supporting a single proposition and another argument supporting a whole cluster of propositions which are to be seen as a whole together.

This abstract schematization makes it clear that it is a serious error to believe that cumulative case arguments are simply arguments which involve an appeal to a series of considerations to support a conclusion. This is true as a general description but it is misleading as an accurate description, for it overlooks the amazing variety of arguments which instantiate this species of argument. Cumulative case arguments differ radically in tone, in style, in structure, in content, and in their outcome. Consider at this point the contributions of Hartshorne and Swinburne.

One does not normally associate Charles Hartshorne with the idea of a cumulative case argument, but, as Viney has recently shown,[5] Hartshorne's account of the rationality of belief in God takes the form of a complex global argument.[6] Overall the argument developed by Hartshorne is a priori in

[5] Donald Wayne Viney, *Charles Hartshorne and the Existence of God* (State University of New York Press, Albany, 1985).

[6] For a succinct statement of Hartshorne's position see his 'Six Theistic Proofs',

that it attempts to work from a series of sub-proofs based on premises which are understood to be logically necessary. By means of deductive inferences one arrives in each of the sub-proofs at a logically necessary conclusion. Thus Hartshorne offers his own formulations of the ontological argument, the cosmological argument, the argument from design, the epistemic argument, the moral argument, and the aesthetic argument. All of these are expressed not as empirical arguments but as a priori demonstrations. Thus, to take one example, the cosmological argument as Hartshorne construes it begins with the claim that something exists. Hartshorne construes this not as an empirical thesis but as a logically necessary truth. From this he then attempts to show that the necessity of something existing is not intelligible apart from the idea of a being which exists necessarily. So the sub-proofs are deductive arguments built on premises which are logically necessary.

It is much more difficult to describe the relation which holds between the sub-proofs in the comprehensive, global argument for belief in God. One way to construe Hartshorne's cumulative case is to see it as beginning with the ontological argument as a foundational argument in the sense that without it all the others fail. All the other arguments in turn buttress the ontological argument. Thus the cosmological argument secures a crucial premiss in the ontological argument by showing that it is possible that there is a necessary being. Likewise the moral argument supports the ontological argument by showing that God, if he exists, is good. From these examples it appears that the cumulative argument taken as a whole is fundamentally deductive in form.

Given the a priori cast of the premises and structure of Hartshorne's global argument it is not surprising that the conclusion is also a priori. The content of the conclusion is generally referred to as panentheism. Thus Hartshorne seeks to show that it is rational to believe that there necessarily exists a divine being who is related to the world in a way analogous to the way in which a person is related to his or her body.

Swinburne's cumulative case argument differs radically from that of Hartshorne in all three of the dimensions already

The Monist 54 (1970), pp. 159–80. This is printed as chap. 6 of *Creative Synthesis and Philosophic Method* (Open Court, La Salle, Illinois, 1970).

identified.[7] Consider the conclusion. Swinburne seeks to show that it is rational to believe in the kind of God generally associated with theism. He goes to considerable trouble to explicate what it is that the theist embraces at this point. The theist, as Swinburne sees it, affirms

the existence of a being with one or more of the following properties: being a person without a body (i.e. a spirit), present everywhere, the creator and sustainer of the universe, a free agent, able to do everything (i.e. omnipotent), knowing all things, perfectly good, a source of moral obligation, immutable, eternal, a necessary being, holy, and worthy of worship.[8]

The claim that such a deity exists is a contingent claim; that God exists is not necessarily true; it is contingently true.

Moreover, the case for this claim is fundamentally inductive rather than deductive in character. The whole argument, both in its sub-elements and in its totality, is cast in terms of a probability calculus which is formally expressed by means of Bayes' theorem. Hence belief in God is interpreted as an explanatory hypothesis which explains the existence of a variety of phenomena by showing that it is probable that they are the effects of the action of a personal agent who brings them about for certain intentions and purposes. The existence of the phenomena constitutes the fundamental premisses of the cumulative case, and the phenomena range from the existence of the universe, its conformity to order, and the existence of animals and humans to the existence of great opportunities for co-operation in acquiring knowledge and moulding the universe, the pattern of history, the existence of evidence for miracles, and the occurrence of religious experience. The probability of theism as an explanation for these phenomena is judged in terms of its prior probability and its explanatory power. Both of these are formally quantified by means of Bayes' theorem.

Clearly Swinburne's cumulative case differs drastically from that of Hartshorne. It works from contingent premisses to a contingent conclusion which is different in content from

---

[7] Richard Swinburne, *The Existence of God* (Clarendon Press, Oxford, 1979).

[8] Richard Swinburne, *The Coherence of Theism* (Clarendon Press, Oxford, 1977), p. 2. We shall not explore here how far Swinburne's position represents a radical revision of classical theism.

that of Hartshorne, and the whole argument is thoroughly empirical and inductive in character rather than a priori and deductive. It shares for the most part, however, one crucial feature of Hartshorne's argument in that it seeks to be thoroughly formal, laying out very precisely the exact logical relation between the various elements in the cumulative case argument. The only exception to this is the treatment of the argument from religious experience, which is construed along perceptual lines. The weight to be assigned to this argument is worked out independently of the use of Bayes' theorem and is only brought to bear in the whole case for theism when the theorem has already accomplished its allotted task.

III

We are now in a position to identify the precise way in which Mitchell construes the cumulative case argument for Christian theism. It differs in several crucial respects from the positions of Hartshorne and Swinburne.

One immediate difference is in the goal of the whole enterprise. Both Hartshorne and Swinburne focus on the truth or falsehood of a single proposition, namely belief in God. It does not matter at this point that they differ on how belief in God is interpreted, that is, whether we interpret God in either semi-classical or neo-classical categories. What is striking about Mitchell's case is that it seeks to establish the rationality of belief in traditional Christian theism. This looks like a rather innocent designation. In actual fact, however, it drastically changes the whole operation, as we shall see presently. For the moment we can note that what is being supported rationally is a whole cluster of beliefs which hang together and which need to be evaluated not just in isolation but as a whole.

It is not initially very clear what Mitchell means by traditional Christian theism. He tells us that it has a distinguished intellectual history and that it has been subject to close critical analysis and careful elucidation. Broadly speaking it is what the ordinary educated person understands by Christianity.[9] This, of course, leaves the conclusion of the whole argument somewhat vague and elusive. Ordinary educated people have

[9] Basil Mitchell, *The Justification of Religious Belief* (Macmillan, London, 1973), p. 3.

very different and conflicting accounts of the intellectual content of Christianity, so it is not clear precisely what elements
in the tangled web of Christian belief are being accepted and
rejected.

This is a revealing omission which can be usefully explored
by recalling how Joseph Butler sums up the meaning of traditional Christian theism. For Butler religion in general and
Christianity in particular contains in it the following elements:

> that mankind is appointed to live in a future state; that everyone will
> be rewarded or punished; rewarded and punished respectively for all
> that behaviour here, which we comprehend under the word virtuous
> or vicious, morally good or evil; that our present life is a probation,
> a state of trial, and of discipline, for that future one; notwithstanding
> the objections, which men fancy they have, from notions of neces-
> sity, against there being such a moral plan as this at all; and what-
> ever objections may appear to be against the wisdom and goodness
> of it, as it stands so imperfectly made known to us at present; that
> this world being in the state of apostasy and wickedness, and con-
> sequently of ruin, and the sense both of their condition and duty
> being greatly corrupted amongst man, this gave an occasion for an
> additional dispensation of Providence; of the utmost importance;
> proved by miracles; but containing in it many things appearing to us
> strange and not to have been expected; carried on by a divine per-
> son, the Messiah, in order to the recovery of the world; yet not
> revealed to all men, nor proved with the strongest possible evidence
> to all those to whom it was revealed; but only to such a part of man-
> kind, and with such particular evidence as the wisdom of God
> thought fit.[10]

Cumbersome as this is, it represents what Butler would
have believed the ordinary educated person to understand by
Christianity. Yet although much of it would be represented in
any modern version of traditional Christianity, it would not
generally be expressed in exactly these terms. The content and
structure would be substantially reorganized. What pondering on this shows is that offering a summary of what constitutes Christianity is itself a major theological exercise which
depends in part on a judgement as to what is and is not rationally acceptable. Thus decisions about what Christianity is and
whether it can be justified may interact on each other in a

[10] Joseph Butler, *The Analogy of Religion* (Clarendon Press, Oxford, 1896),
pp. 16–17.

subtle fashion. As a result the whole conception of a cumulative case argument is transformed from a linear one where one moves from premisses to conclusion to a process of justification which involves a dialectical relation between premiss and conclusion. One does not proceed, as Swinburne does, by first carefully laying out precisely what theism is and then proceeding to argue for it in a formal operation which establishes the probability of a single proposition. Rather, one indicates in broad terms the content of a substantial theological vision and develops the exposition of that vision as one expounds the various pieces of evidence which support it as a whole.

Moreover, personal judgement plays a crucial role in the weighing of the various sub-arguments and in the total weighing of the whole argument. Mitchell makes no use whatsoever of any formal calculus of probability. The argument is, to be sure, broadly empirical in spirit. It is therefore radically different from the kind of cumulative case which is marshalled by Hartshorne. The premisses are treated as contingent truths, the form of the argument is broadly inductive rather than deductive in character, and the conclusion, far from being a necessary truth, is a complex metaphysical or theological vision which is accepted as reasonable because of its ability to illuminate and make the best sense of a whole range of phenomena. Thus it provides an explanation of the existence of the cosmos, of order and beauty, of religious experience, of conspicuous sanctity, and so on. Furthermore, the criteria for a good explanation are far from precise. One certainly tests for coherence, internal consistency, fit with all the known facts, and the like. But these are not quantified in any formal fashion and it is obvious that simplicity, if it is taken seriously at all, does not have the crucial role assigned to it by Swinburne. The whole argument, therefore, takes the form of an extended conversation rather than a chain of formal reasoning. It involves the patient presenting and re-presenting of a network of considerations which together co-operate in favour of a theological vision which to some extent contains elements of irreducible mystery. The interpretation of the vision, the marshalling of the supporting evidence, the weighing of the final outcome, all these involve a radical dependence on a large measure of personal judgement.

Here is one point where we can hear the echo of Newman still sounding in Oxford. He captured the importance of judgement in the weighing of arguments in this way:

It is plain that formal logical sequence is not in fact the method by which we are enabled to become certain of what is concrete: and it is equally plain, from what has been already suggested, what the real and necessary method is. It is the culmination of probabilities, independent of each other, arising out of the nature and circumstances of the particular case which is under review; probabilities too fine to avail separately, too subtle and circuitous to be convertible into syllogisms, too numerous and various for such conversion, even were they convertible. As a man's portrait differs from a sketch of him, in having, not merely a continuous outline, but all the details filled in, and shades and colours laid on and harmonized together, such is the multiform and intricate process of ratiocination, necessary for our reaching him as a concrete fact, compared with the rude operation of syllogistic treatment.[11]

Elsewhere Newman states this same point as follows:

Thus in concrete reasonings we are in great measure thrown back into that condition, from which logic proposed to rescue us. We judge for ourselves, by our own lights, and on our own principles; and our criterion of truth is not so much the manipulation of propositions, as the intellectual and moral character of the person maintaining them, and the ultimate silent effect of his arguments or conclusions upon our minds.[12]

It is important to dwell on this element of personal judgement. As far as Mitchell's work is concerned, it sharply focuses the distinctive way in which he develops the concept of a cumulative case. Although it is arguable that both Hartshorne and Swinburne do at times have to appeal to personal judgement in the layout of their arguments, it is also fair to say that they pay little attention to this fact, and one gains the distinct impression that they share the general philosophical preference for formally rigorous arguments. Mitchell stands very clearly at this point in the tradition of Newman, who had deep misgivings about our ability to capture in a formal fashion the subtlety of some of our rational procedures. Thus Mitchell

[11] John Henry Newman, *An Essay in Aid of a Grammar of Assent* (University of Notre Dame Press, Notre Dame, 1979), p. 230.

[12] Ibid., p. 240.

insists that we recognize a distinct capacity for judgement, which does not in itself consist in the following of rules.[13]

This explains what is surely the most puzzling feature of *The Justification of Religious Belief*, namely the lack of detailed argument for traditional Christian theism. Mitchell's achievement in this respect is self-consciously modest. His aim is to develop a strategy for the defence of the rationality of theism. He makes clear, of course, what that defence would actually look like, yet it is an open question how far that defence can be fully articulated. If, as I am suggesting, we interpret Mitchell as following in the footsteps of Newman, then there are severe practical limits to this endeavour. Given the nature of the case, the balance of probabilities and considerations is too fine, subtle, circuitous, numerous, and various to be captured by any explicit formulation of the argument. Any attempt is almost bound to appear hopelessly artificial, wooden, and inadequate as a rational defence of Christian theism. To borrow again the language of Newman, even the most sophisticated outline of the cumulative case, no matter how sensitively executed, will not do justice to the silent effects of the arguments and conclusions upon the mind.

IV

Thus far in the argument I have sought to highlight the unique way in which Mitchell both understands and deploys the idea of a cumulative case argument. Within this I have drawn particular attention to the crucial role that personal judgement plays in his account of rationality. It is fairly obvious that personal judgement is itself a very complex concept. It is bound, moreover, to excite philosophical controversy, if not hostility. Before turning to objections to it, it is worth pausing to note the attraction and merits of Mitchell's proposals.

For a start, Mitchell's analysis makes intelligible sense of the actual disputes which are carried on between adherents of different belief systems. It explains why they tend to be so intellectually frustrating and interminable. Assent and agree-

<hr>

[13] *The Justification of Religious Belief*, p. 89.

ment are difficult to secure. They have these features because
they range over a whole network of complex phenomena and
because they cannot be fully captured by any formal logical
apparatus. Moreover, it is not enough in the debate simply to
mount a cumulative case against a particular element in the
theistic vision being presented. One must also attempt to set
forth the contours of and arguments for the rival atheological
vision on offer. In fact, if we are to follow Mitchell's model of
argument, the case for atheism should not take the form of a
negative attack of theism. It should also involve the positive
task of articulating and supporting some particular atheological vision of the cosmos, human nature, evil, the future, and so
on. The debate centres on finding out which system makes
best sense of all the available phenomena; hence adherents of
the various alternatives need at some stage to specify and
defend their particular alternative.

Secondly, Mitchell's model makes sense of the kind of conversion, certainty, and tenacity which one commonly finds
among the adherents of rival world-views. Very often the
switch from one cosmic vision to another is a dramatic affair,
involving a drastic shift from one particular vision to another.
Thus the convert to Marxism or to Christianity may find that
he or she undergoes a radical change of mind which seems to
take place in an instant. This is entirely natural, given that the
individual may have suddenly been struck by the force of
some sub-element in the argument, or, as appears more likely,
by the combined weight of all the elements in the cumulative
case which has been mounted by adherents of the vision to
which they are converted. This in turn also explains the level
of certainty expressed. The degree of commitment is bound to
appear unwarranted if we attempt to judge the force of the
argument by the canons of some formal rational calculus. But
if we take into account the silent effects of the total argument
the kind of certainty one commonly finds should not at all surprise us. Likewise, it is understandable that there should be
tenacity. Participation in a particular theological or secular
tradition is inevitably self-involving. It touches deeply personal matters like one's identity and morality and is not likely
to be abandoned at the first sign of trouble. If one is wise, one
will want to go over the relevant considerations again and one

will want to explore the meaning of whatever rival tradition is attractive, together with all the relevant evidence for and against it, with considerable care before one abandons the position one has already embraced.

Thirdly, Mitchell's account, if it succeeds, provides a much better alternative to classical natural theology than the varieties of fideism which have developed in the wake of the demise of the classical arguments for the existence of God. Perceptive religious believers and theologians have long recognized that religious truths do not impose themselves directly and universally on all minds. There seems to be a wide gap, if not yawning chasm, between the evidence and the conclusion, which has been filled in by a variety of options which have sought refuge in what might broadly be referred to as faith. So believing was construed as an act of the whole personality; or, with Pascal, it was held to involve recourse to the 'reasons of the heart'; or, with Kierkegaard, it was thought to involve a 'proof from the emotions'; or, with William James, it was believed to require a 'will to believe' which tipped the scales in a way that was consonant with our emotional nature. Given the repudiation of natural theology which these alternatives embrace, it has never been clear how they can even begin to safeguard the rationality of religious commitment. Perhaps they were never meant to do this, although it certainly sounds as if this is their intention. What Mitchell's analysis suggests is that such endeavours presuppose the principle that arguments for religious belief must take the form of logically coercive demonstrations of a strictly inductive or deductive character. Once this assumption is abandoned and Mitchell's model of argument is accepted then the need to fill the gap between the evidence and conclusion becomes redundant. At one stroke the foundations of most versions of fideism have been shattered.

Despite these attractive features it is obvious that many philosophers and theologians will remain dissatisfied with Mitchell's conception of a cumulative case argument. Many instinctively feel that the recourse to personal judgement is ultimately a sophisticated device which is unintentionally adopted in order to avoid the rigours of hard argument and to conceal from theists their failure to provide adequate support for religious belief. Certainly most philosophers will be tempted to hold that the kind of cumulative case presented by Mitchell should be accepted only as a last resort after formal arguments of a more rigorous kind have been found inappropriate. If at all possible they should be avoided, if not generally ignored.

If this posture rests on the a priori conviction that all arguments must be formal and quantifiable, then it is open to very serious objection. The principal one is that it has not been defended in terms of the canons of its own rationality, for no one has produced either good deductive or compelling inductive arguments to establish that all arguments must be of this kind. In the absence of these, the critic's position is internally inconsistent. We simply have to accept the critic's requirement as a dogma or an article of faith or a personal opinion. It cannot even be a matter of judgement, for it is precisely this that is regarded by the critic as objectionable in any fully rational view of correct believing.

A more moderate and perceptive critic could avoid this problem by requiring that it be shown that the concept of personal judgement is a requirement of any adequate epistemology. To some extent Mitchell has sought to establish this by maintaining that the idea of personal judgement is essential if we are to make rational sense of standard disputes within literary criticism, history, science, morality, and so on. The difficulty with this move is that the critic very often worries whether the examples of argument drawn from these various disputes are themselves genuinely rational. As they stand they appear to beg the question in advance because one may be relying on personal judgement to establish the initial acceptance of these examples as rational. One does not accept, say, that disputes or arguments within astrology are rational and use these as a paradigm for the operation of personal judgement. It would enhance Mitchell's case enormously, therefore, if it could be shown that personal judgement entered into less disputed areas such as mathematics, memory, or perception. I do not believe that Mitchell's position absolutely requires this possibility and I am certain that an adequate epistemology will have to find room for the concept of personal judgement. As yet, however, this remains a major piece of unfinished business in the tradition which Mitchell represents.[14] Be that as it may, there are difficulties in the idea of personal judgement which need to be addressed outside the context of a full-dress epistemology.

V

A recurring feature of Mitchell's position which is disconcerting is the extent to which it makes the actual justification of religious belief thoroughly elusive. As we have seen, the premisses, the structure of the argument, and the actual conclusion form a complex narrative of particulars and probabilities which seems to defy explicit, exacting, and detailed analysis. Note that this is fundamentally a practical or contingent problem rather than a full-scale logical one. This follows from the fact that the particulars of some of the arguments, the general structure of the argument as a whole, and the main elements of the conclusion can be set forth and debated in detail. So the proponent of a cumulative case can clearly make progress on all these fronts. Yet there are limits to this process. This is why the use of personal judgement is so important; it enters deeply at the level of premiss, structure, and conclusion. It seems, that is, to carry much more weight than is desirable or acceptable.

It is understandable, therefore, that informed critics should challenge the idea of personal judgement and seek to restrict its use as much as possible. By its very nature it leaves the argument very elusive and it opens up the door to prejudice, whim, bias, emotion, and other non-rational factors, all of which are bound to have an adverse effect on personal judgement. How might this twofold challenge be successfully addressed?

It does not help very much to try and resolve this problem by developing, as Newman did, the notion of an illative sense. For one thing this smacks too much of some kind of inner faculty or intuition. Initially this kind of inner sense explains nothing. There is nothing wrong in itself with speaking of a capacity to exercise personal judgement, and maybe even the

[14] For an interesting excursion into this domain see Jay Newman, 'Epistemic Inference and Illative Judgement', *Dialectica* 35 (1981), pp. 327–39.

notion of a special kind of sense can have its merits despite the general philosophical antipathy to such language. But such language does not solve the problem; it merely redescribes it. Questions surely arise as to what exactly this special sense guarantees. In addition, it notoriously leads different individuals to radically different conclusions. Thus it led Newman to embrace Roman Catholicism while it leads others to reject that and stay within Anglicanism. In fact the idea can be grossly misleading, for it may lull its proponents into a false security, giving the impression that they are avoiding the exacting task of working through the relevant data, warrants, and conclusions.

Nor is it satisfactory to attempt to solve this problem by saying that one can be trained in the exercise of personal judgement. Generally speaking it is obvious that one can become a competent judge in various areas. One can learn how to weigh evidence in history, literary criticism, science, and the like. This process or set of processes is a complex one, involving initiation into a tradition of argument and debate which can take years to master. It is surely the case, however, that such training is not obviously available for judging the deep disputes which exist between conflicting metaphysical visions. What seems to be required for these is the ability to exercise good judgement across a whole spectrum of fields of inquiry. Thus in evaluating the truth of the Christian faith one is called upon to weigh the merits and relevance of considerations which range from the coherence of the concepts used, the appropriate form of argument to be deployed, and the interpretation of sacred texts to the nature of religious experience, the validity of natural theology, the nature of human existence, the significance of moral and natural evil, the implications of conspicuous sanctity, and all that these involve. It is ludicrous to hold that anyone, least of all the average believer or unbeliever, can have the capacity to judge competently and confidently on all of these issues.

The problem is compounded by the fact that the ability to exercise personal judgement in theology requires the attainment of certain moral and spiritual capacities which themselves appear to require initiation into the Christian faith and are said to be made possible only by divine grace. Thus it is recorded that Peter was able to confess that Jesus was the Son of God only because of personal revelation,[15] and Paul suggests that the gospel makes no sense at all to those who have not been taught by the Spirit of God.[16] In other words, training in personal judgement involves initiation into a tradition of thought and experience. One is introduced to a way of life where certain skills, virtues, and dispositions are cultivated over time. So it is that one learns how to exercise personal judgement. But note what follows: the proper exercise of personal judgement now depends on commitment to a particular tradition. One cannot therefore rely on personal judgement to judge the rationality of that tradition; the books will have already been cooked in advance by the choice of tradition which has been adopted. It is small wonder then that the informed critic fears that the kind of personal judgement to which appeal is made will be deeply influenced by prior prejudice and bias.

This line of argument cuts very deeply into the appeal to personal judgement. It leads Sykes to make the following graphic comment:

Flying by feel is usually preferable to flying by the book, and the reason for this is that the former is more flexible and thus better able to make sudden changes in conditions. But it must also be noted that flying by feel can quickly degenerate into flying by the seat of our pants, and that is where the book is the only thing that saves us. Similarly, intuition is useful in matters of rationality, even suggestive perhaps, but theoretically—and when things go wrong, pragmatically—dispensible.[17]

Clearly this represents a very penetrating and manifold challenge to the kind of cumulative case developed by Mitchell. If successful it surely undermines a central element in his defence of the rationality of religious belief.

VI

This challenge, however, does not in fact succeed. The following considerations cast serious doubt on its fundamental

[15] Matt. 16: 17.   [16] 1 Cor. 2: 12–13.
[17] Rod Sykes, 'Soft Rationalism', *International Journal for Philosophy of Religion* 11 (1980), p. 60.

contentions. Firstly, it is wrong to construe the argument as involving a direct appeal to intuition or to look upon it as flying by feel. One flies not by feel nor by intuition nor even by personal argument. One flies by evidence from beginning to end. The argument is not based on anything but those particular considerations which when taken as a whole constitute the total case which can be made out. To speak of personal judgement is not to speak of a new category of evidence which somehow adds extra weight to the whole. Rather, it draws attention to the way the evidence is recognized and weighed in the scales of rational evaluation. Given this it is misleading to think that there is a measure of personal judgement which can somehow become excessive in nature. Personal judgement simply means the ability to weigh evidence without using some sort of formal calculus. No one can ever have an excess of such ability.

Secondly, it is alarmist to think that our ability to weigh evidence will necessarily be influenced adversely by prejudice, bias, emotion, and the like. It is a simple *non sequitur* to argue that because personal judgement is sometimes biased then it will always be biased. *Abusus non tillot usum.* Given care and an eye for self-deception the sensible person can generally notice when he or she is allowing his or her wishes, predispositions, passions, and the like to tilt the scales in a particular direction. Besides, there are plenty of hostile and friendly critics on hand to point this out when it happens in any particular case.

In this connection it is surely erroneous to look upon the appeal to personal revelation and the work of the Spirit as begging the question in advance in favour of the theist. As Alston has recently suggested, such discourse is an attempt to describe a kind of religious experience which is central to Christianity.[18] To be sure, it appears initially as if this description already presupposes belief in God and therefore automatically disqualifies itself as a consideration in favour of traditional Christian theism. But this can easily be remedied by converting the claim from an internal to an external

---

[18] William P. Alston, 'Christian Experience and Christián Belief' in *Faith and Rationality: Reason and Belief in God*, eds. Alvin Plantinga and Nicholas Wolterstorff (University of Notre Dame Press, Notre Dame, 1983), p. 104.

description. Rather than speaking of personal revelation or the work of the Spirit we can speak of apparent personal revelation and apparent work of the Spirit in our hearts. Thus understood the appeal is in its form consonant with the general appeal to religious experience and has as much right to be taken as evidence as the latter does. In other words, that many people claim to be aware of God in this way is part of the phenomena which has to be either explained by the theist or explained away by the atheist. To do so either way will involve the weighing of that claim in the scales of judgement, and how it will be weighed is not determined in advance.

Thirdly, as the argument stands it claims that the appeal to personal judgement is bound to be circular because its cultivation and therefore its exercise depends on prior initiation into the Christian tradition. This, however, is not the case at all. The nurture of the kind of personal judgement at issue here is carried out not by the Christian tradition but by the network of intellectual skills and arts to be found in those fields of enquiry which are relevant to the various considerations to which appeal is made. Thus in so far as historical considerations are involved, it will require historical judgement; in so far as philosophical considerations are relevant, philosophical judgement will be needed; in so far as general observations are at issue, then good general judgement will be essential, and so on. Moreover, in exploring the kind of judgement involved it is important not to exaggerate the kind of skill which is needed. Ordinary people are given plenty of opportunity to exercise personal judgement of a complex nature in many areas of life. Thus in voting at an election one has to exercise personal judgement in weighing up the merits of competing candidates and parties even though there is no precise formal training in this area. As with the case of religious belief, the weighing of evidence in this instance cuts across a whole network of data and warrants.

It must be conceded, however, that the full articulation of the grounds for our favoured metaphysical vision is unlikely to be executed by any single individual. The informed critic is correct to insist that this is a lasting feature of our epistemic position as pictured by Mitchell's account of cumulative case arguments. Much will have to be taken on trust as regards the content of the vision articulated and the details of the various arguments captured in the final assent. Another way to express this is to claim that our visions, whether they be theological or secular, are instantiated not in a fixed body of absolute propositions but in living, dynamic traditions. In believing that one's chosen tradition embodies the truth, one depends in part on the labour and judgement of others. Take, for example, what Christians believe about Jesus. It is obvious that this constitutes a crucial element in the theological vision embraced, yet it is quite impossible for the average believer to articulate and defend rationally all that is believed historically about Jesus. At this point the believer trusts his or her own judgement or trusts the judgement of some group of scholars who have executed this undertaking. Certainly he or she would be hard pressed to speak competently on the complex issues involved. So there clearly is an element of faith at this point. There simply is no way in which one can be a kind of Renaissance or Enlightenment rationalist who covers all the relevant data and warrants.

In fact the testing of the tradition is something which takes place over time, and is not therefore something to be decided in an instant. The community nurtures within itself a band of scholars and critics who explore the depths and horizons of the faith and report back on their findings. No doubt some in this process will be tempted to be partisan, bringing back only such reports as confirm what is already believed. Whenever this happens it is easy to think that the testing is bogus and that the judgement being exercised is hopelessly biased from the outset. However, the fact is that this does not always happen. Again and again the prevailing expression of the tradition has to be adjusted in the light of new knowledge and fresh testing. Indeed, there are at times crises which appear to rock the whole tradition at its foundations. But if the tradition can be challenged at its foundations then it can also be supported at its foundations, for there is no knowing in advance how exactly the arguments and evidence will fall. It is one of the lasting merits of *The Justification of Religious Belief* that it offers an extremely important account of the rationality of this complex process. I have sought to extend that process by exploring its place in a deep tradition which has yet to be fully mapped and by seeking to defend one of its crucial elements against some penetrating criticism.[19]

[19] I would like to thank Robert Prevost, Leroy Howe, and the members of the Faculty Symposium of Perkins School of Theology for their comments on this paper.

3

The Reasonableness of Christianity

MAURICE WILES

For the last fourteen years, I have had the good fortune to share with Basil Mitchell in the conduct of a series of seminars on the relationship between philosophy and theology.[1] I have learned a great deal from them, but some fundamental puzzles still remain. It seems appropriate therefore in this context to try to articulate what is for me the basic perplexity about how work in philosophy of religion and theology ought to proceed.

My title expresses an aspiration which I believe the philosopher of religion and the theologian ought to hold in common. It is not, of course, original. I did not choose it in order to talk about Locke. But having chosen it, I find that he does in fact provide a possible starting-point. Locke's path to producing a reasonable Christianity was by way of what he calls 'an attentive and unbiased search' of Scripture. Reliance on such a procedure was rendered reasonable by the evidence of prophecy and miracle. Its outcome was the delineation of a set of propositions which God had made a necessary part of the law of faith, and which it is our duty to embrace with docility as truths coming from God. Such a form of revelation, Locke suggests, fits the all-merciful God's concern for men whose hands are used to the plough and spade (to say nothing of the other sex).[2] I call this a possible starting-point only in the sense that it provides a vivid reminder of how different an approach is required of us, with our very different understanding of Scripture, if we in our day are to be able to speak of the reasonableness of Christianity.

Before we consider whether we are in a position to speak in such terms, we need to consider what such a phrase might

[1] A much earlier version of this paper was read to one of our joint seminars. Some of the deficiencies of that version have been eliminated as a result of criticisms by Basil Mitchell and some helpful written comments by Robert Gay.

[2] Cf. Locke, *Reasonableness of Christianity*, preface and section 252.

mean. Two distinctions are worth making at the outset. By 'the reasonableness of Christianity' we might mean either (a) that there are good reasons for being a Christian or (b) that reason is a vital constituent in determining the content of Christian belief. There is no necessary logical connection between those two. It would be possible to claim that there were good reasons (perhaps of a Pascalian wager kind) for assenting to Christianity even though the content of the faith might be determined in some wholly non-rational manner. Alternatively the content of the faith might be determined in a wholly rational manner, like an algebraic system, while there were no good grounds for believing that it related to any reality, this-worldly or other-worldly.

My second distinction is between (a) the claim that there are good reasons for being a Christian and that it is important that there are such reasons and (b) the claim that reason does in fact play a major role in determining whether or not people become Christians. The second may well be false, as I suspect it is; but the first might still be true. Psychological or sociological factors may play a predominant role in determining why particular people become Christian—the accident of birth, some favourable early association with Christianity, or some particular mystical or conversion experience. Reason at that point may not have had any significant role to play. But it may still be important for such people to be able to see their Christian position as reasonable, if they are to stay Christian. Much discussion of the reasonableness of Christianity is *post-factum* rationalization of that kind. Its occurring in that way does not render it valueless.

Historically the attitude of Christians to reason has been varied in the extreme. At one end of the spectrum we have the insistence that Athens has nothing to do with Jerusalem, that reason and faith relate to totally different dimensions of experience, that reason is the devil's whore and has no standing-ground in relation to Christian truth. At the other we have the claim that the existence of God can be demonstrated by a process of deductive reasoning and that the absolute reliability of Scripture can be convincingly proved by the testimony of miracle and fulfilled prophecy. Extreme claims of either kind are in my judgement wholly implausible. Claims of the first kind allow no room for discriminating between equally clamant claims of competing sects to be embodiments of the one true self-authenticating faith. Claims of the latter kind have proved quite unable to stand up to the challenges that philosophical critics have levelled against them. I shall not waste time by going over the arguments once again. I recall those extreme positions only as providing the context within which the serious and difficult problems begin.

But even if we can ignore the largely non-existent 'pure fideists' and 'pure rationalists' we are faced with the immensely difficult task of mapping out an appropriate course through the extensive terrain that lies between those two extremes. To be 'reasonable' is a much broader concept than to be a follower of a set of specifiable rules of logic. The first thing about which we have to be absolutely clear and firm is that we do not have to choose between being 'rational' on the one hand (after the model of the pure mathematician with his wholly deductive proofs) and being 'irrational' on the other (in the sense of being unamenable to reasoning of any kind). As Stephen Toulmin among others has insisted, the form of reasoning appropriate in any particular discipline depends on the nature of that discipline and cannot be taken over without modification from what has proved itself appropriate in some other discipline.[3] Thus the theologian who aspires to be reasonable has no already existing pattern of reasonableness simply waiting to be picked up and applied. He or she has to find the appropriate method and the appropriate norms *in via*. All theologians worthy of the name are in fact engaged in a process of this kind. But it is a difficult and perplexing task. The basic perplexity, to which I referred at the start of this paper, can be very broadly stated in terms of the spatial metaphor used at the beginning of this paragraph. Most philosophers of religion, who ought to be helping the theologians in their mapping exercise, seem to me to keep too close for comfort to either the fideistic or the rationalistic bank—or,

[3] Cf. S. Toulmin, *The Place of Reason in Ethics* (Cambridge University Press, Cambridge, 1953), p. 216. The importance of this general point is well illustrated by some words of Clifford Longley in *The Times* (Mon. 17 Sept. 1984): 'In a theological world pushed to logical conclusions there may be only three sustainable positions: Biblical fundamentalism, strict adherence to the Roman Catholic magisterium, or Cupittism: which may be why most people prefer to be a little illogical.'

perhaps I should say, seem to keep for comfort too close to one of the two banks. The theologian, I believe, needs to travel a more difficult route somewhere nearer to the middle of the stream, and without more help from the philosopher of religion than is actually forthcoming the theologian is hard pressed to steer a proper course. I will try to illustrate what I mean with some more specific examples.

I begin with those who cling to the fideistic bank. The name of Wittgenstein has given a new philosophical status to the fideistic approach to Christianity in recent decades. 'Wittgensteinian fideism' sounds a lot more respectable than fideism *tout simple*. How faithful the various brands of it to be found in the contemporary academic market are to Wittgenstein himself is something I am not competent to assess; nor is it directly germane to my argument. Let me simply give two examples from the American scene of the kind of approach I have in mind. Both explicitly argue that the theism/atheism debate, which is normally conceived of as the basic issue in establishing a 'reasonable Christianity', is misconceived, and that no such debate can reasonably be carried on.

The first is Paul van Buren, probably still best known in England for his *Secular Meaning of the Gospel*, which was based on a strongly positivist account of language. But his later book, *The Edges of Language*, represents a sharp reaction away from his earlier views. In it he makes his main point with the aid of the same kind of topographical analogy that I have been using. 'God' for him is 'a word marking the outer edge of language', and if it is not 'then it falls within our clear, regular use of words and must stand the tests of coherence which rule what I should call the great central plains of our talk'. Here full attention is certainly given to the mysteriousness or (in Ian Ramsey's phrase) the logical oddity of our God talk. But this appears to be done in a crudely dichotomous way. On the one hand is a 'clear, regular use of words' with established tests of coherence; on the other hand are the edges of language where 'the categories of coherence ... simply do not apply'.[4] This sharp dichotomy runs right through the book. Religious language is either language at the limit of its use or it is asser-

---

[4] P. van Buren, *The Edges of Language* (Macmillan, London, 1972), p. 133.

tions;[5] the word 'God' is either a border-marker, a cry as we stumble at the edge of utter nonsense, or it is being understood literalistically.[6] By lumping together every position other than his own as a form of literalism van Buren can make traditional theology appear utterly implausible; but only at the cost of rendering his own wanderings around the edges of language vacuous. Christians do more than simply cry 'God'; they cry 'God' in a sophisticated variety of ways. Van Buren does not help us determine which of those ways are appropriate and why.

My second example is Paul Holmer's book *The Grammar of Faith*. Again the title of the book is significant. Having rightly emphasized the complexity of religious language and the need to take account of the ways and contexts within which it is used, Holmer goes on to speak of doctrines as 'the rules and grammar of the language of faith'.[7] Certainly there are analogies between the way doctrines function in the church and the way conventions of speech and behaviour function in other social groups. But let that analogy dominate one's understanding of Christian belief, and the concept of the truth or reasonableness of Christianity is ruled out absolutely in a way that seems to be wholly unacceptable.

To pick up again my analogy of the stream, such writers (if they have actually left the fideistic bank at all) seem to me to be moving about in the shallows under its lee. I do not think the Christian believer or the Christian theologian should follow their siren voices.

So, as my original choice of title has already clearly indicated, I am more attracted to those who stress the role of reason in relation to belief. But reason, as we have already seen, takes different forms in different contexts. Careful attention needs, therefore, to be given to the way in which reason is understood to function. The two examples that I shall take in this case are two English scholars, Richard Swinburne and Anthony Kenny, one a Christian believer and the other not, who have both published books entitled *Faith and Reason* in the early years of this decade.[8]

---

[5] Ibid., p. 147.　　[6] Ibid., pp. 146, 140.

[7] P. Holmer, *The Grammar of Faith* (Harper and Row, New York, 1978), p. 192.

[8] R. Swinburne, *Faith and Reason* (Clarendon Press, Oxford, 1981); A. Kenny, *Faith and Reason* (Columbia University Press, New York, 1983).

Swinburne closes the introduction to his earlier book *The Coherence of Theism* with these words:

It is one of the intellectual tragedies of our age that when philosophy in English-speaking countries has developed high standards of argument and clear thinking, the style of theological writing has been largely influenced by the continental philosophy of Existentialism, which, despite its considerable other merits, has been distinguished by a very loose and sloppy style of argument. If argument has a place in theology, large-scale theology needs clear and rigorous argument. That point was very well grasped by Thomas Aquinas and Duns Scotus, by Berkeley, Butler, and Paley. It is high time for theology to return to their standards.[9]

That is a noble ideal. But how is it to be put into practice? The primary strategy of both writers is to emphasize the extent to which language about God can be understood in a straightforward, non-analogical sense. This has obvious advantages for the application of rational argument to issues of theistic belief, for, as Swinburne puts it, where words are used analogically the syntactic and semantic rules that govern their use have to be modified with the result that 'the less clear it will be what is being said'.[10]

The point is an important one and it is worth looking in a little more detail at how it works out in their writings. Anthony Kenny's book *The God of the Philosophers* is a careful consideration of the two traditional divine attributes, omniscience and omnipotence. At the start of the book he gives his reasons for concentrating on those two particular attributes.

Other attributes, such as justice, mercy, and love have a more obvious significance for the religious believer; but they are less immediately amenable to philosophical investigation and analysis ... Whatever significance these predicates ['just', 'merciful' and 'loving'] have when applied to God, they cannot be understood simply in the same sense as when applied to human beings. Intellect and power, on the other hand, are intended to be attributed to God in the most literal sense: it is the infinity of the intellect and the limitlessness of the power that makes the difference between the creator and the creature. 'Omniscient' and 'omnipotent' are not predicates which were in use for application to human beings and are then

[9] R. Swinburne, *The Coherence of Theism* (Clarendon Press, Oxford, 1977), p. 7.
[10] Ibid., p. 70.

ascribed in some transferred or analogical sense to God: they express concepts which were devised to represent uniquely divine characteristics.[11]

But is Kenny's argument sound? It may well be true that moral and personal attributes, like justice, mercy, and love, are less immediately amenable to philosophical analysis than intellect and power. But it does not follow from that fact that the two sets of attributes apply to God in different ways. Nor is the etymological fact that 'omniscient' and 'omnipotent' are words applied directly to God of any significance. The OED provides us with 'all-just' and 'all-merciful', of which the same could be said.[12] I see no ground for acknowledging (as Kenny appears to do) the analogical attribution of justice, mercy, and love to God, but not of intellect and power. If that is right, it is of great importance for the assessment of Kenny's argument. For the conclusion to which he is led at the end of his discussion is 'that there cannot . . . be a timeless, immutable, omniscient, omnipotent, all-good being'.[13] But unless Kenny was justified in denying the analogical character of the attribution of intellect and power to God, his argument can be challenged for failing to allow for those modifications of syntactic and semantic rules that govern the use of analogical terms.

Swinburne pursues a very similar line of argument in *The Coherence of Theism*. He too discusses the intelligibility of the divine attributes, omnipotence and omniscience, without appealing to any analogical usage of the terms 'power' or 'knowledge'. He only 'plays the analogical card', as he puts it, very late on in the book, when he comes to speak of God as personal.[14] Since the conclusion to which he comes is 'that it is coherent to suppose that there exists eternally an omnipresent spirit, perfectly free, the creator of the universe, omnipotent, omniscient, perfectly good, and a source of moral obligation',[15] his argument is not open to the same objections as Kenny's. For if the argument holds when the terms are understood in a literal sense, *a fortiori* it will be impossible to dismiss as incoherent any modified analogical (and therefore less precise) interpretation which the theologian may rightly want to

[11] A. Kenny, *The God of the Philosophers* (Clarendon Press, Oxford, 1979), p. 5.
[12] *Oxford English Dictionary*, vol. 1, p. 228.
[13] Op. cit., p. 121.   [14] Op. cit., p. 272.   [15] Ibid., p. 233.

give to such an account of God (whatever other objections his analogical interpretation may be open to).

There is neither scope here, nor have I the philosophical competence, to judge between the substance of their two arguments. I want rather to raise the question of whether their style of reasoning is the most appropriate for a philosopher of religion to adopt. That would clearly be a crucial question for any Christian philosopher of religion who was not convinced that Swinburne's argument held. But quite apart from the outcome of any assessment of the actual conduct of the argument, there are reasons for questioning whether it does represent the form of argument appropriate to the nature of God, as Christians have understood it. In a generally appreciative review of Kenny's *Faith and Reason* Keith Ward argues that he ought to have devoted more attention to the fact 'that God has generally been regarded by classical Christian theologians as a unique kind of being, not just another member of a class of finite objects'.[16] Criticism along those lines seems to me to have force, though it clearly requires careful and detailed substantiation. For our present purpose I want to pursue the implications of the approach followed by Kenny and Swinburne, not so much for the philosopher of religion as for the theologian.

The metaphor with which Swinburne chooses to speak about the impact of analogy on reasoned argument is that of a card game. The appeal to analogy is 'a joker which it would be self-defeating to play more than two or three times in a game'.[17] As we have already seen, he believes the card does need to be played in speaking of God as personal. But the theologian has to speak of God as personal in very concrete ways most of the time. He speaks of a God who loves and saves, who becomes incarnate and makes atonement for human sins. Can he then do so in a way that is amenable to reason? One cannot have a game in which every card is a joker. The theologian is looking for a style of reasoning which can operate with a language about God in which the presence of analogy is not an occasional phenomenon but a fundamental characteristic. The way in which Kenny and Swinburne

[16] *Theology* 87 (Sept. 1984), p. 374.
[17] Op. cit., p. 272.

stress the conflict between analogical usage and reasoned argument does not encourage the theologian in that search. Yet Swinburne exhorts the theologian, and not merely the philosopher of religion, to adopt the way of 'clear and rigorous argument'. How then does he expect the theologian to follow his counsel?

Swinburne's answer emerges most clearly when he turns to more doctrinal concerns in the later sections of his *Faith and Reason*. The more specifically doctrinal work of Christian theology needs a quite different base. It needs 'God's announcement to man of things beyond his power to discover for himself',[18] which can be known to be 'true without qualification' or simply 'because of the prophet's authority'.[19] And for that authority to be known to be God's there must be 'some kind of miraculous signature symbolically affirming and forwarding the prophet's teaching and work'.[20] Paley is adjudged to have been right when he wrote: 'In what way can a revelation be made, but by miracles? In none which we are able to conceive.'[21] The understanding of faith which Kenny chooses to discuss in his *Faith and Reason* is remarkably similar. It is the belief in certain truths not ascertainable by human reason which God has revealed about himself to the human race.[22] His reason for concentrating attention on that understanding of faith is that 'it is the one which was most explicitly articulated to safeguard the concerns of reason'.[23] But since he declares himself to 'have rejected the classical definition of rationality',[24] ought he not also to be ready to abandon this classical conception of faith?

In my initial reference to Locke I spoke of his book as 'a vivid reminder of how different an approach is required of us'. Yet Swinburne in particular (for all his acknowledgement of the difference in detail required by advances in historical knowledge) seems to have led us back to something very like Locke's starting-point. But in leading us back there, he has

[18] R. Swinburne, *Faith and Reason*, p. 183.
[19] Ibid., p. 177.
[20] Ibid., p. 193.
[21] Ibid., p. 192.
[22] A. Kenny, *Faith and Reason*, p. 69.
[23] Ibid., p. 72.
[24] Ibid., p. 25.

not shaken my conviction that it is no longer a possible start-ing-point for us today. I do not see how any theologian who has given serious attention to the work done by biblical scho-lars could begin to pursue the work of Christian theology in the way that Swinburne proposes. Initial misgivings about the appropriateness of the style of reasoning in his own field of the philosophy of religion are reinforced by the conception of faith that appears to be its natural concomitant.

So my perplexity remains. One of the things which as a theologian I hope to gain from philosophers of religion is some guidance as to the appropriate form that reasoning should take in the work of theology. Yet the writings of many of the ablest and most distinguished scholars in that field do not seem to have much help to offer. Nevertheless, I still retain the conviction that there is a route to be found somewhere nearer to the middle of the stream, which combines a full recognition of the indirectness and logical oddity of our religious language with an equally strong insistence on the referential character and the truth claims of Christian discourse and also on the need for appropriate modes of reasoning about those claims. So it is incumbent on me to say something about how I think that path might be followed, even though it was my dissatis-faction with anything I found myself able to say on the subject that prompted my writing this paper in the first instance.

I am convinced that we do need to test our religious utter-ances for coherence and credibility, if we are not simply to be swept giddily on with van Buren along, or over, the edges of language. There is enough religious mystification and double-talk around for this to be a vital task. But I am equally convinced that because of the indirectness of our religious affirmations the task cannot be done as straightforwardly as some other writers suggest. How we are to proceed will depend on how we think our language about God arises. This is a vast and controversial topic in its own right, and all I can do in this context is to spell out briefly my own understanding of the matter and its implications for our present topic. Fundamentally I believe that our language about God is built up by a process of 'symbolization' or 'imaginative construction',[25]

[25] For a fuller discussion see my *Faith and the Mystery of God* (SCM, London, 1982), chap. 2.

that is to say that we take certain fundamental aspects of our human experience and extend them to their limits, in the conviction that that process will provide us with the least inadequate pointers to the nature of that ultimate reality, which is the source and goal of our existence. Thus the fact that we are dependent, not self-created, beings; that we are limited by death; that our knowledge is limited yet always capable of further developments; that we sense ourselves to be challenged to goodness and obligation from beyond ourselves—these things give rise to our speaking of God as creator, as immortal, as omniscient, as perfect. Reflection on this process may convince us that such a way of speaking is rationally defensible, while still leaving open the question of in what precise manner the language is to be understood. But for the Christian believer language about God does not arise simply in this abstract form. In Christian discourse it takes on a much more specific form on the basis of particular historical moments in the prophetic tradition of Israel, culminating in the coming of Jesus, at which such experiences have arisen in especially transparent and transformative ways. In particular such language has taken the form of stories concerning God's revelation in Christ—incarnational, adoptionist, etc.—and stories relating to atonement—a cosmic struggle with the powers of evil, meeting the demands of an immutable law, etc.

Of course, for us this language comes embodied in a well-established tradition. I am certainly not suggesting that each of us individually has consciously built up our forms of Christian speech in this way. But our traditional forms of Christian speech, though well-established, are not uniform or fixed. They come to us in diverse and fluctuating ways. And that is one important reason why it is not enough to regard doctrines as simply the rules of the grammar of faith. There is not just one homogeneous language of the Christian tradition. My reflection on the basic roots of such language was designed to help our consideration of how we ought to go about trying to sort out apparent confusion or conflict within the tradition which we have inherited. To ask what form of the tradition is most coherent is one important test, but it is not enough. Such a purely formal approach is in danger of losing contact with the root sources of our puzzling religious affirmations. So we need also from time to time to trace the language back to its experiential base, and ask again whether we have drawn upon that experience rightly and appropriately in our developed application of it to God. Something like this is recommended by Keith Ward in his book *The Concept of God*, which combines a concern with the ways in which faith in God has actually arisen and does arise together with a concern about the philosophical analysis of the concept of God, in a manner which is rarer than it ought to be in theological writing. He says:

It may be that the concepts which derive from diverse types of experience do not fall together to form one systematic and coherent whole. It may be even they seem contradictory—as with talk of Divine immutability and compassion for human suffering. But if one can show how one comes to talk of God in these ways for different purposes, the difficulties are mitigated.[26]

'Mitigated' is, I think, the right word; the difficulties certainly do not disappear. We ought not to glory in the paradox. We should go on seeking greater coherence in our language and understanding, but not at the cost of riding roughshod over some well-attested aspect of the experiences of the Christian community. We should always regard such paradoxes as provisional, even though they may in fact turn out to be permanent.

But what of the more elaborate story form of developed doctrines of Christology or atonement? Can a similar strategy help us to decide between competing accounts? It would be nice if we could appeal in a more or less direct way to what we sometimes call the 'logic' of the story. But as the gospel parables remind us, though the stories which we are led to tell about God may have their own logic, it is often very different from the logic of prior human expectation. In practice I think that we need to proceed in a way very similar to that which I am proposing for assessing the appropriateness of ascribing particular attributes to God. Despite the difference in the style of affirmation, the underlying issues in, for example, a consideration of the appropriateness of telling the atonement story in terms of God meeting the demands of a law of his own devis-

---

[26] K. Ward, *The Concept of God* (Basil Blackwell, Oxford, 1974), p. 156.

ing are very similar to those involved in the process alluded to by Ward of trying to determine the compatability of ascribing to God both compassion and immutability. Although such stories can never be simply replaced by an equivalent conceptual statement without loss, some approximate translation into conceptual terms is always possible. And both the story and the conceptual terms have roots in our human experience.

So I have no clear-cut recipe to offer of how we may give a reasonable account of faith in God and of Christian belief. Any claim of being able to offer an account of such a kind ought in any case always to be received with sceptical suspicion. As with moral reasoning, what is needed is not a clear process for settling all disputed issues—that is a will o' the wisp—but rather a recognized process of reasoning, even though many substantial differences of judgement may still remain unresolved in the process of applying it.[27] What I have tried to stress is the need for a continuous to and fro movement between the experiential and metaphorical roots of faith and its more direct expression in religious practice and worship on the one hand, and careful and critical reflection at the conceptual level on the other.[28] Neither the precise form of these two activities nor the exact balance between them can be spelled out in advance. Like most comparable skills it is an art that can be learned only by the doing of it. My impression, as this paper has indicated, is that many of our ablest writers attach themselves too exclusively to the one pole or the other. My conviction is that there is a navigable course in the middle of the stream, and my plea is that the imaginative and critical skills of all concerned with the study of religions should be appropriately conjoined in the never-ending search for it.

[27] Cf. W. B. Gallie, *Philosophy and the Historical Understanding* (Chatto and Windus, London, 1964), chaps. 8 and 9.

[28] For an excellent account of an approach to theological reasoning along these lines, see the work of Frank Burch Brown, in his article 'Transfiguration: Poetic Metaphor and Theological Reflection', *Journal of Religion* 62 (1982), pp. 39–56, and more fully in his book *Transfiguration* (University of North Carolina Press, Chapel Hill, 1983).

4

Mystery, Critical Consciousness, and Faith

GORDON D. KAUFMAN

In this paper, I propose an interpretation of religious symbolism and of its criticism. I have a double objective here: to present a conception of the important functions in human life performed by religious symbolism and by its continuing criticism, and simultaneously to show that this understanding is theologically sensitive and appropriate. Although this paper is written by one formed primarily by Western Christian traditions—and loyal to those traditions—it presents a view of religious symbolism which is intended to encourage openness to and appreciation of the great variety of religious traditions which have emerged in human history. It is my hope that these reflections will help in some degree to prepare for, and in that way promote, the newly emerging pluralistic religious consciousness, faith, and community, of which there are increasing signs today.

I

At its deepest level human life confronts us as Mystery. We do not know, and we can see no way in which we will ever be able to plumb, the ultimate meaning of human life—or whether there is such a thing as 'ultimate' meaning. We humans have many questions about ourselves and our world: are some forms or modes of life more 'authentically' human than others? What is a truly 'good' life, and how would one possibly know? Are there some identifiable central problems, or malformations, or diseases of human existence or the human spirit (sin) for which lasting solutions or cures (salvation) are available? Are some religious or philosophical or moral or scientific traditions of more value than others in addressing such matters, or are all in various ways both helpful and misleading, leaving us in a problematic relativism? Should the world, and human life within it, be understood most fundamentally with reference to 'God', to 'material energies', to 'Brahman', to 'life', to 'emptiness'? Or should we try to banish all such questions from our minds and live out our existence, so far as possible, simply in terms of the day to day questions and problems that confront us? This inscrutable Mystery—or these many mysteries—of life provide the ultimate context of our existence. Paradoxically, thus, it is in terms of that which is beyond our ken that we must, in the last analysis, understand ourselves.

From the very beginnings of human life on earth, as far as we can see, men and women have grappled with this problem, though doubtless not always in the self-conscious way we must face it today. As human language and consciousness slowly emerged in the course of evolution and early history, pictures or ideas of the world, and of the human place within the world, began to appear. The earliest versions of these conceptions of the human and its environment emerged in the form of stories and poems and songs, told and sung generation after generation. Important problems to be faced by men and women, and tasks to be performed, were portrayed in these imaginative pictures of human life, enabling humans to gain some idea of the world in which they lived and the powers or beings with which they had to come to terms.

Human life might be presented, for example, as a journey through hazardous territory where one was likely to encounter wild beasts and evil monsters as one sought to get to the safety of home; or it might be portrayed as participation in a great warfare between the forces of light and the forces of darkness. It might be depicted as responsible citizenship in a political order, the kingdom of God, or as but one stage in a never-ending transmigration from one form of life to another. And so on. In the course of history men and women have created many diverse world-pictures, many different conceptions of the place of human existence in the world, of the central human problems and the solutions to those problems. Every great civilization, indeed every isolated tribe, has worked out one or more such conceptual or imagistic ways of understanding and interpreting and orienting human life in face of the ultimate mystery of things; and humans have shaped and reshaped their lives and institutions, their values and practices, in accord with these diverse visions of reality and of the human. Out of primordial visions of this sort have grown the great religious traditions. In their attempt to come to grips with the problems of existence, men and women created and developed these symbolical frameworks and institutional structures, thus finding for and giving to human life the great variety of meanings it has come to have.

II

Understandings of the world, or world-pictures, of this kind provide communities and individuals with order and orientation in life, organizing and interpreting the range and variety of their experiences. No conceptual frame, however, fits all dimensions of experience perfectly, and in consequence there have always been persons like Job and Ecclesiastes, Camus and Sartre, who have cried out against the unintelligibility of what they were living through. Although conceptual and imagistic frames are created as humans attempt to make sense of the main features of the world and of human life, none are ever inclusive enough or detailed enough or profound enough to comprehend and to interpret every feature or dimension of life, anticipating all the novelties life can throw up. It is, after all, the ultimate mystery of things we are up against here. A certain amount of strain, then, inevitably pervades every frame of orientation, and sometimes, in moments or periods of serious crisis or great historical change, the strain may increase to the breaking point: then a new and profoundly different way of understanding the world may be required in order to make sense of things.

At such times the older, more traditional perspective may attempt to muster all its resources, so to speak, in order not to be destroyed. The traditional Christian understanding of life and the world has been involved in such a holding operation for at least the past two centuries.[1] Ever since the period of the

---

[1] It is not only 'religious' world-pictures that are involved in reactionary responses of this sort; for examples drawn from another cultural region—science—see Thomas

Enlightenment there has been strong resistance to the growing criticism of traditional Christian perspectives, and during the first half of the twentieth century a dramatic attempt was made (in so-called 'neo-orthodoxy') to maintain certain central traditional claims by relying completely on the sheer power of the major Christian symbols, whatever the problems raised by modernity. The Christian perspective's mightiest symbolic resource—and simultaneously its most problematic feature (at least for modernity)—is the structure of meaning held together and focused by the name 'God': God is understood to be the ultimate reality with which humans have to do, that than which nothing greater can be conceived, the ultimate point of reference in terms of which all else must be understood, the creator of the heavens and the earth. For those living and thinking within the Christian conceptual frame (as well as for many on the boundaries of Christian faith) God has been conceived of as an absolutely infallible authority. God's truth is perfect truth, and whatever God has revealed is unquestionably valid; since its falsity is inconceivable, it must be believed. Hence, if God has spoken, how can we lowly humans raise any questions, or why should we want to? Like Job, when the Lord speaks to him through the whirlwind, we must bow ourselves down and 'repent in dust and ashes' (42: 6). Even if we cannot understand some of the Christian claims about life and the world, even if they fail to make sense of important features of our experience, and our attempts to adhere to them seem in some respects destructive, these claims may seem persuasive simply because of the great authority behind them. Again, a very moving word from Job comes to mind: 'Though he slay me, yet will I trust in him' (13: 15 KJV). The authority and power and meaning of the symbol 'God' is so great for those caught up in the perspective of 'faith' that it can overcome almost every sort of incoherence, absurdity, or evil.

But it does so at the price of maintaining commitment on the basis of sheer belief, sheer acceptance of overwhelming *authority*, regardless of the highly problematic character, even the seeming absurdity, of such belief. In Protestant neo-

Kuhn, *The Structure of Scientific Revolutions* (University of Chicago Press, Chicago, 1962: rev. edn., 1970).

orthodoxy (as represented by Karl Barth, Rudolf Bultmann, and many others) it was openly asserted that there are no experiential grounds for faith, for acceptance of the Christian world-view; one is simply to *believe*.

The demand for an unqualified fideism of this sort is really a covert admission that the world-view in question has become humanly unintelligible; it no longer makes sense of our experience, evincing its credibility directly in and through its employment in our lives. Because of this failure its claims must increasingly be imposed heteronomously, on the basis of a heavy-handed invocation of God's authority, in the hope that this highest, most powerful symbol still has enough vitality and meaning to overcome the loss of relevance and effectiveness suffered by the conceptual frame. But this is a desperate move, one that cannot succeed for long. For no conceptual scheme can continue to be accepted or used if it fails to do the job for which it was created, that is, provide a framework for explaining and interpreting human life as it is actually lived here and now in this world.

In the period immediately before the full collapse of a frame of orientation, however, it may seem courageous and loyal to remain fiercely committed to it. Thus maintaining one's faith in God, one's commitment to the Christian conceptual scheme (despite all evidence to the contrary), may appear to be a glorious and courageous act in which the few loyal defenders of the faith stand fast against the renegades and deserters who have gone over to the enemy. In this frame of mind, the greater the seeming unintelligibility and absurdity of the faith, the more it may elicit a certain romantic fascination and thrill, along with a sense of virtue and courage as one leaps to its defence; thus a distinctive and powerful sense of meaningfulness in the midst of a world going to pieces may be felt in the hearts and souls of the faithful few—along with, all too often, a strong conviction of self-righteousness.

Twenty or thirty years ago one heard a great deal about accepting the 'paradoxes' of Christianity, about believing 'in virtue of the absurd', about glorying in the 'mysteries' of faith, and Tertullian and Kierkegaard were theological heroes. That mood seems to have passed now, although claims are still made, by both Catholic and Protestant theologians, that theological work must begin with faith, that it is essential to accept the Bible as God's revelation, that the church's fundamental affirmations must be regarded as authoritative for faith and life. All such authoritarian moves, we can now see in the light of the extremism of neo-orthodoxy, express not the vitality of faith but its breakdown. That is, they express the failure of the conceptual frame to make sense of experience, and thus the growing uselessness—and meaninglessness—of that frame, not its significance and truth. For this reason any heteronomous appeal to the authority of revelation in theology should be regarded as a warning flag: the conceptual frame is not working as well as it should, and it needs careful scrutiny and possibly drastic reconstruction. Here the Book of Job can be instructive in a somewhat different way from that suggested above. For this story is really about the breakdown of a traditional frame of orientation, a frame represented by Job's friends but one which Job himself refuses any longer to accept: it simply does not make sense of his experience. Job is the hero of this story not because of his faithfulness to traditional views, but precisely because he dares to question the way in which they interpret suffering and evil in human affairs, even hurling his doubts and objections into the face of God. (In the end, however, he is rewarded in a way designed to satisfy the most ardent defenders of the traditional understanding.)

My point is this: in a time when fundamental religious or theological claims are heavily questioned, when they seem dubious or unintelligible or even absurd, it is a mistake to invoke the *authority* of the major symbols of the tradition as the principal basis on which to do theology. This may appear to work for a while, but in the end it will only produce greater strains in the conceptual frame. Theological work grounded primarily on what is claimed to be 'revelation', thus, is not appropriate today. This is because the idea of revelation is itself a part of the very pattern of concepts and symbols which has become questionable, and it is this overall scheme, therefore, which now must be examined and reconstructed. Doubtless there are some to whom this questionableness is not apparent, or who choose to ignore it. There is certainly nothing wrong with that; people may do theology in whatever way they choose. But for those who find serious difficulties with the traditional Christian understanding of the world, such an approach will not be helpful.

Questions about the fundamental meaning and usefulness of the principal categories of a world-view do not arise when those categories are working properly, that is when they succeed in organizing experience and life into a relatively intelligible whole. At such times there is no need to question the basic metaphors, images, and concepts which constitute the understanding of life. For many persons today notions like 'experience', 'meaning', 'life', 'self', 'universe', 'time', 'nature', and the like all have this kind of more or less unquestioned status, and therefore we use these notions daily in organizing our 'lives' (*sic*) and our 'experience' (*sic*) and in interpreting these to 'ourselves' (*sic*). Certainly interesting and significant philosophical questions can be raised about all these terms: they are ambiguous in important respects, not clearly defined, possibly not entirely coherent, and their precise referents are hard to specify. Nevertheless, we constantly use (and presuppose) these and many others like them as fundamental reference points or anchors which organize and order the complex conceptual web within and by means of which we all do our thinking, understanding, and experiencing; and the conceptual scheme which they help to structure provides us with a world sufficiently intelligible to enable us to live and act and think with some effectiveness.[2]

---

[2] As Wittgenstein points out, if we did not trust the meanings of most of the terms of our common language, and did not trust our memories to make those meanings available to us, we could neither affirm nor doubt, neither think nor act. 'If I do a calculation I believe, without any doubts, that the figures on the paper aren't switching of their own accord, and I also trust my memory the whole time, and trust it without reservation . . . If I ask someone "what colour do you see at the moment?", in order, that is, to learn what colour is there at the moment, I cannot at the same time question whether the person I ask understands English, whether he wants to take me in, whether my own memory is not leaving me in the lurch as to the names of colours, and so on . . . We teach a child "that is your hand", not "that is perhaps [or probably] your hand". That is how a child learns the innumerable language-games that are concerned with his hand . . . The fact that I use the word "hand", and all the other words in my sentence without a second thought, indeed that I should stand before the abyss if I wanted to do so much as try doubting their meanings—shows that absence of doubt belongs to the essence of the language-game . . . I really want to say that a language-game is only possible if one trusts something (I did not say "can trust something").' *On Certainty*, ed. G. E. M. Anscombe and G. H. von Wright (Blackwell, Oxford, 1969), pp. 327, 345, 374, 370, 509.

If and when this world begins to crack apart, as may be happening today, we can go in either of two directions. We can insist that our most fundamental categories—what R. G. Collingwood called our 'absolute presuppositions[3]—in fact stand for and refer to *realities*, to things that are *really there*: 'Time is real; how else could one understand flow and change?' 'Each of us is an individual self; it is unthinkable that our "self-hood" might be just a cultural or linguistic construction.' 'The universe is the totality of everything that exists; what else could it be?' And so forth. Or else we can recognize that our human worlds are *constructed*—that humans have always constructed the world out of just such categories and concepts—and that when these no longer effectively give order to experience and thought, it is not the time to reify them by insisting on their 'objective reality'. Rather, it is a time for reshaping our categories and reconstructing our world. If and as our categorial scheme, our conception of the world, starts to work for us again, its reality and power and meaningfulness will once more seem obvious and no impassioned assertion or defence of it by true believers will be required.

To many it may seem difficult to believe that any conceptual scheme which is being deliberately criticized and reconstructed in the way I am suggesting here could continue to have experience-forming power, particularly for those engaged in the activities of criticism and construction. Indeed, it may be argued, to worship at the shrine of a God, the understanding of whom we ourselves have imaginatively constructed, is the crassest sort of idolatry. What is required now is the emphatic assertion that God *does* exist; Christ *is* God's only begotten son; the Bible *is* God's authoritative revelation; the church *is* God's institutional representative on earth— these all are 'objectively true', and it is the part of faith and of theology to 'believe' them and proclaim them to the world. But these are mistaken suppositions, based on a misunderstanding of the way in which our conceptual frames work. I would like to present two sorts of arguments on this point, one largely anthropological, the other more specifically theological.

---

[3] See *An Essay on Metaphysics* (Clarendon Press, Oxford, 1940).

III

First, the anthropological considerations. As we noted a moment ago, it is simply not true that concepts like 'experience', 'meaning', 'self', 'universe' lose their meaning (*sic!*) and cannot be used when they are recognized as purely human constructs with highly problematic features. All of us are aware that these concepts (along with all the others available to us) have been created by women and men seeking to understand and make sense of various dimensions of their lives. Moreover, although these particular concepts seem to us to designate 'realities' of some sort, we must admit they are realities which we never directly perceive: however important they may be as points of reference in terms of which we appropriate our existence and seek to understand it, they clearly do not refer to specific 'objects' somewhere out in the world. Many cultures, in fact, do not have these concepts at all; and the meanings which they hold for us today are distinctly modern ones, the historical development of which can be traced. Philosophers, poets, and others have long scrutinized these terms, criticizing them in various ways and reformulating them. In the future, doubtless, they will come to have meanings significantly different from those they now bear.

All of us are aware of these points, but they do not prevent us from using these concepts daily to make sense of our lives and to give order and structure to our world. We are quite capable, then, of living in a world even while it is being reconstructed, and of ourselves participating in the reshaping of our concepts and categories at the very moment we are using them to order our experience and give it meaning.

Experience is always in this way dialectically interconnected with our reflection on it. We take in the events of life and the objects of experience in terms of concepts and categories inherited from our culture, even while we participate in the remodelling and remaking of these very categories and concepts so they will better fit that experience, that is so they will enable us better to anticipate its diverse features, absorb their richness and fullness, and direct our activities in response to them. Some of us, of course, are much more sensitive than others to the lack of fit, to the confusions and distortions, of our symbols and concepts: these are the prophets poets, and philosophers calling us to re-examine ourselves, see things in new ways, direct our lives down different paths. Most of us simply live out of the conceptual frame inherited with our religion and culture, paying little attention to its peculiarities and problems until, perhaps, some tragic event occurs which wracks us with pain and suffering; or the slow monotonous running down of life at last confronts us with the meaninglessness of it all; or a hopeless dilemma in which we find ourselves leads us to break down in despair. Then we realize how desperately we need a new faith, a new frame of orientation, if we are to go on. Such a new frame of orientation is never simply spun out of thin air. It is always the product of rebuilding, transforming, reshaping the old categories—or those among them which still, to some extent, provide a way of grasping our situation—enabling them better to interpret life as we now experience it. This is a precarious and danger-ous project, repairing and rebuilding the very boat which keeps us afloat. But of course it is even more dangerous simply to sit complacently in that boat as it sinks, or to oppose or otherwise obstruct those seeking to rebuild it. If it has ven-tured into waters which it cannot manage, something must be done.

To understand better how such reconstruction is possible, let us distinguish three significantly different moments in the human consciousness or awareness of meaning. First, there is the *moment of naïve awareness* in which meaning seems to be simply there, something directly given and to be accepted. In this moment of consciousness our speech about, for example, the value and significance of God and Christ—or of democ-racy, justice, truth, our nation, etc.—is taken to refer to objec-tively given realities, realities in terms of which life must be ordered. In virtually all our unreflective use of such concepts as these, their meaning impinges on us in this 'objective' way. It is hardly surprising, then, that in cultures that are largely tradition-bound, as well as with more or less unreflective indi-viduals in all cultures, the objectivity of the (network of) meanings within which life is carried on is largely taken for granted.

Human consciousness, however, is capable of transcending in some degree the meanings within which it lives and of subjecting them to criticism and creative transformation. We must, then, secondly, take note of the *critical moment* in consciousness in which our concepts and categories seem in some ways questionable and problematic. Sometimes this critical moment becomes sufficiently widespread and powerful to call into question large complexes of cultural meaning, as with the sophists (and Socrates) in ancient Greece, or in some segments of modern culture since the Enlightenment. It then becomes apparent that, far from being simple representations of 'objective realities' with which humans must come to terms, these structures of meaning are humanly created cultural artefacts which have grown up in a history and which can be transformed in further history. This conception of meaning has been worked out systematically in modern times by Feuerbach, Marx, Nietzsche, James, Freud, Dewey, Foucault, Derrida, and others, and it has become very influential in the contemporary intellectual world. In many ways it has been destructive of the power of major symbols which for generations have provided significant orientation in the West. Since those symbols, instead of presenting 'objective realities' with which humans must come to terms, were now seen to be simply human creations—perhaps even corrupt and destructive ones—one could take them or leave them as one chose; and one would probably be the wiser to leave them behind.

It is important to recognize that human beings are not able to live entirely and exclusively in this critical moment of consciousness. Without some accepted conception of the world and of the human place within the world—a symbolic frame of meaning for the orientation of life—we can neither think nor act. After critical consciousness appears on the scene with its destructive questions, therefore, it is necessary to make some response. Two distinctly different moves can be made: (a) One may confine critical scrutiny and questioning to certain specific domains of meaning—such as traditional religious symbols—while actually orienting one's life by other meaning-complexes (a Marxist conceptual frame, a Freudian one, a positivist one) which are left uncriticized and which are, thus, taken (more or less naïvely) to present the actual 'realities' with which humans must come to terms; thus the moment of naïve awareness of meaning returns in full force, but now with respect to a somewhat different symbolic scheme. Or (b) one can move into and live out of a third stance, one rooted in what we shall call the *reflective* moment of consciousness. This moment includes awareness both that symbolic meaning is indispensable to human life and that every actual structure of meaning is humanly created and must be subjected regularly to scrutiny and criticism.

When abstractly formulated in this way, this moment may seem possible only for certain intellectual elites; but that is a misunderstanding. The reflective moment of consciousness is as much a function of the dialectical structure of certain idealizing symbols as it is of the degree of sophistication possessed by some groups or individuals.

It may be quite widely recognized within a society, for example, that symbols like 'justice' or 'truth' or 'God'—which have fundamental orienting significance within that society—escape every attempt to grasp or understand their full meaning: no articulation of them, no practice or institution developed in connection with them, can be regarded as adequate, and each must be continually revised, reformulated, reconstructed in light of the (never fully realized) ideal which the symbol suggests. Symbols of this sort, it could be said, manifest a continual strain toward self-transcendence—a feature of great importance to human life, since it keeps these symbols (and lives oriented by them) open to new experience and to unanticipated possibilities. Such symbols present themselves as having power to draw us beyond our present selves, to bring us to a deeper understanding or humaneness and thus a more profound self-realization; this is part of their great attractiveness to human beings. It is important to note that the values and meanings to which symbols of this sort call us continue to shine through them even when we are aware that every version of them is limited and inadequate: who does not feel real force in cries for *justice* or demands for *truth*, however problematical each of these notions may seem? Such idealizing symbols can manifest their power to a critical consciousness quite as well as to a more naïve mentality, and they often provide the basis for criticism of traditional practices and institutions.

This third reflective moment of consciousness, thus, though aware that any particular meanings are always human constructions, is also aware of the importance of such symbolic meaning both for drawing humans forward and for constraining them; in short, for orienting human life. It is this, I suspect, that Paul Ricoeur is trying to articulate with his notion of a 'second naïvete' within which life today must be carried on.[4] But that expression is misleading, because this reflective moment is anything but naïve: it is a consciousness even more critical, in certain respects, than moment two, which may nihilistically—and naïvely—suppose that humans can live without significant commitment and value and meaning.

We have been trying to understand how human life can go on in face of the profound mystery within which it finds itself: I have argued that it is through the creation of symbolic meaning, symbolic frames of orientation, that humans address this issue. But our structures of meaning may function in quite diverse ways with respect to this ultimate mystery. In what I have called the moment of 'naïve awareness' of meaning, the ultimate mystery of things becomes obscured, or even tends to dissolve away, since the meanings carried in tradition are taken to represent 'objective reality'; thus, we *know* how things ultimately are. Every fundamentalism, religious or secular, lives out of this kind of naïve certainty. In contrast to this self-assurance, the second or 'critical' moment of consciousness arises out of a renewed awareness of the pervasiveness and inscrutability of mystery. Hence in its criticism it calls into question the structures of meaning to which people are committed, and in so doing it easily becomes either a new dogmatism or else nihilistic. We should note, now, that although both these moments of consciousness express certain definite faith-commitments, neither is grounded in a *deliberate* or *self-conscious* faith, for both know too much: the moment of naïvety supposes itself to know how things really are; the moment of criticism knows that we can never know this.

In contrast, the third or reflective moment of consciousness is connected with a radical kind of self-conscious faith. For it involves commitment both to the meaning of our most profound orienting symbols as well as to the meaningfulness of

[4] *The Symbolism of Evil* (Harper and Row, New York), pp. 350 ff.

our activities of criticizing and reconstructing those same symbols in full awareness of the ultimate mystery of life: in a reflective consciousness of this sort we live out of a trust which enables us to continue acting creatively and constructively even though we do not know with finality who we are or where we are going. With such a faith, such a consciousness of the profound mystery of life combined with confidence in the possibility of living creatively within that mystery, life can go on, however problematic our particular conceptual frame may have become. Thus it becomes possible to engage in criticism and reconstruction of our conceptual schemes, even while we are living and thinking within them.

IV

Our argument has begun to move us beyond general anthropological considerations (about the role of conceptual frameworks in human life and how they change) to more specifically theological concerns about the grounding of human life in faith. Let me, then, conclude these reflections by considering in more explicitly theological terms the central issue with which we are here concerned, the fact that our lives unfold within a context of ultimate mystery which makes questionable all our symbols and ideas.

In Western religious traditions the mystery of and behind human existence is usually identified as God, and in affirmations that God is 'infinite' or 'absolute', 'transcendent' or 'incomparable', believers have reminded themselves that this one whom they worship must be understood ultimately to be a mystery. This is a highly dialectical point, and it has important implications for our understanding of theology: it implies, for example, that we should acknowledge that all our theological ideas and images are, as I like to say, human imaginative constructs.[5] Let me explain this point.

On the one hand, the image/concept 'God' is intended to symbolize that—whatever it might be—which brings true human fulfilment; that is, in speaking of 'God' we are seeking to attend to the mystery in its aspect as source and ground of

---

[5] For further elaboration of this claim about the 'imaginative' and 'constructive' character of theological work, see my *Essay on Theological Method* (Scholars Press, Chico, Calif., 1975; rev. edn., 1979); and *The Theological Imagination* (Westminster Press, Philadelphia, 1981), esp. chaps. 1, 9 and 10.

our being and our salvation, as that on which, therefore, we can rely absolutely. But, on the other hand, as genuine mystery, God is taken to be beyond our knowledge and understanding. This implies and requires an acknowledgement of our *unknowing* with respect to God, an acknowledgement, that is to say, that we do not know how the images and metaphors in terms of which we conceive God apply, since they are always our own metaphors and images, infected with our limitations, interests, and biases. (For just this reason we dare not claim that they have been directly revealed by God.) It is only in and with such acknowledgment that the symbol 'God' can turn us—by indirection—toward that which, as the ultimate source and context of our humanity, completely transcends us, our ideas, and our control. Thus, precisely in and through our recognition that all our theological concepts, symbols, and methods are our own imaginative constructs, are we enabled to acknowledge God as *God*.

The difficult dialectic on which we are here attempting to focus is not merely of intellectual interest: it is an expression of something which has always been regarded as central to religious piety, namely repentance. Repentance is certainly a human act (or attitude), but it has the peculiar dialectical character of being an act of giving up, an act of renouncing our own claims. This must include, I want to emphasize now, our claims to knowledge and certainty. If we try to overcome and control the mystery within which we live, for example through our theological ideas or our religious practices, we sin against God, for we are trying to make ourselves the ultimate disposers of our lives and destiny. We must, then, repent: we must turn around from this posture, which we all too easily take up, and move toward a recognition that our destiny is ultimately in God's hands not ours, that is that it remains a mystery to us. Repentance for this order of sin is very difficult for us, perhaps impossible when we are hardened in our ways. It is, doubtless, only as we actually fail to accomplish our purposes—for example, our religious or theological purpose to 'know God'—only as we are broken in our attempts to achieve, that 'grace' breaks through the mystery that establishes and sustains us, creating in us the new modality of existence which is faith. Piety of the sort we are discussing here may or may not involve verbal prayer: to insist that it must would presuppose we know more about God than we possibly can. But prayer in the sense of expressing ourselves, of coming to full consciousness and intention, of giving ourselves over to that beyond the human which constitutes us as human, is certainly central.

With this emphasis on our faith in and dependence on what is ultimately mystery, I do not mean to suggest that we do not in many ways continue to create and sustain ourselves; we certainly do this, especially in and through our religious activity, including our theological reflection. My contention that our religious symbolism is our own construction is intended to emphasize just this point. But simultaneously (as I have just tried to show) this emphasis deepens our consciousness of the inscrutable mystery within which we live and which gives us our being as human. The forthright recognition that our theology is our own work, our own doing, can thus open us to what has traditionally been called God's grace and mercy. That is, by clearly indicating what is our own activity it indirectly opens us to that beyond the human sphere of knowledge and control, that which, ultimately, constitutes us as human and which (we may hope and believe) will further our humanization.

To the extent that Christians have insisted that certain formulas and practices known in the church are alone saving for humans, they have expressed, unfortunately, a piety of law not gospel: the dialectic in the concept of God seems to require an agnosticism, not a dogmatism, with regard to all such matters. Not a cynical agnosticism, of course, that is destructive of everything that humans believe in and need, but that agnosticism which indirectly opens us to what is beyond our world, to that which we do not yet know but which will be creative of our future. Faith is the 'letting go' (Kierkegaard) of all attachments including specifically and especially our religious and theological attachments, because it is just these idolatries which shield us from—and thus close us off from—that ultimate mystery in which both our being and our fulfilment are grounded.

The contention that our theology is always our own construction reminds us that there is a sphere which we humans can (and should) control, and that our theological work takes place within that sphere. But just this recognition raises indirectly the question about that which we do *not* control, that which we do not and cannot consciously or deliberately construct, the ultimate mystery which we (in faith) call 'God'. Traditional theology sought to express the insight that we are beyond our proper powers when attempting to speak of God by maintaining that biblical and traditional symbols, said to be 'God's revelation', must be held inviolable to our criticism and reconstruction. But that was a wooden and misleading way of making the point; it was subject to demonic uses and it led to a heteronomy of religious tradition. The dialectic at stake here is expressed more adequately in the understanding that all theology (including that in the Bible) is human imaginative construction. This conception straightforwardly expresses the religious awareness that gives rise to theological reflection: everything is ultimately in God's hands, is mystery—and just for this reason every expression of faith (including this one), being our own human construction, must be questioned and criticized.[6]

---

[6] Anyone familiar with Karl Barth's commentary on *The Epistle to the Romans* (Oxford University Press, London, 1933) will recognize how heavily I am indebted to him for essential elements of my reflection here. I hope, however, that I have succeeded in avoiding the serious dialectical errors into which Barth fell (as it seems to me) in much of his all too definite and confident talk about the 'wholly other' and about Jesus Christ, revelation, and salvation.

5

Reason Restored

J. R. LUCAS

Hume rubbished reason. Kant's critique did little to restore its standing in the eyes of philosophers, and in the subsequent two centuries academics and intellectuals of all sorts have had only a fragile faith in the power of reason to guide them into all truth, and many truths, especially those of religion and morality, have been relegated to the realm of feeling or fiat. Only the natural sciences have been exempt. No failure of noetical nerve has prevented the scientists from speculating, conjecturing, and theorizing about the nature of things, and from advancing the boundaries of human knowledge with no more than a polite nod in the direction of philosophers' fears that they might be outrunning the powers of reason and over-reaching the bounds of possible experience. Scientists are sure of the cognitive standing of their subjects, but other thinkers, and especially philosophers of religion, have been unmanned by doubts whether they are engaged in a rational activity at all, or whether they are just expressing their emotional preferences or merely avowing an arbitrary leap of faith.

The consequences for the philosophy of religion have been disastrous. It has been fighting a war on two fronts, and losing it on both. On the philosophical front natural theology has been unable to resist the corrosive acids of Hume's scepticism, and against the claim made by some scientists that science has shown that no theistic world-view is tenable, it has been unable to counter the confident dogmatism of the atheists by bringing to bear against them the doubts the philosophical sceptics have raised against theology. Yet at least one of these counters must be possible. If science is possible, Hume must be wrong. And if it is reasonable to enquire into the rationality of religion, it must be reasonable also to enquire into the rationality of science, and to conclude that the findings of science are not unquestionably the only ones worthy of credence by a rational man.

Hume attacks reason on many grounds. He attacks inductive reasoning on the grounds of its not being deductive, reasoning to unobserved entities on the grounds that it is neither deductive nor inductive, moral reasoning on the grounds that it transcends moods. Each form of reasoning is faulted for being something else. It is an expedient often made use of by modern reviewers.

It is pertinent to point out what the sceptical strategy amounts to, and it may lead us to doubt its cogency. Once we recognize that there are many different forms of reasoning, and many different types of cogent argument, we shall turn a less than sympathetic ear to the sceptic who complains that moral, or philosophical, or theological, or metaphysical argument is not some other form of argument. Instead of lamenting that metaphysics is not mathematics, we may be led to reflect on the nature of metaphysical argument and develop criteria for distinguishing good arguments from bad. Basil Mitchell often does this, especially in *The Justification of Religious Belief*, and points to the parallel between the arguments of the theologians and those of the lawyer or the literary critic. But although a detailed exegesis of theological reasoning is of great value, it is not a conclusive defence and will not convince the sceptic. It is like the philosophy of history. Much insight has been gained by the careful philosophical exposition of the ways in which historians reason and the aims they hope to achieve, but Henry Ford is unimpressed, and still maintains that history is bunk. In the same way, many post-Humean sceptics are not interested in how theologians reason, holding that any argument which fails to conform to their canons of reasoning is simply invalid and unworthy of credence. Against such a claim it is not enough to maintain, as Strawson and Wittgenstein have done, that since we do, as a matter of fact, reason in certain ways, these ways constitute the standards of what should count as good reasons. That would be to make reason immune to rational scrutiny. And while the presumption that any form of reasoning widely practised must be cogent is strong, it is not incontrovertible. After all, astrology is much practised.

The most telling objection against the sceptics's claims is that they cannot be argued for without thereby showing them false. For arguments are normative. A valid argument indicates what must be acknowledged, if the premises be granted. If the only derivations are deductions, and we cannot deduce an 'ought' from an 'is', then clearly no conclusion can be adequately grounded about what sorts of argument we ought to be guided by. If, however, inductive as well as deductive arguments are admitted, then it might seem possible to make an inductive inference that all patterns of reasoning which were actually valid conformed to the canons of deductive or inductive argument. But before drawing such an inference, we should have to examine putatively valid inferences, and discover that only deductive and inductive inferences were actually valid. And this we could not do without some other test for validity. We cannot appeal to an inductive inference to give us a generalization which we shall then use to rule out possible counter-examples as not being inferences at all. If I am drawing merely inductive inferences about patterns of argument, then I must examine *all* patterns of argument, and I shall find that there are many arguments we use—moral arguments, political arguments, philosophical arguments, and historical arguments—which do not fit Hume's formula. Indeed, they are counter-examples to Hume's thesis. And, therefore, Hume's thesis cannot be established as a valid generalization about patterns of valid arguments by inductive argument alone.

The sceptic's position cannot be coherently argued for, but could conceivably be true. Sextus Empiricus and Wittgenstein likened the sceptical argument to a ladder one could climb up but must then jettison. Although the sceptic himself cannot argue that we ought to be guided only by arguments conforming to his criteria, he may nudge us into adopting that position, and if once we have adopted it, or even reckon that at least it is a tenable position, then we shall be hard put to it to see how, if we were to adopt it, we could be led to abandon it. And, of course, we cannot be forced to do so. By limiting the types of reasoning recognized to be cogent, the sceptic limits also the range of arguments which can be brought against him. In particular, if only deductive arguments are allowed as cogent, no position can be shown to be untenable unless it is actually self-contradictory. The sceptic's position can thus be made secure—but unappealingly vacuous. If the only cogent arguments are deductive arguments, then very few arguments are available either against or for any philosophical position. Any substantial thesis is one which makes some claim, and which can therefore be denied without self-contradiction. So, in the absence of some self-evident principle which can serve as an indisputable premiss, no substantial philosophical thesis can be refuted or established by argument. Argument, on the sceptic's view, becomes irrelevant to philosophy. The sceptic cannot be argued out of his position; but equally nobody else can. Hume's disciple is impregnable in his unbelief; but so too is Plantinga in his belief. Once he has shown that there is no inconsistency in Christian theism, the believer has done all he need, or can, do. Any position that can be stated without self-contradiction is tenable, and reason, if it is confined to deductive reason, is powerless to decide between differing positions. If the sceptical thesis be true, not only is there no reason why we should adopt it, but there is no reason why we should not adopt any other position that tickles our fancy.

The claim that only deductive arguments are valid has drawn much strength from the example of mathematics. Mathematics has been taken as a paradigm of rigorous reasoning. Only if we argue *more geometrico* can we be sure that we are reasoning properly. But the absolute clarity of mathematical argument has become cloudy in the course of this century. A divergence has appeared between a formal definition of deduction in terms of axioms and rules of inference, and an incompletely formalizable notion of deduction in terms of models and intended interpretations. We can capture the spirit of the former in what has come to be known as First-order Logic (or to be more precise, First-order Predicate Calculus with Identity). First-order Logic behaves itself. Theorems can be proved, *more geometrico*, and each theorem is true under every interpretation of the calculus in which the logical constants have their usual sense; moreover, each formula which is true under every such interpretation is a theorem and can be proved. That is to say First-order Logic is not only sound, but complete. It captures all, and only, those inferences that a computer could be programmed to carry out. But it is not adequate for mathematics. For that, we must either use Higher-order Logic, as Frege did, or adjoin to First-order Logic some extra postulates, for example Peano's five postulates for Elementary Number Theory or Zermeloz's and Frankel's axioms for Set Theory. In either of the latter cases the resulting system is incomplete. There are some formulae which are true under the intended interpretations but which cannot be proved and are not theorems. A comparable result ensues if we follow Frege, and ground mathematics in Higher-order Logic. In that case we do not have to adjoin extra postulates, and we escape certain other infelicities of First-order Logic, but find that our Higher-order Logic is not completely axiomatizable: we cannot formulate a set of axioms and rules of inference which will be sufficient to prove all and only those formulae that are true under the intended interpretations of the system. Either the axiomization will not be sound—we shall be able to prove as theorems formulae which are not true under all intended interpretations—or it will not be complete—some formulae which are true cannot be proved as theorems in that axiomatization. It is reasonable to discern in the history of mathematics a succession of principles being recognized as true although not deducible from hitherto established axioms: for example, the principle of mathematical induction, the axiom of choice, the continuum hypothesis, the generalized continuum hypothesis. How exactly we recognize these as true is a matter of great dispute. Gödel himself was a Platonist, but few mathematicians are happy with Plato's perceptual metaphor. It is, perhaps, better to say that we establish them by reason, but if so not by a formal proof-sequence. Either we give a formalist account of deductive argument in terms of formal rules of inference finitely formulated and unambiguously applied, in which case mathematics is not entirely deductive, or mathematics is a deductive discipline, but deduction is not finitely axiomatizable. If the sceptic takes the former course, he is not letting himself in for much in allowing deductive inference as a cogent form of argument, but he is obliged to be sceptical about even the widely accepted propositions of mathematics. If the sceptic takes the latter course he can avoid having to profess unconvincing doubts about mathematic truths, but he is no longer able to be confident that he has not landed himself with more than he bargained for.

Few sceptics confine themselves rigorously to deductive argument alone. Most, including Hume in some of his moods, acknowledge inductive inference too. But it is unclear what the bounds of inductive reasoning are. If all the swans I have ever seen or heard about are white, it is plausible to infer that the next swan I see will be white too. This is a paradigm minimal inductive inference, which Hume tried to explain in terms of a conditioned reflex, and many philosophers would allow as valid. But if it is in these circumstances rational to conclude that the next swan I see will be white, it is rational also to conclude that the next one after that will be white, and the next again, and so by similar reasoning that every swan is white. The latter proposition, however, is of a different logical form, and instead of arguing from particular propositions to particular propositions we are arguing from particular to general. Such arguments are commonly accepted as inductive, but they are of a significantly different form. 'The next swan is white' is not only a particular proposition, but a tensed one. 'Every swan is white', or, equivalently, 'All swans are white', is not only general, but tenseless; we can infer from 'Every swan is white' and 'Leda was a swan' the conclusion that 'Leda was white'. Such an inference would not be valid if the 'is' of the first premiss were a present-tense 'is'. It is, rather, an omnitemporal use of the verb 'to be' which is put into the present for lack of a better tense to put it into. Such a use of the present tense is sometimes indicated, following a suggestion of J. J. C. Smart, by italics. So we write 'Every swan *is* white' or 'All swans *are* white' to indicate that the grammatically present tense is being used in a logically tenseless way. Such a use is entirely unobjectionable. But it heightens the profile of induction. Induction does not merely argue from particular to particular in the ordinary tensed indicative mood to general in a different, tenseless mood. The mood is clearly different, not only because it does not conjugate like the ordinary indicative mood, but because it yields counterfactual propositions, such as 'If Zoe were a swan, she would be white', which the ordinary indicative mood does not. It then becomes difficult to disallow, as also a species of inductive inference, arguments from actual instances to natural laws and from observed phenomena to unobserved entities. We argue from the regular whiteness of swans to a rule that they must be white, and from white appearances to a genetic make-up that accounts for them. Such inferences, although rejected by Hume, have commended themselves to scientists ever since. We seek generality, integration, unification, and explanation in our account of the world, and it seems reasonable so to seek. Although quarks, psi-functions, and wavicles all transcend the bounds of possible experience, we form some sort of concept of them, and succeed in saying things about them which can be significantly affirmed or denied. Nobody makes out that Special Relativity, General Relativity, and Quantum Mechanics are plain sailing. They are difficult, and it is easy to be confused and talk nonsense about them. But it does not follow that rational argument about science is impossible, or that reason must acknowledge that such knowledge is too high for it, and it cannot attain unto it. The arguments Hume put forward for ruling out altogether knowledge of unobserved entities or explanations of the universe as a whole, would, if they were cogent, rule out all sub-atomic physics and cosmology. But, while many thinkers fear—or hope—that they are cogent when deployed against natural theology, few seriously suppose they cast any aspersions on the reputability of modern science.

The transition from minimal inductive inference to more general and generous types of inductive inferences may be resisted. It would be reasonable to reckon that the next lottery ticket I encounter, and indeed any particular lottery ticket I consider, will fail to win a prize, and yet it would be false to conclude that every lottery ticket will. The next raven I meet will be black, and likewise the next after that, and the next, and the next, but no biologist familiar with the phenomenon of albinism would dare claim that all ravens are black; and if there can be albino ravens, it would be prudent to reckon with the possibility of non-albino swans. Hydrogen atoms with atomic number 1 (i.e. protium atoms) have been observed to be very stable, and it would be foolish to take at all seriously the possibility that the next, or that any particular one will decay spontaneously: but shall we then conclude that none ever will? That would be foolhardy indeed. A general proposition, beginning with the words 'All' or 'None', extends far, far further than any particular proposition does, and is therefore exposed to a far greater risk of being falsified, so that a canny man should play cautious, and refuse to move from the relatively safe ground of particular predictions to the much more dangerous terrain of generalization.

But it is difficult to be consistently cautious. The very examples cited depend for their plausibility on the prior acceptance of the calculus of probabilities and the general canons of inductive inference. Granted these, we can construct counter-examples to the generalizing policy, just as Bertrand Russell did with the Michaelmas goose. An inductive inference always can—in the deductive logical sense of 'can'—prove mistaken, and once the principle of inductive reasoning is established, we develop much more subtle rules of application: and then it will be possible to devise special cases in which, granted some generalizations already accepted, the rationality of the one inference would not establish the rationality of the other. But we are concerned only with scepticism about principles, and if we can in principle always argue to any particular swan's being white we can in principle argue also to every swan's being white. For no counter-example is possible, granted the validity of minimal inductive inference. If it were not the case that every swan was white, then there would be some swan which was not white. And yet for this swan the minimal inductive inference applies, and shows that it is white. And hence the argument from Any to All holds, and the minimal inductivist is led to allow, as also valid, inductive generalization.

Some residual discomforts remain. They are due in part to an unclarity about the nature of inductive inference and the ways it can be justified, as well as to a special, logician's reluctance to concede the validity of the inference from Any to All. Some justifications of induction have been in terms of Confirmation Theory, and we often say that inductive inferences are 'merely probable' to distinguish them from deductive ones. And then, if there is a finite probability of any particular instance of a propositional function being false, the probability of their all being true is small indeed. But Confirmation Theory is not the only way of justifying induction, and it is in fact dubiously applicable to most inductive inferences, and the sense in which it is only probable and not absolutely certain that the sun will rise tomorrow is very different from that used in the calculus of probabilities. Moreover, even in the natural sciences, our generalizations are not quite as hard as logicians make out, and can tolerate the occasional anomaly or 'sport'. In human affairs we are very ready to say, with Aristotle, that generalizations hold only for the most part, only ὡς ἐπὶ τὸ πολύ (*hos epi to polu*), and the sciences are much more exacting than that. But they are not absolutely exact, and the occasional monstrous birth, and even the one-off spontaneous disintegration of an atom of protium, would not actually falsify a sufficiently well-confirmed generalization.

The sceptic who allows minimal inductive inferences but balks at inductive generalisations is difficult to argue with because we often justify minimal inductive inferences by appeal to some principle of generalization, some law of the uniformity of nature, rather than vice versa. We are inclined to say to him 'You cannot justify minimal inductive inferences unless you have already accepted inductive generalization', but although many justifications of minimal inductive inference presuppose the validity of inductive generalization, it is not true that all do. And in any case the sceptic may refuse to justify, and simply say, like Hume, that minimal inductive inference is a habit he has happened to form, and he sees no need either to justify it or to extend it.

Some such line can be held—just—but is, once again, unappealing. The argument from Any to All can be resisted without full-blooded inconsistency. I can, in some systems of formal logic, prove that for each number a property can hold of it, and yet prove also that it does not hold for all. Such systems are not full-bloodedly inconsistent, but, rather, ω-inconsistent. And formal systems can likewise be ω-incomplete. But these are defects of particular formal systems, not merits in a serious logician seriously concerned to know the truth. A sceptic who did not mind being convicted of something like ω-inconsistency or ω-incompleteness could not be proved to be inconsistent or inadequate in any more straightforward sense. But the onus is on him to show why the bounds of reason should be drawn at just this implausible place, rather than on us to show that they cannot be. After all,

we do naturally and normally accept inductive generalizations. Once it is no longer maintained that no non-deductive
argument can be valid and it is allowed that some sort of
inductive arguments—minimal inductive inferences—are
valid, then some reason is required to justify the claim that
these alone among inductive arguments, and no others, are
valid. And no such reason is forthcoming.

Once it is recognized that inductive inferences can lead
from a tensed 'was' to a tenseless 'is' or 'be', it becomes hard
to maintain as a matter of logical principle that we cannot
derive an 'ought' from an 'is'. We may not be able to *deduce* an
'ought' from an 'is'—any more than we can deduce a 'will be'
from a 'was'—if we take care to define our 'ought's and 'is's
carefully enough. But it is a very evident fact that we do argue
about morals, and pass judgement on what we ought to do
and ought to have done. To claim that we cannot do, or cannot properly do, what we do do needs arguing for. And, as we
have seen, such arguments cannot be available, in as much as
they would have to be based on some sort of 'is'—facts
(perhaps metaphysical facts)—and would lead to some sort of
'oughts'—values, norms, precepts (perhaps logical 'oughts' or
logical 'ought nots').

Moral arguments in particular and practical arguments in
general differ from deductive and inductive arguments in that
they have much weaker canons of relevance. Questions about
mathematics and natural science are 'academic'. They do not
have to be decided. If we cannot produce a cogent deductive
or inductive argument, we suspend judgement. We do not
have to decide whether Goldbach's conjecture is true, or
whether Quantum Mechanics is complete. Much as we may
want to know the answers to these questions, if we cannot
obtain one according to the relevant criteria, we may simply
have to say that we do not know. We can afford to be choosy
about what counts as a mathematical or scientific argument
because we always have the option of not reaching a conclusion. It is otherwise in practical life. Decisions have to be
taken. Not to decide is in effect to take a particular decision.
The option of suspending judgement is not open. Our information may be imperfect, our reasoning ill-considered, but we
must do the best we can in the time available and in the light

of what we know at the time. Practical reasoning is thus messy, and especially moral reasoning, which has a certain ultimacy about it that precludes complications being ruled out by custom, convention, or fiat. The messiness of practical reason shows up especially in the two-sidedness of the arguments, some being for and others against a particular decision. Two-sidedness is not peculiar to practical reasoning. It is vestigially present in inductive argument—no matter how many white swans I have seen, if I have seen a black one, that constitutes a decisive argument against the claim that all swans are white. It is none the less in practical argument that two-sidedness is dominant. Almost all practical arguments have two sides, and we have to weigh them and strike a balance between them. Our decision will depend not only on the strength of the arguments on one side, but on the weakness of those on the other. Many arguments are cogent in the absence of counter-considerations, and we often state them explicitly with this proviso, 'other things being equal', *ceteris paribus*, 'in the absence of special circumstances', 'as a general rule', 'ὡς ἐπὶ τὸ πολύ (*hos epi to polu*). The logic of practical reasoning is not one of incontrovertible proof-sequences but of prima-facie arguments and counter-arguments, of rebuttals and objections, of exceptional circumstances and special cases; and the fundamental connective is not 'therefore' but 'but'.

The two-sidedness of practical reasoning not only imposes a dialectical structure on our deliberations but gives a key to our knowledge of other minds and our understanding of the humanities. Besides making up my mind about what I shall do, I can consider what I should do if circumstances were different; and although in the present circumstances I must override and reject some considerations in accepting and acting on others, I can fully appreciate how I might in other circumstances act on them, and so I can appreciate also how you in your circumstances might act on them. Because I know what I shall do in the actual situation, I can know what I should do in hypothetical situations, and so understand what I might do if I were you. Empathy is possible because I experience in my own deliberation the conflict of argument and feel the force of factors inclining me to act in various ways.

I never have murdered any of my colleagues or pupils: fortunately the sixth commandment has always retained sufficient
sanctity in my eyes to restrain me; but I have been tempted,
and so can understand the minds of those who have found the
temptation irresistible. Equally I can enter into the minds of
historical agents or those portrayed in literature, and although
sometimes their reasoning and reactions will be entirely
opaque to me, often there will be enough resemblance between their situation and my actual or possible deliberations
for their response to be one of which I can see the rationality. I
do not have to suppose, counterfactually and sometimes
implausibly, that I *would* in the event respond in the same
way, but only that I *might*—only that there would be *some*
reasons for so acting, in the absence of weightier considerations against. And that supposition is one that is much easier
to make. I can understand what makes other people tick
because of the many-sidedness of what goes on in making up
my own mind. The messiness of practical reasoning, and the
many decisions it partially leads me to take, gives me a width
of understanding I could never otherwise obtain, and a partial
entrée into the minds of all sorts and conditions of men far
beyond my actual ken.

Theological reasoning, as Mitchell has persuasively argued,
has the two-sided structure typical of practical reasoning in
the humanities. That is only to be expected. For one thing, it
carries moral consequences. If God exists, it matters what we
do, and if God is a God of Love, our response should be a
response of love too. And, secondly, if theism is true, the fundamental category of the universe is personal, and the fundamental category of reason should therefore be personal
reasoning. Although the sciences are useful to the Christian
apologist as a shield against Hume's scepticism, they do not
provide perfect paradigms of theological reasoning. History
and literary criticism offer better parallels. The theologian
should not expect to prove his case with the conclusive finality
of a chemist or physicist, but having put it forward more ten-
tatively after the manner of a critic offering an interpretation
of, say, *King Lear*, should consider possible objections and how
they may be countered, and only then, in the absence of sustainable objections, come down in favour of his interpretation.

It is a matter of *sic et non* rather than of definitive proof. But although in this way theological reasoning has fewer resources for compelling assent than has mathematical or scientific reasoning, it has a wider range of reasons that may win acceptance. The theologian can press much harder the question 'What is the alternative?' Although any decision he takes about the nature of the whole universe is taken under conditions of imperfect information, and so is one that always could conceivably, and sometimes more than conceivably, be wrong, it is a decision he has to take, since the way he is to live his life depends on it, and life cannot be postponed. The Either/Or of practical decision-making extends backwards into the way in which the world is to be viewed, and the theologian is entitled to adduce in favour of his world-view not only direct arguments for but also arguments against the available alternatives. If the only alternative to Christian theism is some form of materialism, and no form of materialism can adequately account for consciousness, conscience, rationality, or the thirst for truth, then the rational unappealingness of materialism is to that extent a consideration in favour of theism. Of course, we must be careful. It is all too easy to pose the alternatives wrongly, and to engage in theological ping-pong, where both sides are right in what they say against each other, but wrong in assuming that theirs are the only alternatives. It is important, but difficult, to identify what the alternative world-views that are seriously available really are. But these are difficulties in practice, not insuperable difficulties in principle. In principle theological reasoning is not ruled out, and is likely to have the two-sided, dialectical character typical of practical argument and reasoning in the humanities, in which we seek out and meet objections, weigh considerations, and are guided by the cumulative weight of the arguments on either side.

Reason is much less circumscribed than Hume or Kant supposed. There are no good arguments for supposing that we cannot reason about religion, or that statements of theology lack cognitive status. Nevertheless, we should be wary of too extreme a rationalism. Although human beings are rational agents, each has a mind of his own which he has to make up for himself and which he is capable of making up differently from other people. Although we share a common rationality, and can very largely agree on what constitutes reasons for or against some course of action, we often disagree exactly how the balance is to be struck between conflicting reasons. Nor is it evidently the case that there is always only one right decision. Different people may differ in their assessment of the weight of argument on either side without either being definitely wrong. The hard guidelines of the Decalogue and Christian morality are relatively few, and leave much scope for the Christian to do his own thing in his own inimitable, but recognizably Christian, way. It is the same with God. If God is personal, he is rational, but not merely rational. Hence the sense of his hiddenness and inscrutability, from which in turn stems the need for revelation. It is characteristic of persons to be not rationally transparent but to have some privacy of intention and some privacy of thought. I cannot tell what you are going to do until you have made up your mind, and avowed your intention. So too with God. We cannot see through him, but must wait on his choosing to share his thoughts with us, and show us what he has in mind. Reason is not opposed to revelation, but requires it to complete our knowledge of a rational, but personal, God we are led by reason to believe in. Instead of being led, as was supposed, to the conclusion that we must abolish knowledge to make room for faith, we are being shown that the God of the philosophers cannot be just the God of the philosophers but must be also the God of Abraham, Isaac, and Jacob, and the Father of Jesus.

6

The Displacement of Truth

ROM HARRÉ

I

The Strict System and its Limitations for the philosophy of science

Philosophers of science have, for the most part, taken the task of the analyst of the knowledge-garnering activities of science to be explicable in terms of the concepts of truth and falsity. The way these concepts have been understood has been determined by their behaviour in two rather different contexts. One such context is that created by an interest in the logical structure of scientific discourse. In this context the behaviour of the concepts 'truth' and 'falsity' is controlled by powerful principles such as the Law of Non-contradiction. Included amongst the principles that dominate this context are the truth-preserving transformation of logical entailment, institutionalized in the traditional truth-tables. In this context the syntax of the concepts is determined. The other context is that of the assessment of the descriptive or representational adequacy of statements which purport to refer to all kinds of extra-linguistic matters, such as the state of the natural environment, and even the moral hegemony of the Divine order. In this context the meaning of the concepts is determined.

For the purposes of traditional philosophy of science the concept of truth has usually been taken strictly, marking a (perhaps unattainable) perfect match between the sense of a statement and the corresponding state of the world. In the 'strict' system any degree of imperfection in that match is enough to merit the judgement 'false'. This is the sort of assessment scheme typical of those philosophies which take the problem of truth to be concerned with how it is possible for something symbolic (linguistic) to refer to any non-symbolic state of the world. (The coherence theory of truth, which takes thought and world ultimately to be of the same nature, has not been popular with realists, since its way with truth depends on a background idealism). If 'truth' and 'falsity' are used to mark different degrees of 'fit' of propositions, one with another and with meaningful manifestations of the world, of a propositional sort, the mutability and potential variety of the latter seem to clash with the idea that there is only one world and the task of science is to describe it. Thus arises the commonsense objection to the permissive relativism of Rorty's *Philosophy and the Mirror of Nature*.

In recent times the analysis of scientific thought has proceeded as if it was obvious that scientific knowledge was built up by creating and refining a *discourse*. But discourse is only one of many modes for the public display of cognition. I will have in mind a more inclusive class of informative entities which I will call 'cognitive objects'. When knowledge is expressed in the iconic mode as a diagram or model, representational accuracy and inaccuracy (faithfulness, etc.) replace 'truth' and 'falsity' as the main ways of expressing and assessing epistemic worth. A notion like 'representational quality' is obviously better adapted to a less strict dichotomizing of assessments than are 'truth' and falsity'. Likenesses can be more or less faithful, drawings and diagrams more or less accurate portrayals. But to use picturing as the model for perceiving will not do, since it institutionalizes the idea that the percept is not the object. The qualified judgement 'more or less accurate' is certainly easier to analyse than the puzzling idea of degrees of truth. Truth and falsity seem to be polar or terminal concepts which do not easily admit of degrees. I shall call the assessment system which is based on a polar reading of 'truth' and 'falsity' and which is controlled by the above principles the 'strict' system. Within that system we can find a place for deduction as truth-preserving entailment, and for logical necessity and possibility.

It is ironical that studies of the workings of the strict system as a presumed general philosophy of science have revealed all kinds of 'problems'. These emerge as clashes between the basic properties of the strict system and well-founded intuitions about the way the assessment concepts of the epistemology of science actually behave. I propose to treat these problems as *reductiones ad absurdum* of the strict system. They are reasons for rejecting it as a basis for a philosophical analysis of scientific activity. I do not think that they are intellectual puzzles to be resolved in the interests of maintaining the hegemony of the strict system. For example, Hempel's paradox of the ravens shows that some strict entailment relations, that is relations which are the result of truth-preserving logical operations, do not transmit empirical confirmation in all cases in which they transmit truth. So while all forms of contraposition preserve truth, some, namely those which lead to a statement about the complements of the original subject and predicate classes, do not preserve empirical confirmation. While 'All electrons are negatively charged' entails 'All positively charged particles are non-electrons', the instantial confirmation of the latter by the discovery of the existence of those particles we call 'protons' does not transfer to the contrapositive. The discovery of the existence of positively charged non-electrons neither confirms nor disconfirms the claim about electrons. For instance there may be no electrons. Studying the properties of protons does not, of itself, help towards discovering the laws of electrons. The qualification 'of itself' must be entered, since theory may be comprehensive and integrated enough for physicists to be able to work out the necessary properties of electrons on the basis of information about other particles, taken from some natural ensemble. But this kind of reasoning is not available to a philosopher whose technical analytical apparatus is confined to the concepts and relations of the strict system.

But there are more fundamental difficulties with the strict system. They appear in the readiness with which sceptical doubts as to the possibility of achieving any reliable knowledge of the natural world arise out of an examination of the conditions for the application of the concepts of the strict system.

Consider scope and depth scepticism: the truth or falsity of statements which 'go beyond experience' can never be determined. For instance, we can never be sure of the truth of universal statements such as 'All past, present, and future electrons will be negatively charged' unless these statements are being used to inform the reader of a defining or criterial property of the natural kind in question. Similarly we can never be sure of the falsity of existential claims such as 'There are creatures with eyes in their chests' unless the space-time region for the search is strictly bounded. The possibility that universal statements can be shown to be false through the experimental demonstration of the falsity of a logical consequence of the statement in question remains open. So does the possibility of showing general existential claims to be true by the discovery of an instance of the kind in question. I will discuss these 'remainders' in the next section.

We still owe to Hume the most thorough and most influential investigation of the possibility of using the strict system as a basis for the assessment of claims to possess scientific knowledge, that is as a real working system. Hume's famous arguments can be separated into an examination of the scope of claims to have empirical knowledge of the properties or existence of unexamined particulars in nature (the problem of induction) and a critical discussion of 'deep' claims to knowledge, that is knowledge of the unobserved (and unobservable) causes of observed patterns of events. The latter is closely linked with an attack on natural necessity and on the alleged empirical standing of the concept of 'causal power'. The only modality of which scientific knowledge admits is pure contingency.

(a) *Scope*: any claim to have proved the truth of a law of nature on the basis of the kind of evidence that could be turned up by any human project is shown to be spurious. To reach from particular items of evidence to laws whose scope is supposed to be universal by the exercise of reason would require some general and incontrovertible principle (the 'uniformity of nature' for instance) whose actual empirical standing is easily seen to be too weak to provide the level of support needed. It is only too well known that this weakness is thought to derive from the need to invoke the very principle under consideration in any attempt to recommend it by finding supporting empirical evidence. This argument, be it noted, does nothing to show that it is unreasonable to accommodate our beliefs to the results of our experiments and systematic observations. Only if reasonableness is made to coincide with having the kinds of reasons for belief that only a deduction of a verbal expression of that belief from incontrovertible premises would provide, would it be unreasonable to accommodate our beliefs to what limited evidence we have. In this sense of 'reason', as Hume showed, we can never have reason for the kinds of beliefs that are the substance of scientific knowledge. I believe that these considerations show that the strict system of assessment cannot justly be used in scientific contexts. And thus far I am with Hume. But this admission does not preclude the possibility of developing some other weaker but more defensible scheme by which a scientific community can distinguish general principles, theoretical prescriptions of so far unobserved entities, etc., which, in the light of their studies, should be thought worthy of belief, from those which are merely plausible or should be abandoned. Nor need we be driven to a psychological or sociological account of why one hypothesis is accepted and another rejected.

(b) *Depth*: Hume's arguments against the use of concepts like 'substances', 'power', and 'causal efficacy' in scientific discourse, other than to express psychological states like expectation, depend on the same metaphysical scheme as do his arguments for inductive scepticism, namely an atomistic, phenomenalist analysis of experience. If there are no real relations between events, *a fortiori* there can be no productive relations between events. Locke had already expressed a similar worry about depth in his use of the concept of 'nescience'. Material things must have real essences. According to the corpuscularian philosophy the real essences of particulars are arrangements of particles. These are the physical properties by means of which real things are able to produce the effects they do on sensitive creatures like ourselves, and to engender consequential physical changes in other material beings. But the human perceptual system is so constituted that we cannot experience any such properties. Amongst other sensory deficits we lack microscopical eyes. There can be no place in our *science* for real essences. This does not make it wrong for Newton and Boyle to have made the attempt to describe the 'arrangements of parts in the superficies of bodies' as the hidden causes of their appearances, but it does mean that we can have no more than opinion concerning them.

II

The Ambiguity of Experimental Results and Technical Observations

But could we not finally ground the truth and falsity of science in the results of competently used experimental and observational techniques? Studying scientists at work soon makes it clear that experimental results are made germane to the assessment of laws and theories by decisions as to which part of the complex of metaphysics, auxiliary theories, and conceptual relations involved in treating any experiment of observation as a test should be taken to be vulnerable to its outcome. There is ultimately no non-arbitrary way of making that decision, I believe. How it is made in particular cases will be determined by power-relations in the thought-collective, the social order obtaining amongst this or that group of scientists. Hence any claim to have established the truth of an existential hypothesis or the falsity of a universal claim by reference to the result of experiments or observations is defeasible. This point is sometimes thought to be a modern discovery, but it can be traced back at least as far as Kepler's remarks on the epistemological status of astronomical hypotheses. In the introduction to Darwin's *Origin of Species* the author cites a variety of evidence which throws into doubt the utility and plausibility of the traditional conceptual distinction between varieties and species as a real metaphysical demarcation. Darwin lets the evidence speak against the then current metaphysics. But the defenders of *infima species* could and did use the same evidence to demonstrate (speak for) the rich proliferation of varieties.

Experimental results are not data in search of a hypothesis, but by virtue of our willingness to entertain this or that hypothesis or theory an observation becomes fraught with significance. Only then does it become germane to the question of whether we should accept or reject a hypothesis. We find this most beautifully exemplified in the reasonings of Galileo. By the conceptual transformation of the idea of motion from a 'process of change requiring a sustaining cause', the Aristotelian conception, to a continuous, self-maintaining state, Galileo *provided himself* with an enormous range of diverse evidential anecdotes. Taken within his new framework, certain phenomena with which everyone was capable of becoming acquainted, but which had scarcely been noticed as significant, became potent items of evidence for Galilean physics. For example, once one has in mind the idea of the uncaused persistence of motion, then the hitherto unemphasized fact that a rider can throw up his spear and catch it again, while at the gallop, takes on a strong evidential quality.

From an exhaustive catalogue of the multiplicity and diversity of motions to be observed in the world nothing unqualified could generally have been induced. An Aristotelian could advance the fact that a rolling ball soon comes to rest, that a coasting ship soon stops moving, and so on as facts evidential for the principle that without a sustaining cause motion soon ceases. This is why Koyré's epigram 'For it is thought, pure unadulterated thought, and not experience or sense-perception, as until then, that gives the basis for the "new science" of Galileo Galilei'[1] fails to capture the true beauty of Galileo's method. It is not that Galileo makes 'no appeal to experience'[2] in discussing how a ball will fall when dropped from the mast of a ship. His whole procedure works by the demonstration of the power of his physical hypotheses *to provide themselves with evidence culled from experience.* Theory becomes a device for focusing our attention. Theory precedes fact, not because *necesse* determines *esse* as Koyré would have it, but because a theory determines where, in the multiplicity of natural phenomena, we should seek for its evidence. Science is empirical because we may fail to find what we want. The task of reconstructing what were the perfectly correct observations which had served as evidence for the Aristotelian point of view, when that was how we looked at the world, can be postponed. Once we have been led to attend to the horseman and his spear, and to see that as the significant fact, our attention is, so to speak, distracted from such matters as that other horse which was needed to keep the exemplary cart in motion. The fact that carts soon stop without horses to pull them then ceases to be a

[1] A. Koyré, *Metaphysics and Measurement* (Chapman Hall, London, 1967), p. 13.
[2] Koyré, loc. cit.

fact of any significance. Accommodating the 'old facts' is not achieved by finding a cunning way of deducing them from the new theory as the deductivists would have it. We don't bother with them, any more.

In fairness to Koyré it is worth remarking that in a later chapter in the work cited above he comes much closer to the position just sketched. He sees quite clearly that experiments are not, indeed could not be, the inductive grounds for hypotheses, but that it is hypotheses which endow certain experiments with significance and thus transform their results into 'evidence'. 'Experimentation', he says, is an 'interrogation which presupposes and implies a *language* in which to formulate the questions, and a dictionary which enables us to read and to interpret the answers'.[3]

Consider now modality. Hume's famous argument against causal necessity—that there is no contradiction in conjoining a description of a cause with the negation of a description of its usual effect—is surely valid. But what does it show? At best it shows that causal or natural necessity is not logical necessity. Indeed, that was how Hume seems to have taken the argument, since he went on to give an account of causal necessity in terms of the psychological phenomenon of a habit of expectation formed through exposure to repeated instances of a concomitance of similar pairs of events. The argument certainly does not show that a statement like 'An unsuspended body in a gravitational field *must* fall if released, *ceteris paribus*' is incoherent. And, of course, despite Hume's argument there are all sorts of other possible accounts of the concept of causal or natural necessity that is expressed in the modal vocabulary of scientific discourse than the psychological interpretation he proposes. The actual system of assessment involves a repertoire of modal words which are used to mark certain quite important distinctions. Hume's argument is important since it shows that these uses are not explicable in terms of the concepts of the strict system.

Finally, it is worth noticing that general existential claims can be shown to be unfalsifiable within the system of strict concepts. Yet the scientific community becomes convinced, and rightly, that certain particular entities and certain kinds

[3] Koyré, p. 19.

of beings do not exist. After the debate is over the community will accept no further claims concerning them. The actual system then cannot be isomorphic with the real system, nor can its use be illuminatingly analysed in terms of the concepts of that system.

III

A Sketch of the Actual System

To find accounts of the actual system of assessment in use in science one must bypass the study of printed scientific texts. These texts are written within the conventions of a certain rhetoric, or, if we look at the matter historically, within a sequence of different rhetorics, each of which 'secretes' its own philosophy of science. Failing one's own research corpus gleaned from recording the conversations of everyday life in laboratory and common-room and grubbing around for the remnants of early drafts of scientific papers, one must turn to the literature of the microsociology of science in which the actual system is described. This literature is frequently enlivened with quotations in *oratio recta*. I will illustrate something of the way the actual system works with descriptions of two main processes: the use of judgements of personal character in deciding on the reliability of the results of research, and the asymmetry in the way data is treated when it is used to support one's own ideas and when it is quoted in support by a rival.

In the actual system personal character is taken as an epistemic warrant. The most striking feature of the actual system is the extent to which assessment of a great variety of factual claims is rooted in judgements of persons rather than in the quality of the experimental researches. These include both what claims should be accorded the status of observational/experimental *results*, and this includes even quantitative data, and the deeper theoretical interpretation of results, for example what molecular structures such and such results indicate. 'Results' do not stand freely, so to speak, as the bench mark

against which reliability is routinely assessed, but are themselves judged pretty much on the basis of the character of the
person who produced them. As Latour and Woolgar[4] show,
'results' and 'interpretations' are not neutral decontextualized
propositions, but come qualified by the name and so by the
reputation of the person who obtained them (or under whose
aegis they were obtained). Instead of true and false results we
are presented with Green's and Brown's results. In a way the
qualification by name is a kind of 'epistemic equivalent' of
assessments of truth and falsity, since citing some results as
Green's means they can safely be accepted, while citing some
other results as Brown's means they should be treated with
scepticism. To illustrate this, Collins[5] quotes the following:
'[Quest and his group] are so obnoxious, and so firm in their
belief, that their approach is the right one and that everyone
else is wrong, that I immediately discount their veracity on
the basis of self-delusion.' The moral status of persons determines the epistemic status of their results. As Latour and
Woolgar put it, 'this kind of reference to human agency
involved in the production of statements is very common.
Indeed it was clear from the participants' discussions that *who*
made this claim was as important as the claim itself.'

But is this any more than a specialized form of traditional
inductive reasoning? Is the 'who' important as grounds for the
assessment of these data as worthy of belief because that
person's results have, in the past, turned out to be, in some
traditional way, better than the results of others? In their
discussion of these points Latour and Woolgar do seem to
confuse the question of whether one would wish to collaborate
with someone ('No—she's super-competitive!') with whether
results, labelled as that person's, should be counted as reliable
and thus be incorporated into the discourse as facts. The only
non-inductive element in their discussion[6] is their reference to
unfavourable assessments based on the principle that if people
are too pushy and anxious they will tend to accept sloppy
results or indulge in wishful thinking. This is a principle not

---

[4] B. Latour and S. Woolgar, *Laboratory Life* (Sage, Los Angeles, 1979).
[5] H. M. Collins 'Son of Seven Sexes: the Social Destruction of a Physical Phenomenon', *Social Studies of Science* 11 (1981), pp.33–62.
[6] Latour and Woolgar, pp.162–5.

very different from what is implicit in the quote from Collins above. But the concept of 'sloppiness' seems to make sense only against the background of a quite traditional epistemic concept like 'accuracy'.

The strict system treats of an inductive process from true (or false) singular statements to confirmed (or disconfirmed) hypotheses of greater generality, as if it existed as an impersonal schema, the value of which was independent of the persons who used it or of their social position in the community of scientists. The actual system has no place for non-inductive singular true statements. The indexicality of the reliability of singular statements to the person who made them or to the laboratory in which they are represented as a discovery, or to the apparatus one or more of whose states such a statement describes, only makes sense as inductions from past performances of that person, laboratory, or apparatus. But these are *inductions from prior inductions*, for example that Green was a pupil of Black and Black's results were always reliable. There is no point in this regress at which the naked fact reveals itself to provide a foundation in terms that would be recognized within the strict system. (This point has been taken up by Popper in his late revisions of the notion of basic statement.) I will call this 'inductive indexicality'.

But more can be said about the grounds for the personal reputations upon which 'inductive indexicality' depends. It is clear from detailed studies made by Latour and Woolgar, and others, that in the realm of fact-stating discourse certain kinds of raising of the standards of experimentation were important in the grounding of reputations. This goes back at least as far as the work of Berzelius in developing standards of experimental work that transformed the accuracy of quantitative chemistry. This is quite a complex matter. Standards of experimentation are task-dependent. Set a new task and new, sometimes more but sometimes less stringent standards are called for. Latour and Woolgar note that one effect of adopting a new task definition from a field and of raising the standards, whether by changing some intrinsic attribute of research such as the accuracy demanded of some physical measure or by proposing a research programme that will cost large sums of money, is to eliminate some of the competition.

But the idea of 'raising the standards of experimental research' would be in need of explication even if there were no other workers in the field. Compare 'We have found a substance which does what is expected, that is, is biologically active' with 'We have discovered the structure of the substance which exhibits this level of biological activity.' According to Latour and Woolgar, the shift from a research task defined in terms of an attempt to substantiate the first claim to one intended to substantiate the second transformed the conditions under which the claims of the protagonists of different points of view were readable as 'stating the facts'. They quote the following statement:[7]

Everybody knowing the field could make deductions as to what TRF was . . . their conclusions were correct but it took ten years to prove it . . . To this day I do not believe they had ever seen what they talked about . . . There is no way you can postulate the amino-acid composition of an unknown substance. (Quoted as a remark by Guillemin.)

For the latter much more stringently controlled chemical techniques are required and a much greater investment of time and money. The successful scientist in Latour and Woolgar's moral tale certainly seems to have thought both the practical and the moral consequences of the shift of the task definition were relevant to his claim for hegemony.

If we look a little more closely at the actual discourse in which these claims are made the moral element becomes very clear. The exertion of effort is claimed as a mark of moral virtue. For instance, someone called Schally is quoted by Latour and Woolgar[8] as saying 'the only way is to extract these compounds, isolate them . . . Somebody had to have the guts . . . now we have tons of it.' Of a colleague Schally remarks with a notably arrogant lack of charity 'of course, he missed the boat, he never dared putting in what was required, brute force'.[9] Further studies of social construction of 're-liability' and 'credibility', particularly in these curious personalized moral terms, can be found in Pickering.[10]

---

[7] Ibid., p.121.   [8] Ibid., p.118.   [9] Ibid., p.119.
[10] A. Pickering, 'Constraints and Controversy: the Case of the Magnetic Monopole', *Social Studies of Science* 11 (1981), pp.63–93.

IV

'*Us*' and '*Them*'

In the actual system there is a marked asymmetry in the criteria by which one judges one's own hypotheses and those which are used to undermine the credibility of those of a rival. Gilbert and Mulkay's[11] results are used in a creatively equivocal way in discussions of the belief-worthiness of putative claims to knowledge. In supporting one's own ideas experimental results are cited as robust data, and a traditional inductive schema is invoked as the rationale of the claim. But when a scientist is discussing the ideas of an opponent 'experimental results' are treated as labile, their supporting role as seen by the opposition appearing merely as self-deception. The critic has little difficulty in finding an alternative interpretation of the result of his rivals. In this new guise the data no longer support and perhaps even undermine the rival's claim to knowledge. The critic shows no inclination to do similar work on his own results and treats them as if they were 'picked directly from nature'. They are presented as capable of only one interpretation, namely that under which they support his claim. In the critical phase an epistemological doctrine rather like that of Whewell[12] or Hanson[13] is emphasized. Considerable weight is put on the way pre-existing beliefs and theories are involved in the creation of 'data' out of mere 'results'. In neither of the cognitive practices I have described, that is 'inductive indexicality' or the 'us and them asymmetry', do the traditional concepts of 'truth' or 'falsity' seem to play any part. Instead we get phrases like 'confirmed as being correct over the entire range';[14] 'S did beautiful experiments which were convincing to me mostly';[15]

---

[11] G. N. Gilbert, and N. Mulkay, 'Warranting Scientific Beliefs', *Social Studies of Science* 12 (1982), pp.383–408.

[12] W. Whewell, *The Philosophy of the Inductive Sciences* (Johnson Report, London, 1967), bk. 1.

[13] Norwood Russell Hanson, *Patterns of Discovery* (Cambridge University Press, Cambridge, 1969).

[14] Gilbert and Mulkay, p.390.

[15] Ibid., p.391.

'it is very hard to get your hand on these things you are work-ing on';[16] 'these experiments demonstrate that . . . is real';[17] 'see what certain molecular chains are doing . . .';[18] 'N's numbers agree with what S wants',[19] and so on.

V

Strict Assessment and the Moral Order

The work of Latour and Woolgar and others has shown that there is a rhetorical use of the terminology of the strict system in the debates through which epistemic assessment of scien-tific claims are decided, pro tem. The 'logical' properties of discourse such as entailment and consistency (as the avoid-ance of contradiction) are used as part of the criteria by which scientific productions are assessed in the community's system of credit. They appear as essentially moral properties of an agonistic scientific discourse or debate. We can look upon it as one of the many language-games that make up this form of life. I propose in the light of these observations that we should reinterpret the activities of traditional philosophy of science. When philosophers carry on their discussions of science in terms of the strict system they are not describing either the cognitive or the material practices of the scientific community, even in ideal form. They are touching on its moral order.

If we read the realist manifesto 'Scientific statements should be taken as true or false by virtue of the way the world is' as a moral claim it would run something like this: 'As scientists, that is members of a certain community, we should apportion our willingness or reluctance to accept a claim as worthy to be included in the corpus of scientific knowledge to the extent that we sincerely think it somehow reflects the way the world is.' Put this way the manifesto has *conduct-guiding force*. It

---

[16] Ibid., p.393.
[17] Ibid., p.397.
[18] Ibid., p.398.
[19] Ibid., p.399.

encourages the good and the worthy to manifest their virtue in trying to find out how the world is. Seeking truth is a hopeless epistemic project, but trying to live a life of virtue is a possible moral ambition. Those who promulgate their ungrounded opinions as if they were proper contributions to the corpus of scientific knowledge are roundly condemned as immoral. Moral principles are those maxims which would guide our conduct were we people of unimpeachable virtue. The moral version of the manifesto cited above would enjoin the carrying out of careful experiments, the avoidance of that kind of wishful thinking which leads to the fudging of results, and so on. The moral force of this kind of principle comes through very strongly in the discussions reported by Latour and Woolgar concerning the early work on TRF cited above. The practice of science is what it is because the morality of the scientific community is strict. Looked at this way the study of the epistemology of science must begin with philosophical reflection on the actual practices of the community if as philosophers we wish to know what scientific knowledge *is*. Failing to follow this ordinance can lead us to confuse the demands of the moral order of the scientific community, the thought-collective, with the possibilities of the achievement of some ideal form of knowledge, given the existing practices. Anthropologists have learned that when they ask a member of a community for an account of the local kinship system, they are as likely as not to receive an account of the moral order rather than a description of the vagaries of actual practice. Between the stringency of the moral order and the laxness of real life lies an idealization of the latter, made with an eye on the former, and it is this third *via media* that is usually the guiding system for the decisions of everyday life.

The effect of translating the work of a philosopher out of epistemology into moral philosophy can be illustrated with the case of Popper's 'fallibilism'. It can comfortably be reinterpreted as a cluster of moral principles, a 'Rule' for the conduct of daily life in a community, a scientific community. As epistemology Popper's ideas have proved rather easy to criticize. For example, there is no way conclusively to falsify a universal hypothesis or the theory of which it forms a part. Even if there were a rejection of a hypothesis, just because it had been falsified by an instance would be irrational without some version of the principle of the uniformity of nature as support. But fallibilism can be a guide to 'good conduct'. The morality of the scientific community appears in principles such as 'However much personal investment one has in a theory one should not ignore contrary evidence' or 'One should seek harder for evidence that would count against a theory than that which would support it', and so on.

Adherence to these and similar principles will help one to resist temptations, such as self-deception. But why is self-deception counted a vice in the moral order of the community of scientists? In the general morality of everyday life self-deception is perhaps a failing but hardly a sin. For an explanation we must return to the idea of a moral order based on trust. Scientific knowledge is a public resource for action and for belief. To publish abroad a discovery couched in the rhetoric of science is to let it be known that the presumed fact can safely be used in debate, in practical projects, and so on. Knowledge claims are tacitly prefixed with a performative of trust. Interpreted within the moral order of the scientific community, 'I know . . .' means something like 'You can trust me that . . .'; 'You have my word for it.' If what one claims to know turns out to be spurious then on this reading one has committed a moral fault. One has let down those who trusted one.

This is connected with another moral distinction, that between pretending to have a good reason for stating something when one has not and being genuinely mistaken. Epistemologically they are on the same footing, but morally they could hardly be more distinct. Popperian fallibilism, if interpreted as a moral position, a kind of 'Rule', would differentiate them clearly. In the first case I do not have contrary evidence because I have not bothered to look for it, or have not heeded it, while in the second I have just not happened to come upon it despite genuinely trying to find it. The trust that scientists claim from lay persons entails a commitment to intellectual honesty, to having made attempts to substantiate claims in the way that claims are substantiated in the community. The same argument which transforms epistemology into the communal 'Rule' would apply to any intellectual community whatsoever, for instance the community of theologians.

What then should be the major concern of such studies as philosophy of science, or philosophy of religion for that matter? From the considerations advanced in this paper it seems that a description of the moral orders of such communities must play an essential part in the philosophical project. But one can go further. If one could develop an idealized version of the actual system of assessment of candidates for belief, one might be able to explain why the use of the actual system does produce material that is valued in those moral orders, and why the strict system is an expression of that morality. We should be able not only to show why the claims of magicians should be taken as less trustworthy than those of engineers, but also why the moral order of the scientific community makes this kind of moral distinction. To accomplish the latter we would need to discuss the morality of science against the background of an idealized version of the cognitive and material practices of that community. There is no need to struggle with the impossible task of trying to prove that the actual practice of science truly realizes an epistemic state of affairs deemed desirable within the scientific community. So the attempt to *define* scientific realism in terms of the principle of bivalence, that scientific theories are true or false by virtue of the way the world is, is a mistake, confusing an ethical thesis about honesty of endeavour with an epistemological thesis about how to achieve the highest standards of representational quality for scientific cognition. Scientific practice could never produce cognitive objects to which the strict dichotomy 'true or false by virtue of the way the word is' could be applied in the epistemic mode.

In philosophy of science we want to be able to explain how imperfect representations can be the basis of trustworthy belief and practice that is 'good enough'. The practices of mankind are very diverse and what is to count as 'good enough' can hardly be given a universal definition. At best we can say what is good enough for a test of a drug, good enough for the design of a bridge, and good enough for the tuning of a symphony orchestra. I have already mentioned the discussion by Latour and Woolgar of the way that standards of assaying can be changed and of the moral advantage of redefining them 'upwards'. For example we could try to show how fulfilling the conditions for 'plausibility of a theory' makes the material practice of looking for exemplars of theoretically prescribed classes of unknown beings a sensible policy. It is worth reminding ourselves that the scorn that has been poured on the naïvety of the D-N 'model' of explanation was justified only in the context of what scientists actually did. If this was what scientific explanation had to be then that kind of explanation was impossible of achievement by any flesh and blood scientist. But is it so absurd as a moral ideal?

To my mind the importance of the strict system lies not in epistemology, but in the fact that it represents the most perfect and generally sustained moral order ever created by mankind. Alongside the history of the moral force of the order within the scientific community the minimal success of 'Love thy neighbour' makes a regrettably ironic contrast. Philosophers of science who chose to follow the spirit of the above remarks would be setting out to construct an idealized and abstract version of scientific cognition and its actual assessment modes. But would such a version be normative? Well, it would not be the whole story. It would bring out that part of the normative background of science that regulates it as a material practice—what someone who joins this community ought to do (just as the 'Rule of St Benedict' enjoined on Benedictines certain daily observances). One should classify the beings presented by nature and try to establish their natural kinds. One should seek for exemplars of the beings whose description has been adumbrated in theory. One should be willing to accept only those laws which are covariant under the Lorentz transformation, and so on. But the total normative background also involves that which I have called the strict system, the moral maxims that masqueraded as epistemological categories in traditional philosophy of science. As an epistemological doctrine 'Seek the truth and reject falsehood' is worthless, but as a moral maxim it figures a good deal in one way or another in the occasional sermons that scientists preach.

There is another kind of discourse, the theological, where terms from the strict system are cheerfully bandied about, and meet much the same fate, the encouragement of scepticism.

No theological statement of which 'God' is the putative referent could be known to be true or to be false. But there is an
obvious reading of the strict system in this context too as a
cluster of moral maxims, part of the 'Rule' that regulates the
theological community.

VI

Simple Truth

But, it might be said, surely you cannot be denying that the
common-sense notions of 'truth' and 'falsity' have no place in
the epistemology of natural science? Indeed not. In the sense
that what you say is true if I, now occupying your standpoint,
and sharing with you the bulk of a conceptual scheme relevant
to the matter in question, were to give a similar account of
what can be experienced from that standpoint, then what you
said was true, otherwise not. The comparison is between your
discourse and mine, apropos of a common referent. It cannot
be between the relation my discourse has to the common referent and the relation that yours does, since those relations
could not become objects of comparison within a single field of
knowledge. The comparison of discourses has the flavour of
the old coherence theory of truth, while the mention of a common referent reminds one of the correspondence theory.

From a philosophical point of view this account of the role
of true and false in the discourse of science leaves at least two
questions unanswered:

(a) How do I know that we are noticing something about a
common referent? The material practice of locating referents
in space–time relative to other referents is not enough.
Perhaps I can know we are noticing the same things only if
our discourses are similar.

(b) How do I know that our discourses are similar? Clearly
there can be no case by case comparison to decide the question. It may be that we can do no better than to notice that as
members of the same community we manage to coexist and
co-ordinate our practical activities in a common form of life,

including common rights and duties and a morality in which sincerity of reporting is a common good.

In general, I think, we have to admit that there are no clear-cut procedures for determining that what you see I see, what you mean I understand, and so on. Only our long-term participation in a common form of life shows that for all practical purposes we inhabit a common world of material things and conversational practices. The use of the concepts of the strict system in their literal acceptation would require a vantage-point outside our community and its practices from which aspects of nature could be compared with fragments of discourse as if they were mutually independent of one another. There is no such vantage-point, nor could there be. But there are co-operative practices and long-standing communities with their moral orders. It is to these that we must look, if anywhere, for the foundations of knowledge. But these foundations are not factual but moral.

7

Theological Realism

JANET MARTIN SOSKICE

Esperanto. The feeling of disgust we get if we utter an *invented* word with invented derivative symbols. The word is cold, lacking in associations, and yet it plays at being 'language'. A system of purely written signs would not disgust us so much. (Wittgenstein in *Culture and Value*.)

Dr Johnson, defending against a critic the practice of quotation, 'No, Sir, it is a good thing; there is community of mind in it' (in Boswell's *Life of Johnson*).

> God is our rock.
> Jesus is the lamb of God.

What should we say of these Christian affirmations? Are they metaphorical or not? Let's try two more:

> God is our father.
> Jesus is the son of God.

Are these metaphorical or not? There can be something unsettling to many Christians about saying 'yes' to both these questions. Perhaps one might feel happy about saying 'yes' to the first but hesitate over the second. Let us look at the extent of the problem.

Virtually all Christians can agree that most of our talk about God is figurative. To assent to this has no bearing on one's theological conservatism or radicality—there are few true literalists who believe that mention in the Bible of God's 'mighty arm' or 'the earth, his footstool' means that God has physical limbs. The God of the Jews and Christians is known as 'He who Is', the cause of all things yet apart from all things. No 'name', as Jacob discovered when he wrestled with the angel, can capture him. But here is an ancient tension: if God cannot be described then how is 'theology' possible? Since

ancient times the answer has been that we do not speak of God
directly but by means of tropes and figures.

Perhaps it may surprise us that Judaism, a religion hostile
to any form of visual representation of God, provides in its
sacred texts so extensive and so unlikely a gallery of verbal
icons. God is compared to a lion, a king, a rock, stars, dew,
clouds, fire, and a breast-feeding mother. Hosea goes so far as
to say that God is 'like a moth of Ephraim, and like dry rot to
Judah' (Hosea 5: 12). But on reflection this flamboyance is
just what one would expect. Indeed, given God's radical
otherness the more extreme the image the better. No one is
going to make the mistake of thinking God is a moth. That, as
Wittgenstein might remark, is too big for a blunder. It would
show you didn't know how to play the game.

It seems uncontroversial, then, that our speaking of God the
Creator is highly figurative, but what shall we say of our talk
about Jesus? He was, or so Christians hold, not only true God
but true man, and as a man many things might be predicated
literally of him, for example that he was a Jew, that he lived
about two thousand years ago, that he was crucified, and so
on. Might we have here the basis for theology which kept clear
of metaphor? But the task of ridding Christology or any other
branch of theology of figurative speech must be a thankless
one. We may be able to say a good deal about the man, Jesus,
in a literal way, but the picture changes when Jesus is spoken
of as more than man. The earliest 'Christologies' we have,
going right back to the Bible itself, are ineliminably metaphorical: Jesus is the son of God, our High Priest, the King,
shepherd, lamb of God. He gave his life in 'ransom' for us.

Should we feel inclined to overlook the extent to which doctrinal formulation depends on models, it is useful to be
reminded of the many models that either didn't make the
grade or, alternatively, enjoyed popularity at one time and
were tactfully abandoned at another. For example, the early
church made far more use than we do of the model of Christ as
physician, claiming scriptural warrant from the healing
miracles and the parable of the Good Samaritan. From this
followed reflections on the sacraments as healing medications.
Hippolytus, again employing a Biblical image, compared
Christ's humanity to a bridegroom's cloak, which presumably

might be slipped on or off.[1] Another, odder expression of Christ's atoning work was the metaphor of Jesus as the 'bait' for God's fish-hook.

> The purpose of the Incarnation . . . was that the divine virtue of the Son of God might be as it were a hook hidden beneath the form of human flesh . . . to lure on the prince of this age to a contest; that the Son might offer him his flesh as a bait and that then the divinity which lay beneath might catch him and hold him fast with its hook.[2]

The unsuitability of this model of the atonement may seem obvious. But it is not obvious that the models we use at present are entirely satisfactory either, and indeed in the history of theology models and metaphors come and go. While it is true that many come from the Bible, different epochs favour different scriptural models, and develop the same scriptural models in different ways.

Since the time of Athenagoras at least, the good theologian and insightful faithful have recognized the language of both popular devotion and formal theology to be highly metaphorical and not found that to be particularly problematic. Why then should the modern believer feel discomfited, as many do, by the questions with which this article began? One reason may be that we tend unreflectively to think that the fact a claim is made metaphorically means it's 'merely metaphorical', where this is understood as unfactual, untrue, and unnecessary. We need to be cautious with this phrase 'merely metaphorical' and its even more slippery associate, 'merely metaphorically true'. Claims are made true or false by circumstances and not simply by their manner of expression. If I say to a competent speaker of the English language that 'Herbert is eaten away with anxiety' and circumstances bear that up, it is Pickwickian of someone to add, 'but of course that is only metaphorically true'. 'It is true if it is true!' we want to say. Truth and falsity are assessed at the level of intended meaning, not at that of so-called literal word meaning. Metaphor is a kind of language use and not a kind of truth.

Nevertheless, not all the malaise of the modern believer can

---

[1] J. N. D. Kelly, *Early Christian Doctrines*, fifth rev. edn. (Adam and Charles Black, London, 1977), p.149.

[2] Rufinus of Aquileia, cited in Henry Bettenson (ed.), *Documents of the Christian Church* (Oxford University Press, London, 1943), p.49.

be dismissed with a linguistic qualification, although in this case a good deal might. We are circling about a very real and important debate in modern theology when we consider metaphor, and this debate centres not on *whether* religious language is ineradicably metaphorical, but *what follows* if this is so. To put this in an extreme form, some theologians and philosophers of religion who agree that talk of God is metaphorical may be reflecting, in the mode of the prophets, psalmists, and mystics, on the inability of human thought or speech to comprehend the Diety, while others mean something much more like 'Christian language is merely metaphorical, a powerful if somewhat archaic system of images but not to be taken as somehow speaking about a world-transcending God in any traditional sense.' In this extreme form then, both the mystic and the contemporary atheologian (one who wishes to dispense with traditional theism altogether) can agree that talk about God is metaphorical. We might say, though, that agreement here is spurious.

My suggestion is that mere acceptance of the same set of words here glosses over the real issue of whether those speaking are theological realists or theological instrumentalists. By theological realists I intend here those who, while aware of the inability of any theological formulation to catch the divine realities, none the less accept that there *are* divine realities that theologians, however ham-fistedly, are trying to catch. By theological instrumentalists I intend those who believe that religious language provides a useful, even uniquely useful, system of symbols which is action-guiding for the believer but not to be taken as making reference to a cosmos-transcending being in the traditional sense. Feuerbach and his latter-day followers would be clear candidates for the second camp, but many other, less obviously radical theologians put forward ideas whose implications are much the same.[3] Not surprisingly, instrumentalism in both its theological and non-theological applications (notably in the philosophy of science where debate between realists and instrumentalists has raged for some time) is associated with criticisms of the possibility or necessity of metaphysical explanations.

Realism is attractive because it seems undeniable that

[3] For a latter-day follower of Feuerbach see Don Cupitt, *Taking Leave of God*. For a

Christians and Jews traditionally have been realists of some sort. The difficulty is that, since Locke, Hume, and Kant, it has been assumed by many to be philosophically indefensible. One can see why; with traditional metaphysics given short shrift theologians have judged there to be limited scope in claiming to speak of that which we cannot comprehend.[4]

The perceived weakness of natural theology has added strength to the instrumentalist case. Religious language does not tell us about God, on their account, but evokes response to God. The difficulty, as always, is Response to what? Belief in what? Instrumentalism all too easily reduces to a position where religious language is in no sense more than a life-enhancing means of discussing the human condition. For many it is difficult to find any resemblances between that and traditional theism.

To meet instrumentalism, the realist must attempt to say how religious language can claim to be *about* God at all, given that naïve realism in these matters is unthinkable. This task, I suggest, is bound up with giving some good account of how metaphor works in religious language.

The terminology of 'realist' and 'instrumentalist' is not, of course, native to philosophical theology but borrowed from debates which have taken place in the philosophy of science. Ian Ramsey, as Nolloth Professor of the Philosophy of the Christian Religion at Oxford, did much to popularize comparisons between the philosophy of science and the philosophy of religion, and stimulated a debate about the use of models in theology as compared to those in scientific theory construction. Philosophers of religion since have drawn comparisons between the use of models in the two fields, emphasizing, for example, the need for a multiplicity of models, all of which have a tentative descriptive status, and other supposed shared features such as simplicity, elegance, and extensibility. For the most part these comparisons have been inconclusive, amounting at best to a 'companions in guilt' argument of the form

less obviously radical position with some of the same implications see Sallie McFague, *Metaphorical Theology*.

[4] For just two influential theologians who have suggested that metaphysical arguments are either impossible or unhelpful for theology see Robert King, 'The Task of Systematic Theology' in *Christian Theology*, ed. Peter Hodgson and Robert King, and John MacQuarrie in the introduction to *Principles of Christian Theology*.

'Religion need not be ashamed of its reliance on models if science proceeds in the same way'. This does not constitute much of an argument, however, unless the philosopher of religion can demonstrate why these perceived similarities are significant, and here accounts have been weak. Committed as they often are to a hearty, if uncritical, realism *vis-á-vis* the role of models in scientific theory (in order to affirm the necessity of models to scientific practice and thus justify their presence in theology), the philosophers of religion have, with some regularity, drifted into non-cognitivist positions when they apply their ideas to theology; religious models are seen to be challenging, unifying, evocative, and morally valuable. This ghostly gain may be better than no gain at all, but it is far from the promise of cognitive stability which, presumably, was the attraction of the analogy with the philosophy of science in the first place.

Yet we can see why this happens. Scientific realists who place a high value on models do so because they view them as descriptive of states and relations which, while going beyond our powers of direct observation, none the less are in important senses independent of the construction we put upon them. The models, then, if qualified and limited, are nevertheless held to be descriptive. Yet the very idea that the theologians' model describes God as He is in Himself must be (and rightly) anathema to most philosophers of religion.

Despite these difficulties, or indeed even because of them, the comparison between models in science and religion should continue to interest us, not at the level of individual models (light 'waves' and heavenly 'fathers'), but at the more fundamental level of what constitutes model-based explanation in the two disciplines.

I take it that the theological realist has this much in common with the scientific realist; they both want to preserve their models and the metaphorical terminology to which these give rise, and want to preserve them not as convenient fictions for the ordering of observables but as terms which somehow provide access to states and relations which exist independent of our theorizing about them. So the scientific realist wants to say that speaking of the brain as a computer and talking of feedback, programming, and so on really is talk about brain activity, and the theological realist that talks of God as father or the vine-dresser of Christ the true vine really is talking about God's relationship to humanity. But neither of these realists wants to claim privileged and unrevisable knowledge of their unobservable subject-matters. Indeed, models and the metaphorical terminology to which they give rise are prized in these contexts precisely because of their adaptability; they are always tentative, always qualified. Were this not so they would not be models.[5] But here we come to a problem: how can these metaphorical theory terms claim to be in some sense descriptive or, as I prefer to say, reality-depicting, prior to and without definitive knowledge?

It is here that the would-be scientific and theological realist might seek help from recent studies of reference, particularly those of Saul Kripke and Hilary Putnam. Starting from studies of proper names, Kripke and Putnam have come to challenge traditional theories as to how terms like 'cow' and 'electricity' refer. For example, traditional theories associated with Bertrand Russell suggested that the reference of a proper name is identified by the application of a definite description. Kripke, on the other hand, argues that reference can take place independently of the possession of a definite description which somehow 'qualitatively uniquely' picks out the individual in question and can even be successful where the identifying description associated with the name fails to be true of the individual in question. In one of his examples, a speaker who says that Columbus was the man who discovered America and proved the world was round really refers to Columbus, even though Columbus did neither of these things and even if that is all the speaker 'knows' about Columbus. And the reason the speaker refers, even though all his particular beliefs about Columbus are incorrect, is because the relevant linguistic competence does not involve unequivocal knowledge but rather depends on the fact that the speaker is a member of a linguistic community who have passed the name from link to link, going back to the man, Columbus, himself.[6]

---

[5] The exception, of course, is replica models (homeomorphic models), like modern trains. But these, for obvious reasons, are the least interesting kinds of models for theory construction.

[6] 'Naming and Necessity' in *Semantics of Natural Language*, ed. Donald Davidson and Gilbert Harman (D. Reidel, Dordrecht, 1972), pp. 295, 301.

Kripke's point is in part an amplification of a more modest observation about reference which another writer makes as follows:

successful reference does not depend upon the truth of the description contained in the referring expression. The speaker (and perhaps the hearer) may mistakenly believe that some person is the postman, when he is in fact the professor of linguistics, and incorrectly, though successfully, refer to him by means of the expression 'the postman'. It is not even necessary that the speaker should believe that the description is true of the referent. He may be ironically employing a description he knows to be false or diplomatically accepting as correct a false description which his hearer believes to be true of the referent; and there are other possibilities.[7]

The point here is that reference depends, in normal speech, as much on context as on content and that reference is an utterance-dependent notion. This, we might note, is what makes metaphor and various other forms of figurative epithet possible; given the right context it will be perfectly clear to your auditor that by 'that rose amongst the thorns' you are referring to your favourite politician.

By extension and not uncontroversially, Kripke and Putnam argue that the reference of natural-kind terms like 'gold' and physical magnitude terms like 'electricity' need not depend on definitional conventions in the form of lists of attributes, for example 'gold is a malleable, yellow metal'. Rather, they argue, reference may be fixed by a kind of 'dubbing' or 'baptism', such as 'gold is whatever this substance is' (pointing), or 'electricity is what caused this needle to jump'. We can fix a reference prior to and apart from any knowledge of the essential properties of certain states and relations and yet claim that, when we used the terms, we were referring to the kinds as constituted by those essential properties, whatever those properties might be. Furthermore, if the reference of a term like 'electricity' is fixed not by some set of properties but by a 'dubbing' or some similar procedure, then the fact that the description associated with the term may change across theories is yet compatible with continuity of reference.[8]

[7] John Lyons, *Semantics* (Cambridge University Press, Cambridge, 1977), pp. 181–2.

[8] I am aware here of dealing with a complex argument in a summary way. Readers who wish to pursue it might refer to *Metaphor and Religious Language* by Janet Martin Soskice (Oxford University Press, Oxford, 1985), especially chapter seven.

In a most interesting article, Richard Boyd develops these comments on reference to support a realist construal of the role of metaphorical theory terms in scientific theory construction.[9] In the past it has been said that metaphors simply lack the precision necessary to science. Over and against this stands clear evidence that actual theory construction is sometimes heavily dependent on metaphorical terms. Boyd's suggestion is that the old vision of scientific precision is chimerical and, following Kripke, that the 'existence of explicit definitions is not characteristic of referring expressions', nor even 'a typical accompaniment to sustained epistemic access'. If this is so, then, he argues, we have the leeway necessary for a realist interpretation of metaphorical theory terms. Indeed, model and metaphor are ideally suited for providing flexible networks of terms which, while not necessarily directly or exhaustively descriptive (their very status as metaphors alerts us to that), can none the less claim to be reality-depicting.

In the right circumstances, even a substantially false description may put one in the right relationship to a causally significant situation and make genuine epistemic access possible. For example, consider a phenomenon called 'rose replant disease'. Despite this nomenclature of 'disease', I understand that no one is quite sure what it is; what is certain is that roses planted in soil where other roses have recently grown fail to flourish. It is not known whether this is because one rose may pass infection to another through the soil or whether the first rose depletes the resources of the soil in some way that cannot readily be met by top-dressing with fertilizer, or something else entirely. Yet the designation 'rose replant disease' successfully refers to the phenomenon whatever its cause, and the language of 'disease' provides the focus by which we may attempt to isolate the causes. It is epistemic access that is important to referring expressions, especially in the sciences. As Boyd puts it, reference is an epistemic notion.

The argument so far has tried to demonstrate how it is that terms may be judged to be reality-depicting prior to definitive

[9] Richard Boyd, 'Metaphor and Theory Change: What is "Metaphor" a Metaphor for?' in Andrew Ortony (ed.), *Metaphor and Thought* (Cambridge University Press, Cambridge, 1979).

knowledge and thus vindicate the use of metaphor in theory construction, thereby strengthening the realist's case.

Before attempting to apply these arguments to the religious case we should emphasize two things. First, the realist programme outlined is a cautious one: the realist is not claiming that the particular account of the world which he or she favours is the only or even the best one. Indeed, models change, theories move on, and descriptive vocabularies accordingly come and go. This descriptive flux, far from debilitating the realist's argument, is exactly why he or she feels the need to make one. Some explanation must be given for the continuity of access which makes scientific investigation possible. The account given of metaphor and theory construction goes some way to clarifying how descriptions can change while maintaining that that which is described need not. As Richard Boyd puts it, the world informs our theories, even though our theories never adequately describe the world.

Secondly, this realism has a significantly social face, so much so that the arguments of Kripke, Putnam, and Boyd, at least in the way in which I've made use of them, might best be described as 'social' (rather than 'causal') accounts of reference and reality depiction. As Putnam insists, it is not words which refer but speakers using words *who* refer. The realism under discussion emphasizes rather than conceals contextuality, by emphasizing that descriptive language, while dealing with immediate experience, will be language embedded in certain traditions of investigation and conviction. For example, the Western geneticist takes it for granted that trait inheritance is not the result of magical spells or configurations of the planets at the time of birth and is due to some biochemical mechanism which he or she explains by the best model available in the tradition in which the investigation stands, that of Western medicine. The descriptive language the geneticist uses is forged in a particular tradition of investigation and a context of agreement on what constitutes evidence and what is a genuine argument. While theories may be reality depicting they are not free from contextuality, both historical and cultural. This point, that reference is linked to particular contexts of enquiry, is one which any realist should welcome.

How, then, might we apply this to the religious case? Any

argument analogous to the ones made in the philosophy of science must involve the claim that we are causally related to God. This seems perfectly acceptable, indeed it is a basic tenet of most theistic religions that we are so related, but how can this relationship be described? We might propose that God relates to us causally through religious experience: to take a famous example, God is that which on Monday 23 November 1654 from about half-past ten until half-past midnight, Pascal knew as 'Fire. God of Abraham, God of Isaac, God of Jacob, not of philosphers and scholars. Certainty, certainty, heartfelt, joy, peace.'

Religious experiences like this one, and also of a more diffuse kind, are of considerable importance to the way in which theists claim to speak of God, a point to which we will return. We should not feel too embarrassed at considering the religious experience of individuals in attempts to ground our talk of God, for even the experiences on which scientific investigations rest are, at some descriptive level, the experiences of *some one*. None the less there is a clear disanalogy here with the scientific case, because religious experiences cannot be repeated under controlled circumstances, and using them to fix a reference involves a commitment to the validity of the experience as reported by the experiencer.

We might then try a designation on which there is general agreement that if it designates anything it designates God. Consider Anselm's 'God is that than which nothing greater can be conceived.' This comes near to what we seek, for it is a formula which does not wish to describe so much as to give a designation which, if it designates anything, designates only that which is called God. The wider proof, despite many defenders, is not generally thought to be successful, but this is of no matter here since our object is not to prove that God exists but to provide some designation which, if it designates anything, designates God. The difficulty, however, is that the abstract nature of the formula 'God is that than which nothing greater can be conceived' gives us no suggestion of a causal relation to the world. If religious experience seems too intimate and Anselm's formula too abstract, we might try the more experiential 'God is the source and cause of all there is'. This formula, fundamental to the cosmological argument, retains the kind of epistemic agnosticism we want—God is not described in terms of some set of essential properties, but pointed to as the source of the universe. Now this does not demonstrate that there is such a unified source or that, if there is, it is the God of the Christians; but this possibility of error, even of being radically mistaken about that which is, is a risk the realist takes. This amounts to being willing to admit that the Christian God might not exist, and many Christians admit freely that this is a possibility, however much their own experience leads them to think that this is not the case.

Now let's re-examine attempts to ground our speaking of God via religious experience. We sometimes fail to remark that the religious experiences which are significant are not simply one's own—many religious people never have dramatic religious experiences like that of Pascal. As important or even more important to the overall composition of a religion like Christianity is the experience of what one might call 'authoritative others'. What this means is that if Pascal has such an experience, and if I'm inclined to trust his judgement about it, then I too can say 'God is that which appeared to Pascal on 23 November 1654'. I use Pascal's experience to ground my reference. But here note that this reliance on 'authoritative others' is not unique to religion. What I refer to on the basis of my own immediate experience is a rather small set of things but what we speak of on the basis of our relationship to others is vast (that is one of the points we can take from Kripke's 'Columbus' example). I have no immediate personal experience of Napoleon, or the current President of the United States, or of quasars. I speak about them in virtue of my connectedness, through language and various structures of communication, to others who I consider do have some kind of access to these persons or entities. The astrophysicist is, for me, an authoritative other when I want to speak about quasars or 'black holes' in space.

In religious matters, of course, people come to be seen as authoritative for reasons other than what they say—we may know of their great devotion, their disciplined life of prayer, or their concern for the loveless and poor, we 'sense' a kind of sanctity in what we hear, see, or read of them. Pascal, Dr Johnson, or one's great-aunt might all count for an individual as authoritative others. Ezekiel or St Paul might count for large groups of people, for whole religious traditions, as authoritative others. But how do we get from the bare experience of individuals to the complex story and formal teachings of, say, a religion like Christianity? We can imagine a situation like this. Such a person has an experience which they take to be 'of God' and, often with a struggle and usually hesitantly, describe it, characteristically by using metaphor. This may be a novel metaphor or one culled from the particular tradition in which the individual stands. 'That which appeared to me so is God.' Once they have introduced the description we, or those who regard them as authoritative, may use it to designate 'He who Is'. This is one possible account of what Christians call 'revelation'.

We are not considering religious experience simply in the restricted sense of one's own personal religious experience or lack of it, but also in the broader sense in which it is also the experience of a community as seen through a particular interpretative tradition. Religion, too, makes claims based on experience, different in kind from that on which scientific judgements are based, but experience nonetheless, and as in the scientific case this experience is understood in a context of shared assumption and shared models, and discussed in terms of a descriptive vocabulary which has been built up by a community over a period of years or even, in the Judeo-Christian case, over millenia.

My suggestion is that a good deal of the language of what Christians consider divine revelation develops in this way: metaphors capture someone's experience, for example Hosea's vision of Israel's relationship to God as like that of wife to husband. Subsequent writers in the tradition then pick up the model and in recounting their own experience extend it, as did Ezekiel in an extreme way with the 'marriage' model. In the Bible, revelation cannot be separate from tradition (whether literary or devotional or both), for it is pre-eminently within a continuous stream of reflections that models for God's activity have been developed and maintained. Ian Ramsey's studies of the 'wind/spirit' model for divine activity shows this admirably.[10] It is the claim of the theological realist

[10] See his *Models for Divine Activity* (Oxford University Press, Oxford, 1964).

that the models and the metaphorical terminology, while clearly arising in particular cultures and contexts and modified over time, may nonetheless be reality-depicting.

Now if this case for realism is convincing, it has a number of implications for the theologians: firstly, as I've argued, it is perfectly respectable to use metaphors to speak of a God who 'cannot be named'. Secondly, as above, the models used will inevitably be linked to particular historical and social contexts. On my argument this isn't a vice but the very foundation of a realist case: having a shared descriptive vocabulary and a tradition is one's only chance of being able to say anything at all, in theology, science, ethics, or any other field of interest and endeavour. A shared and matured descriptive vocabularly gives the possibility of sustained reflection which goes beyond the necessarily limited experiences of each individual. Thirdly, and finally, change in models and descriptive vocabularly is wholly to be expected, but none the less the realist can still argue for continuity of access. Again we must remember that it is not words which refer, but speakers using words who refer. With natural language it is not that individual terms somehow 'latch on to' the world, but rather that whole networks of words, practices, and beliefs represent it. Perhaps this is what Wittgenstein was getting at in expressing his 'disgust' at Esperanto in the quote with which we began.

'The realist explanation, in a nutshell,' says Putnam, 'is not that language mirrors the world but that *speakers* mirror the world; i.e. their environment—in the sense of constructing a symbolic representation of that environment.'[11] When we consider religious language we should regard the particular models or, more accurately, sets of counterbalanced models which a given culture or group finds valuable as 'housing' something important to the faith, even if no one particular formula is, or even could be, wholly satisfactory.[12] These 'conclusions' in the philosophy of religion are merely starting-points for Biblical and doctrinal studies. What, for instance, is housed in the talk of God's 'messengers' who appear in the

[11] 'Realism and Reason' in *Meaning and the Moral Sciences* (Routledge and Kegan Paul, London, 1978), p. 123.
[12] This is not to say that we have a mysterious pre-linguistic content which, at intervals, we clothe in new terms. Experience and interpretation are inseparable here.

New Testament as angels? Is the fact that many twentieth century Christians, even quite conservative ones, make little mention of angels (or of demons) a matter of not believing in them any more? Or is the story and the language game much more complex? Do we judge that these ways of speaking housed insights that we prefer now to express simply by speaking of divine presence and human frailty? These are things for systematic theology and Biblical studies to discuss.[13]

'It seems that from the very beginning this religion (Christianity) has been committed to the possibility of expressing the same faith, the same teaching, and the same doctrine in diverse ways', says George Lindbeck.[14] It has been the attempt of this defence of metaphor and theological realism to add credibility to this ancient desire for continuity in change, and underlying unity within diversity of expression. Much remains to be spelled out. But what we are dealing with is not just a modern problem, it is also an ancient insight—the insight that cataphatic theology is made possible by apophatic, that we speak for the most part metaphorically of God, or not at all.

[13] Two recent theological studies which move interestingly in this direction are George Lindbeck's *The Nature of Doctrine* and '*Christus Victor* Revisited: A Study in Metaphor and the Transformation of Meaning' by Colin Gunton, *Journal of Theological Studies*, vol. 36, pt. 1 (April 1985), pp. 129–45.

[14] *The Nature of Doctrine* (SPCK, London, 1984), p.92.

8

Conspicuous Sanctity and Religious Belief

GRACE M. JANTZEN

Natural theology is traditionally defined as dealing with those truths about God and his relations to the world which can be arrived at by means of natural human faculties, without the aid of divine revelation. Theologians have, of course, differed as to which, if any, truths can be so obtained. St Thomas Aquinas believed that at least the existence of God as the First Cause could be proved by human reason, and offered the famous Five Ways to support his claim. Other theologians, like Karl Barth, have been much more sceptical about the possibility of natural reason to arrive at any truth whatever about God. Since it is systematically distorted by the effects of the fall, any God which could be found by human reason would be a false god.

Whatever we make of this, the definition of natural theology as it stands presupposes that we can tell the difference between natural human reason and divine revelation. This means that we must be able to identify a revelation, to know what counts as a revelation. As both St Thomas and Karl Barth use the terms, the contrast is primarily between such truths as emerge in the process of reasoning about the world and its contents on the one hand, and Sacred Scripture and (possibly) ecclesiastical tradition or preaching on the other. The latter is revelatory, the former is natural.

But where does religious experience come in? Should it be considered part of revelation? It would be natural to do so if we were to think of religious experience as special communications of religious truths in voices and visions and the like. Yet although that is the sort of thing that writers like Mackie[1] and Gaskin[2] evaluate when they discuss the evidential value of religious experiences, it is hardly what most believers mean by

[1] J. L. Mackie, *The Miracle of Theism* (Clarendon Press, Oxford, 1982).
[2] John Gaskin, *The Quest for Eternity* (Penguin, Harmondsworth, Middx., 1984).

it. A great many Christians would say that they continue in their faith in God because, in spite of all the problems (intellectual and otherwise) which attend on religious belief, they would be fundamentally untrue to their own experience if they abandoned their faith. But in this appeal to religious experience they are not usually appealing to voices and visions and ecstasies. Rather, they are indicating the sense of the presence of God in their daily, ordinary lives, giving purpose to routine, providing courage, comfort, and hope, strengthening and deepening their moral commitment and sensitivity, leading them to worship and praise.

Even the mystics, often considered to be the vision-mongers of Christendom, are on the whole much more cautious about experiences in the 'voices and visions' sense than popular opinion—or philosophers like Mackie who take their whole analysis of mysticism from the valuable but outdated and one-sided chapter on 'Mysticism' in William James's *The Varieties of Religious Experience*—would suggest. To cite only two examples from many: the most strident sceptic could hardly outdo St John of the Cross in his systematic debunking of such experiences as a source of information about God and his relations to the world,[3] and Julian of Norwich, though she was much more tolerant of visions as sources of revelation, is nevertheless emphatic that 'I am not good because of the revelations, but only if I love God better . . . for I am sure that there are many who never had revelations or visions, but only the common teaching of Holy Church, who love God better than I . . .'[4] And it is this, not the vision, which is important.

This daily, ordinary loving obedience to God is certainly experiential; it is not merely an intellectual assent to a set of credal propositions, though as in all continuing experience the intellect must be integrated into the whole. And it is obviously religious. Is it then religious experience? Surely it is; and it is, I suggest, what is commonly meant by Christians who appeal to their personal experience of God, rather than some earth-shattering one-off ecstasy—even when they have *also* experienced this.

---

[3] Cf. *The Ascent of Mount Carmel*, Bk. 2.
[4] *Showings*, eds. E. Colledge and J. Walsh, Classics of Western Spirituality (SPCK and Paulist Press, London and New York, 1978), p.191.

Well, then, is this garden-variety religious experience to be categorized with natural theology or with revelation? Hardly with revelation: there is not usually a claim to any new truths being communicated, though there is often a personal appropriation of truths that had formerly been accepted at only an intellectual level. Yet it is also decidedly odd to put it with natural theology and its reliance on ordinary human faculties. Its whole character is somehow to transcend these faculties, not in the sense of obliterating them, but perfecting and enhancing them. What I mean is illustrated by comments like 'Only the steady awareness of God's presence made it possible for me to bear those years of drudgery', or 'I'm sure I wouldn't have troubled to listen to him had not God sensitized me to his needs.' Whatever we make of comments like these, the sort of things to which they refer are the nuts and bolts of everyday Christian experience, and are often spoken of by reference to such theological concepts as divine grace or the indwelling, sanctifying Holy Spirit.

Natural theology can of course include such experiences among the phenomena which it considers. Thus for instance Basil Mitchell speaks of conspicuous sanctity as an important ingredient in the cumulative case for theism,[5] and Patrick Sherry gives a sensitive account of the way in which many people feel that in an encounter with a saintly person they are confronted with God more decisively than in the best of arguments.[6] But including them in this way is obviously different from saying that the experiences themselves are nothing more than the ordinary working of human faculties. If that is how they were assessed, then such assessment would be a way of excluding their relevance to natural theology, rather than seeing them as a part of it. They can be a part of natural theology—part of a case for the existence of God—only if they are thought to be in some sense at least possibly supernatural.

So must we after all think of them as revelatory? Not, I have said, in the sense of providing new theological truths. In one sense, of course, a Christian believes that all of creation and human history can be taken as the revelation of God; but if the concept of revelation is broadened to that extent, then it can

---

[5] *The Justification of Religious Belief* (Macmillan, London, 1973), p. 41.

[6] *Spirits, Saints and Immortality* (Macmillan, London, 1984), pp. 34–5.

no longer serve as a contrast to the concept of natural theology. Thus ordinary, continuing religious experience, the personal heart of Christian faith, seems to cut across the time-honoured distinction between natural and revealed theology, and by not fitting into either category raises questions about the categories themselves.

The epistemological value of such ordinary religious experience is often ignored by philosophers of religion. Even when they do discuss religious experience, the tendency is to turn quickly to the phenomena of voices and visions and ecstasies to assess their evidential value, on the assumption that if these most intense cases offer little to a cumulative case for theism, the calmer, continuing experience could hardly offer more. I think that this is mistaken, as I hope to show. As a preliminary to doing this, it is interesting to probe an assumption upon which all the arguments of natural theology, positive and negative, are based. This is the assumption that the existence or non-existence of God is an important issue.

What does it matter whether God exists? The question may sound outrageous, even blasphemous, and too obvious to require attention. Yet surely the task of philosophy is to probe the obvious, to discover and question our assumptions and presuppositions. The idea that it is important whether or not God exists certainly qualifies as one such assumption. For theists, clearly, it is central to their framework of beliefs and values; but non-theists, too, even when they consider religion of negligible or negative value, would, I think, on the whole agree that if, contrary to their beliefs, God did exist, this would be of great importance.

But important for what? To whom? *Why* does it matter? The obvious place to look for an answer is in those books on philosophy of religion which I have already cited which evaluate the case for and against religious belief. Yet even here answers are not easily forthcoming. Some philosophers simply dive into the arguments, assuming their importance without further ado.[7] Others, like J. L. Mackie in his *The Miracle of Theism*, explicitly affirm the paramount significance of the question 'whether there is or is not a god'. He says 'This is a

[7] See for example Richard Swinburne, *The Existence of God* (Clarendon Press, Oxford, 1979).

genuine, meaningful question, and an important one—too important for us to take sides about it casually or arbitrarily.'[8] Yes, but why? Mackie considers this too obvious for further comment; he moves directly to assessment of the arguments.

This, I suggest, is very odd philosophical procedure when we stop to think about it. What, after all, is the point of expending vast intellectual energy evaluating the pros and cons of a proposition unless we are quite clear why its affirmation or negation matters? I suggest that when we stop to consider why the question of the existence of God is important, new insights emerge into the relationship between natural theology and religious experience.

An initial response to the question might be that the existence of God (or his non-existence) is a fact, and normal human rationality wishes to ascertain the facts. The arguments and counter-arguments of natural theology are efforts to decide what should be counted as facts in relation to the question of God; it is important as all facts are important. This response, however, will hardly do, not because the existence or non-existence of God is not a fact, but because many facts are utterly trivial. Not even a statistics-mad society considers all statistics, even if correct, as having equal significance: a person who kept a meticulous record of the number of blades of grass in his back garden would find no market for the publication of his 'facts'.

The putative Loch Ness Monster, by contrast, has a perennial fascination for many people, who are willing to spend time and money on books about her. Yet even here the question of the existence of God is taken to be of an altogether different order of importance. Most people, believers or not, would consider it in rather poor taste if the BBC News ended with a light-hearted tale of a new effort to prove theism, the way it occasionally ends with a report of a new attempt to find Nessie. It might be felt that such an account would trivialize that which many people consider to be of the utmost significance. But now we are back at the beginning. Clearly the existence of God does not hold its importance simply because it is a fact, but because of the kind of fact it is. So we must ask again, *why* is it so important?

[8] Op. cit., p. 1; cf. Gaskin, p. 9.

We might want to reply that if God exists, this alters our whole conception of the universe. It is not a chance combination of elements but has come into existence through purposive creative activity. If, on the other hand, God does not exist, then the universe as we know it is in the end a brute fact, perhaps one in a series of hot Big Bangs. Thus our cosmological understanding is affected by the answer we give to the question of God's existence.

Yet it would be a mistake to pin too much on this. Astronomers and cosmologists do not have to settle the question of God's existence before they can get on with their work, nor do their religious beliefs affect the methods and techniques appropriate to their science. In this sense, the facts about the existence of God 'leave everything as it is'. This shows that the fact of the existence or non-existence of God is in some respects different from scientific facts. If there is a God who is in some sense the cause of the universe, then he is (in that sense) the cause of *all* facts about the world. He is not a fact among other facts, but of a different order altogether. At the level of scientific investigation, it is possible for practitioners to disagree about their religious beliefs while being professionally of one mind.

Suppose now that natural theology were to discover a sufficiently strong case to put beyond reasonable doubt that there exists a God, a being who is personal at least in the sense of being wise enough and powerful enough purposely to bring about the universe. This would have significance in terms of ultimate cosmological theory, and in that sense would satisfy intellectual curiosity and affect our overall account of the world. But by itself it would hardly make a difference to scientific procedure, let alone be of profound significance for everyday life.

For this to be the case, we would have to know not merely that there is a God, but that this God is one to whom we may personally or corporately relate, and that consequences attend upon this relationship. It is difficult to see how natural theology could ever come to this awareness; it would seem that if there were no revelation taken into account, then the God arrived at by natural theology would be irrelevant to all except cosmological theorists. There would be no basis to suppose that this God was interested in human beings unless he in some way revealed such interest. But then we have moved away from natural theology in the strict sense towards some variety of revelation. Natural theology cannot in principle, even if totally successful, discover a religiously significant God; or, better, it cannot arrive at the religious significance of any God it discovers. This would not have come as a surprise to St Thomas, of course. He held that there are many truths which reason by itself can never discover, and that at least some of them are necessary for salvation. Most important among these is the truth of God's desire for relationship with us, and his revelation of it paradigmatically in the Incarnation of Christ.[9]

I should like to suggest, however, that without religious experience even such revelation of propositions about God would be devoid of religious significance. We might have expected that revealed theology would take us very much further than natural theology in its answer to the question 'Why does it matter whether God exists?', and so, in a sense, it does, for it emphasizes the need and the means of salvation, a concept which natural theology on its own could hardly have developed. Historically, of course, much of what passed for natural theology was greatly taken up with considering what was necessary for salvation, but that is because much of it was not natural theology in the strict sense but rather critical assessment of the putative truths of revelation, without which the idea of salvation could hardly have arisen.

It has been regularly held that by means of revelation we are informed that this life is part of a much greater life, extending after death into everlasting bliss or everlasting torment. The Incarnation and death of Christ reveal (some would say 'make possible') the forgiveness of God, so that belief in him ensures our salvation—heaven after death. Thus whether or not God exists is of utmost importance because it involves our everlasting destiny.

There is no doubt that many people have thought along these lines, and tried to organize their lives so that they will be candidates for one kind of future rather than the other. But

---

[9] *Summa Theologiae* I, Q1, a1; cf. Q2, a2, reply Obj. 1.

when it is put this starkly, it is clear that on this account the significance of the existence of God is not religious at all, but prudential. It may matter for my everlasting destiny whether or not God exists, but it does not matter for its own sake. It is only that if God exists I may have certain hopes or fears for myself and others, and take certain precautions, which would otherwise be pointless. Putting it another way, if this very same God had revealed that there is no life after death, or that it is the same for everybody no matter what they believe or do, then God would be irrelevant, even if we were quite convinced that he exists. On this account, then, God himself would be without religious significance, though not without prudential implications.

What we should draw from this, however, is not that the existence of God is a matter of no religious importance but rather that this concept of salvation is utterly inadequate. Salvation is not (or at least not primarily) about our future destiny but about our relationship to God and the gradual transforming effect of that relationship in our lives.[10] Many Christians have echoed sentiments attributed to a great Muslim mystic:

> My God, if I love thee out of fear of hell, burn me in hell.
> If I love thee out of desire for Paradise, exclude me from Paradise.
> But if I love thee for thyself alone,
> Grant me a share in thy everlasting beauty . . .

To love God for his own sake, to share his everlasting beauty: now we have indeed entered the realm of religious significance. And at the moment we do so, we also enter the realm of religious experience. The two are not separable. This need not of course be the realm of religious experience*s*, voices, visions, and ecstasies; but as we have seen, this is not in any case what most Christians mean by the term. If religious experience is centrally the sense of the loving presence of God, gradually helping people to reorient and integrate their lives in accordance with their love for him, is this not precisely what salvation is? Salvation must, surely, be religious experience if anything ever is: not in the sense of being a single climactic

---

[10] I have argued for this in more detail in 'Human Diversity and Salvation in Christ' in *Religious Studies* 20, pp. 407–13.

experience, though for some people the initial reorientation of their lives may have this traumatic character, but in the sense of a gradual opening of all life, all of experience, to the whole-making love of God. Many Christians believe that this has ramifications beyond bodily death, and I am not denying that possibility. But whether it does nor not, that is not what is centrally important. Salvation in Christian thought is the transforming experience of God percolating through life. It follows that salvation is not 'all or nothing' like a possession which one either has or does not have; rather, it is a process, a 'way' of salvation, along which one can go forwards but also backwards. Those who can identify a particular time when they began to turn to the love of God—perhaps their baptism—may well refer to this as the time they 'were saved', but, speaking strictly, this is the time when they *began* to be saved in a process that still continues. Salvation, here, is not primarily from 'hell-fire', but from the fragmentation of a life not integrated in the whole-making love of God.

But what is the epistemological value of such religious experience? If what I have said so far is correct, then we have in religious experience a knowledge of God that goes beyond anything obtainable through natural theology or even through propositional revelation. At their best, these can give us only knowledge *about* God, the facts of his existence, nature, and activity. Religious experience purports to be knowledge *of* God, knowledge by acquaintance rather than knowledge by description. Even if this is true, it does not belittle the need for knowledge of facts, of course, since unless the main propositions of natural and/or revealed theology were true, knowledge of God in experience in the sense I have described it would be illusory. Nevertheless, religious experience may offer a means both of coming to those facts and testing them; and those who speak most profoundly of experience of God claim to know him in so intimate a sense that natural theology seems to them like intellectual gymnastics.

This sense of complete certainty, characteristic of many of those regarded as giants of Christian spirituality, is frequently noted by those who assess the evidential value of religious experience for natural theology. But two mistakes often vitiate the consideration of certainty. The first is that it is often assumed that the certainty is a concomitant or result of cataclysmic mystical phenomena—experience*s* rather than continuing, much more prosaic, experience. I have already argued that this focus is distorted. Once one has opted to focus on the allegedly soul-shattering mystical phenomena, it is a very short step to the second mistake, which is to suppose that the mystics did not distinguish between feeling certain and being certain—psychological and intellectual certainty. It is only to be expected that such traumatic events will have deep psychological effects—the mystic can hardly help but *feel* certain of the truth of the vision—but of course that is no guarantee of the veracity of its contents, let alone of the whole religious system in which it occurs and is understood.[11]

As with many philosophical pronouncements about mysticism, however, a careful study of primary texts yields a quite different account. In the first place, many mystics explicitly drew the distinction between feeling certain and being certain, and spent a great deal of effort warning against the pseudo-security of the former.[12] Furthermore, it was usually of the psychologically cataclysmic phenomena that they were most sceptical and least certain.[13] In order to come to any useful assessment of their certainty and its epistemological status, therefore, it is necessary to look again, and to ask two basic questions: what were they so certain about? And how did they arrive at this certainty? To focus the discussion, I propose to take as a case study St Teresa of Avila's teaching in her book *The Interior Castle*.

Teresa writes that a person who has advanced to a certain stage of spirituality experiences union with God which, once experienced, can never afterwards be doubted.

God implants himself in the interior of that soul in such a way that, when it returns to itself, it cannot possibly doubt that God has been in it and it has been in God . . . a certainty remains in the soul, which can be put there only by God.[14]

---

[11] See for example William James, *The Varieties of Religious Experience* (Collins, London, 1977), pp. 407–13.

[12] For one amusing account see *The Cloud of Unknowing*, chaps. 52–3.

[13] See Walter Hilton, *The Scale of Perfection* 1, 10–11 and 2, 26; also John of the Cross, *The Ascent of Mount Carmel*, bk. 2.

[14] *Interior Castle* 5, 1; English trans. E. Allison Peers (Sheed and Ward, London, 1946), vol. 2, p. 251.

As the quotation indicates, there is a sense of self-loss and a definite period of time in which this union is felt to take place: it sounds rather like a climactic experience (in the narrow sense of the word) after all. But the context makes clear that Teresa is not talking about a vision or any sort of physical or quasi-physical sensation. She is rather talking about a period of intense psychological awareness of what has been happening as the soul turned resolutely and steadily to God, a moment of *recognition*. Although the psychological intensity of the recognition passes, the individual can never again doubt that what she has recognized is true about herself.

A non-religious parallel can make this clearer. Suppose an individual whose life has been marred by a negative self-image works gradually to change that self-concept. It may have been intellectually repudiated for a long while, but it is nevertheless still a fundamental attitude. Then one day comes the liberating recognition: 'I am a worthwhile person after all.' The intensity of this may well be overwhelming at first, but that soon fades. Yet if the recognition has had depth and reality, and is not merely a form of words or a theory, then even though the intensity fades, that is not what matters. The liberation is there, there is a new perception of oneself, of which one is certain and no longer has any doubts—in spite of the fact that it may take a long time to work out the insight in practice. In one sense the intense experience does not matter at all, nor is that what generates the certainty. What is important is the new insight of self-worth; and if it had grown slowly and calmly rather than coming in a rush of emotion it would be none the worse for that, nor would it carry any less certainty.

Similarly, Teresa is talking about a union with God which has been developing for a long time, though there may come intense moments of realizing what is happening. And once it has been realized, it can never be denied again, though the immediate awareness may well fade. Teresa continues, 'If anyone has not that certainty, I should say that what he has experienced is not union of the whole soul with God.'[15] Although a vision or a voice may be psychologically compelling at the time of its occurrence, it can and should be doubted

---

[15] Ibid., p. 252.

afterwards, not gullibly accepted. But the recognition of union with God is different. Why? Is Teresa simply moving in circles: if it really is union with God then we will have certainty, and if we have certainty, then it really is union with God?

I think not; but to see why not it is necessary to look at the broader context of her work. Teresa in this book is describing what happens in prayer, dividing it into stages from the first rudimentary beginnings to the heights of 'spiritual union', as she calls it. She takes as her overarching metaphor the image of the soul as 'a castle, in which there are many rooms (or apartments) . . . some above, others below, others at each side; and in the centre and midst of them all is the chiefest mansion',[16] which is where God dwells. The progress of prayer is the progress through the various rooms of the castle, moving from the remote outer rooms filled with darkness and reptiles and foul things towards the centre and the presence of God. The imagery must not be pressed too hard; Teresa herself jumbles it with other metaphors in characteristic abandon. Nevertheless it provides a vivid framework for her sustained exploration of prayer.

Fundamental to her metaphor is the insistence that growth in prayer is growth in self-knowledge. The interior castle is the soul; exploration of it is therefore exploration of ourselves.[17] The journey to God is at the same time the journey inwards. In company with many other mystics, Teresa speaks of God at the centre of the soul, so that increasing knowledge of God requires increasing self-knowledge. She says

It is no small pity, and should cause us no little shame, that, through our own fault, we do not understand ourselves, or know who we are. Would it not be a sign of great ignorance, daughters, if a person were asked who he was, and could not say, and had no idea who his father or his mother was, or from what country he came? Though that is great stupidity, our own is incomparably greater if we make no attempt to discover who we are . . .[18]

Thus Teresa encourages her readers to enter into this castle of

---

[16] *Interior Castle* I. I; p. 202.
[17] This is a theme permeating Western spirituality at least since St Augustine's *Confessions* to such an extent that spirituality is often simply called 'the interior life'.
[18] *Interior Castle* I. I; pp. 201–2.

self-exploration. But here she finds her metaphor betraying her. She exclaims,

I seem rather to be talking nonsense; for, if this castle is the soul, there can clearly be no question of our entering it. For we ourselves are the castle: and it would be absurd to tell someone to enter a room when he was in it already![19]

Further consideration, however, convinces her that the problem is only one of expression. Although in one sense it is indeed ridiculous to talk about entering into ourselves, the quest for deeper self-knowledge is anything but ridiculous, and it is this which Teresa is advocating. Her account of the movement through the various rooms of the castle is an account of coming to terms with ever-deeper layers of oneself. Though she stresses that there are many differences between people, and that her own experience must not be made into a Procrustean bed, she does think that at least in general outline there will be similarities between people's self-exploration, so that her account will be useful to other people who are going through it. Her writing, therefore, is not intended as a mere narration of her own life, but as a guide to others, based on the presupposition of a broad similarity in the human psyche. We might note in passing that without this presupposition no psychology would be possible: it may be here, in the broadest sense of 'religious experience', that we should look for similarities between world religions, rather than seeking a mystical core of religion in the phenomena of mystical experiences. The fact that Teresa is writing her book as a guide for others should count as yet another warning against the tendency to take her writing as a narration of unique individual experiences which can be totted up in an overall weighing of the probabilities of theism. She is not interested in that. Instead, she is inviting her readers to pursue self-exploration, and is offering her own insights as a guide.

This, however, means that the method of assessment of the insights arrived at will be rather different from methods appropriate to evaluating other sorts of propositions, say legal or scientific ones. When can one be sure that an insight about oneself is true? The first thing is that the insight must be

[19] Ibid., p. 203.

personal, must be 'owned'. It is of no use for my self-exploration if someone else has insights into me which I don't have,
even if they are correct—and indeed even if at an intellectual
level I acknowledge that they *are* correct. If it is to be any good
for me, I must come to recognize it for myself, to own it at a
deeper level than a purely intellectual one. But once I do, then
I am *sure* of it. This is not a matter of testing probabilities but
of *recognition*—looking at old familiar material and really
seeing it for the first time.[20] It is much more like suddenly (or
gradually) recognizing the point of a poem, perhaps a poem
we had read many times before, than like checking a
hypothesis; more like fitting the pieces together to make a
discovery than like conducting an experiment.

But of course alleged discoveries can be mistaken, and
'eureka' insights can misfire; there is always the possibility of
self-deception. That is why testing and retesting are of such
crucial importance. Teresa suggests that the insights of self-
exploration must similarly be tested, and offers three connected ways of avoiding self-deception, ways which themselves facilitate the efforts toward self-knowledge. The first is
prayer, the second humility, the third is obedience.

This sounds quite hopelessly pious—not to mention ques-
tion-begging—until we see what Teresa means by them.
Starting with prayer, Teresa certainly does not mean merely
'saying prayers', repeating religious exercises: in her view
such mere uttering of pious phrases is more likely to foster self-
deception than to correct it. What she means is summed up to
be the word 'meditation', and she is thinking of meditation on
Christ and Christian doctrine. But what does this have to do
with increasing self-knowledge and avoidance of self-deception? Teresa knows that self-knowledge cannot come about by
sheer introspection: self-preoccupation is the opposite, not the
correlate, of self-possession. Efforts that are simply introspec-
tive would almost certainly end up either in narcissism or in
self-flagellation. Self-knowledge, like many other forms of
knowledge, can best be learned indirectly.

[20] For some psychological aspects of this, see Don Browning, 'Faith and the
Dynamics of Knowing' and Leland Elhard, 'Living Faith: Some Contributions of the
Concept of Ego-Identity to the Understanding of Faith'; both in Peter Homans (ed.)
The Dialogue Between Theology and Psychology (University of Chicago Press, London and
Chicago, 1969).

Again, a non-religious parallel is helpful: consider what it is to teach philosophy. The function of a philosophy teacher is not so much to impart information as to foster learning skills so that the students will learn to gather and evaluate information for themselves; the goal of a teacher is to make himself or herself dispensible. But this cannot be done directly. Giving students information *about* learning skills is not the same as developing those learning skills in them; that can only be done by teaching something else—arguments about the existence of God, or the history of philosophy, or logic—and engaging them in the actual practice of learning, so that little by little they acquire the techniques and skills for themselves, and eventually apply them of their own accord. In this way students are learning not only the content of philosophy but how to be philosophers, and indeed neither could be properly learned without the other.

Trying to know oneself without any other reference point would be like trying to develop philosophical skills without any content: it would be self-defeating. Prayer, in the sense of meditation on Christ, gives a reference-point. Here is a life and a death, a set of values, by which other values can be measured. By sustained reflection on Christ's life and teaching we come to greater self-knowledge than by sheer introspection. Teresa is of course writing as a committed Christian for whom Christ is God Incarnate, but her analysis at this point does not depend on acceptance of that doctrine: she herself mentions meditation on the saints as well as on Christ. The point is that if we set ourselves to ponder the lives and teachings of anyone to whose values we pay lip-service, we will become more in touch with those values and thereby more aware of ourselves: Christ is a paradigm of such a model.

Sometimes this growing self-awareness is by way of contrast; at other times it is by recognition of what really attracts us. Teresa describes it like this:

As I see it, we shall never succeed in knowing ourselves unless we seek to know God . . . There are two advantages in this. First, it is clear that anything white looks very much whiter against something black, just as the black looks blacker against white. Secondly, if we turn from self towards God, our understanding and our will become nobler and readier to embrace all that is good: if we never rise above the slough of our own miseries we do ourselves a great disservice.[21]

By meditating on Christ and measuring ourselves against him, we come to see more clearly what our values really are, as opposed to what we like to think they are, and are thereby forced to relinquish self-deceptions about them. This is part of what Teresa means by prayer, and demonstrates how prayer can be a source of self-understanding as well as a test for its validity. And up to this point at least, what she has to say is not restricted to Christian believers, either in the sense that only Christians can profitably ponder the values of Christ, or that only Christ is worth pondering.

The second test of insight is humility, and it is closely linked to the first. By 'humility' Teresa does not mean being a door-mat for people to tread on: such an exhortation would in any case scarcely be consistent with her own vigorous reforming campaign in which church dignitaries, the leaders of the Inquisition, and even Philip II were on occasion treated to a taste of her forthrightness. Humility has much more to do with courage than with a negative self-concept: it is the willingness to face squarely and without pretence the insights that come in self-exploration. Unless accompanied by continuous will-to-honesty and renunciation of hypocrisy, one could meditate forever to no profit. Humility is the willingness to own up to the truth as it presents itself, whether it commends, rebukes, or challenges. Humility and integrity are closely related.

Part of what is involved here is also the willingness actually to embark on this demanding process, and making the time and space to do it. Teresa emphasizes the importance of this, and says that anyone who is serious about this spiritual progress will be well advised to put aside unnecessary affairs:[22] she does not of course mean that one must become a monk or a nun, but she is aware that we can become so preoccupied with all our activities that they become a hindrance or even a defence against being in touch with ourselves, to the extent that when we do manage to create some external silence for

---

[21] *Interior Castle* 1. 2; p. 209.
[22] Ibid., p. 211.

reflection, our heads are buzzing with other things and there is insufficient internal silence to 'hear ourselves think'. Serious and long-term commitment to exploring the interior castle may be a costly business and may require reorganization of our lifestyle: part of humility lies in accepting this. The practicalities involved here are once again fruitful for deepening self-knowledge, a test of our self-concept, and an exposition of self-deception.

This could sound as though it were one long exercise in self-indulgence, albeit of a rather peculiar sort. Teresa's emphasis on obedience corrects that impression. She is writing in a monastic context, where obedience is in the first instance to one's superior. But there is a much more fundamental sense of obedience underlying this, and that is praxis in accordance with increasing self-understanding. Self-exploration as Teresa speaks of it is never simply recognizing facts about oneself; rather, in this recognition, there is developing integration. As we discover who we are, we become what we discover: we do not merely find what is there already, but are changed by what we find. This may sound paradoxical, but is really a truism: a person who comes to recognize for the first time that he or she is really worthwhile after all is profoundly changed by that recognition. Yet this must still be thoroughly assimilated in the hard work of putting into practice, learning to act in accordance with the new self-knowledge, with many a blunder along the way.

So for Teresa it would be mockery to meditate on the values of Christ and measure ourselves by them without any intention to do something about the patches where we don't measure up. She states flatly,

All that the beginner in prayer has to do—and you must not forget this, for it is very important—is to labour and be resolute and prepare himself with all possible diligence to bring his will into conformity to the will of God . . . You may be quite sure that this comprises the very greatest perfection which can be attained on the spiritual road. The more perfectly a person practises it, the more he will receive of the Lord and the greater progress he will make on this road; do not think we have to use strange jargon or dabble in things of which we have no knowledge or understanding . . .[23]

[23] Ibid., 2. 1; pp. 216–17.

The spiritual life for Teresa does not consist in fancy phrases or pleasant experiences, whether or not these occur, but in the prosaic putting into practice of those values which we learn to know more deeply in meditation. The path of self-knowledge is thus the path of self-transformation, and the project is that of a lifetime. Actually learning to live by deepening self-understanding requires consistent deliberation and commitment; it has nothing to do with sporadic pious impulses on the one hand or with conformity to externally imposed rules on the other. Teresa along with many mystics is emphasizing union of the *will* (not the emotions, which fluctuate) with the will of God—the deliberate adoption and internalization of the values of compassion and sensitivity arrived at in meditation. Whether one also has sensations of emotional or ontological merging with the divine is simply not important.

We can now see how it is that Teresa can speak of certainty, and at the same time we can see the inadequacy of the distinction between being certain and feeling certain. A person who is systematically developing self-knowledge, working through the layers of the psyche and striving for integrity and integration, can hardly help but be acutely aware from time to time how his or her values are changing. Putting it another way, he or she is discovering values which had been there all along, latent and hardly recognized, perhaps buried under a rubble of hurts and defences. And these growing insights are of a different status than hypotheses about oneself whose probabilities are to be assessed. They have an immediacy and certainty which can, indeed, be deepened and tested in the ways described; but that is a different sort of testing than is appropriate for hypotheses. In this sense it does indeed make sense to speak of it as psychological certainty; but that label must not then be equated with 'feeling' certain and contrasted with 'being' certain, as though the certainty is nothing more than an emotion or a sensation. It is rather the sort of certainty which underlies one's whole reflective self-concept, more like the certainty of direct acquaintance than the certainty of correct description.

It remains to be asked, however, how one can pass from this immediate acquaintance with oneself to talking about immediate acquaintance with God. Why should one suppose that a journey inward really is also a journey beyond oneself? We may well grant that working through the successive layers of the psyche, the rooms of the interior castle, helps us in self-awareness and integration, and furthermore that the values of compassion, justice, and so on are discovered, not invented: they have an objective status.[24] But by what right does Teresa see this as the will of a personal God? How do we move from the ethical to the religious?

Teresa in company with many other men and women of prayer testifies that as one deepens in self-understanding and obedience to the values one owns, these are increasingly experienced as personal, as themselves the expression of love and generosity not our own. As one seeks, one finds that one is being sought. The integrated self transcends itself—and indeed without so doing it would not achieve integration. Again, this does not mean that there must be moments of ecstacy; rather, deepening self-awareness brings deepening awareness of a gracious and personal other, God, at the centre of the soul. Union with oneself leads to and becomes union with God.

But how do we *know*, we insist? On what *grounds* can Teresa make that sort of a move? Her response would be that this simply is what does happen, and that there is not a difference in *kind* in the certainty with which we gradually come to know ourselves and the certainty with which we gradually come to know God as the imminent One whose generosity makes the self-discovery possible and worthwhile. If one makes sense, she would say, so does the other: it is a fact of experience testified to by those who take the journey.

How are we to assess this response? One way is to take account of it as a basic datum for a programme of natural theology: the fact that deeply integrated people of conspicuous sanctity bear testimony to this experience of God as the foundation for their experience of themselves must surely be of very great significance in a cumulative case for religious belief.[25] But it seems to me that while this is important, Teresa's claims raise a deeper question: what counts as 'natural'? What is natural to a human being? In her view, it is natural (though

---

[24] Cf. Steward Sutherland, *God, Jesus and Belief* (SCM, London, 1984).
[25] Cf. Richard Swinburne, *The Existence of God* (Clarendon Press, Oxford, 1979).

not easy) for a human being to move through layers of the psyche to the supernatural: the gulf between them is not so deeply dug as the traditional distinction between natural and revealed theology would suggest, and religious experience is the bridge. She would furthermore say that speculation about the existence of such a bridge is idle if one is not planning ever to cross it anyway; even if it exists, it would only be one more fact about the world. It becomes relevant only if one's path will take one to its edge. And the path is one that we ought to take anyway: the point of increasing self-knowledge and deepening moral integrity would not be vitiated even if we found no bridge after all.

9

Knowledge from Experience, and the Problem of Evil

RICHARD SWINBURNE

I

The deductive argument[1] attempting to prove the non-existence of God from the occurrence of evil runs as follows: (1) 'If there is a God, he is omnipotent and perfectly good', (2) 'An omnipotent being can eliminate any evil, if he chooses', (3) 'A perfectly good being will eliminate evil in so far as he can', whence (5) 'If there is a God, there is no evil'. But (6) 'There is evil', whence it follows (7) 'There is no God'. I understand by 'omnipotent' in (1) 'able to do anything logically possible for him to do' (that is, able to do any action the description of which involves no self-contradiction).[2] That being so, the argument is undoubtedly valid. (7) follows from the premisses (1), (2), (3), and (6). Anyone who wishes to avoid the conclusion must deny one of the premisses. (1) is definitional of the Christian God, and while my way of understanding 'omnipotent' in it is, I believe, that of only the vast majority of Christian theologians, the same conclusion follows if a stronger sense of 'omnipotent' (for example as able to do both the logically possible and the logically impossible) is adopted; very few Christian theologians have been prepared to accept a weaker sense of 'omnipotent' than mine—God would not seem to be God if there were limits to his power beyond those of logic. That being so, (2) does seem fairly evidently true. Understanding by 'evil' not simply the absence of good, but the suffering, physical and mental, of conscious beings, and their evil acts, there is nothing logically impossible in an agent eliminating

[1] I have represented the atheist's arguments as deductive. In so far as it turns out that his premisses are dubious and he needs to give inductive arguments for them, the argument does of course become inductive in character.

[2] The sense in which the description involves no self-contradiction does however need careful spelling out. See my *The Coherence of Theism* (Clarendon Press, Oxford, 1977), chap 9.

evil, and hence an omnipotent being could do so—he could eliminate suffering and eliminate the ability of agents to cause it. (6) seems evidently true. What could be more obvious than the fact of much human suffering and wrongdoing? But note that it cannot be taken for granted that (6) is true unless even God cannot in future make it the case that humans do not now suffer. If it is logically possible that agents can make things to have happened, then an omnipotent being could in future make it not to be the case that men now suffer and do evil. Now I think, and I expect that most of my readers think, that this is not logically possible, because it is not logically possible that causes follow their effects. But it is important for me, for reasons which will appear later, to bring this out into the open, that (6) can only reasonably be taken as a premiss if (8) 'It is not logically possible that causes follow their effects' is true. The problem for theism only arises if (8) is true: for if (8) is false, God could in AD 3000 make it the case that there never has been evil, and so the argument would lose a crucial premiss and fail to be cogent.

Given all this, if the theist wishes to avoid the conclusion, he must deny (3); and that is what most theists do. They point out that much evil is a means to greater good, and that we remain perfectly good if we make no attempt to eliminate any evil which is a means to greater good. On a human level that is obvious. There is nothing wrong with a parent allowing a dentist to give his child a filling and so in the process suffer pain if that is a necessary means towards the child's future well-being. But the atheist will claim that in all such cases, although humans may not be able to do so, an omnipotent being could eliminate the evil without eliminating the greater good. God could give children healthy teeth without their needing to suffer pain at the dentist in order to get them. So a more plausible premiss which the atheist argues will serve him better is (3'), 'A perfectly good being will eliminate evil in so far as he can do so without eliminating any greater good.' But then it is not nearly as obvious as it was that (5) follows from its preceding premisses. For although an omnipotent being can change the laws of nature, what he cannot do on my understanding of omnipotence is change the laws of logic. And it may well be that there are greater goods for the occurrence of which allowing some lesser evil to occur is a logically necessary condition.

Some well-known defences of theism argue that this is in fact so. The existence of evil, or at any rate the existence of a natural possibility of evil, is logically necessary if certain kinds of good are to be possible. Argument along these lines is characteristic of the best-known theistic defence, the 'free will defence'. The free will defence is sometimes stated simply as a claim that it is good that men should have free will in the sense that the man who chooses is the ultimate source of his choosing this rather than that; that choice is not necessitated by prior causes. But simply stated thus, the free will defence will not account for the existence of evil, for free will in this sense would exist if men had free choices between equally good states of affairs—a natural possibility of evil is not necessary to provide it. So what the defence must state is that it is good that men have a free and responsible choice, in the sense that they are aware of different morally good and evil alternatives open to them which make significant differences for good and evil to the world and to the experiences and opportunities open to themselves and their fellows in future, and that they are aware of them as morally good and evil alternatives. It is good, I suggest, that agents other than God have a share in moulding the world and each other, and the deep responsibility that that involves. But if men have a free and responsible choice, they may well choose to do evil; and a God who gives them that choice takes the inevitable risk of their doing so. It is not logically possible that in the sense stated God could give to men free and responsible choice and also make it the case that they did not choose to do evil. The possibility of men doing evil is a logical consequence of the good of their having free and responsible choice.

An action would not be intentional unless it was done for a reason, that is unless it was seen as in some way a good thing (either in itself or because of its consequences). And if reasons alone influence actions, that regarded by the subject as most important will determine what is done; an agent under the influence of reason alone will inevitably do the action which he regards as overall the best. If an agent does not do the action which he regards as overall the best, factors other than reason must have exerted an influence on him. In other words, desires for what he regards as good only in a certain respect, but not overall, must have influenced his conduct. (I understand 'desire' in the ordinary language sense which is much narrower than the sense in which it is used by some philosophers. An agent desires to an action in so far as doing the action comes easily and naturally to him, quite apart from what he believes about its moral worth.) Now if an agent is to be able knowingly to choose evil rather than good, he must have a desire for what he rightly believes to be not overall good (although good in a certain respect). Agents need a certain depravity, in the sense of a system of desires for what they correctly believe to be evil. This depravity is itself an evil which is a necessary condition of a greater good.

Now this argument, as it stands, can only be used to account for what is called moral evil, the evil produced or constituted by humans choosing to do what they know to be evil. And much evil in the world is moral evil. Much of the suffering of the world is either caused deliberately by men or, through negligence, allowed by men to occur, in the knowledge that it is evil. However there is much other evil, which I will group together under the umbrella title of 'natural evil'. The main part of this is the evil unpreventable by man, such as much of the suffering produced by disease and natural disaster. (Much but by no means all such evil, for quite a bit of the suffering produced today by disease and disaster could have been prevented by men, if they had chosen to take the trouble to prevent it.) But 'natural evil', as I shall understand it, also includes evil caused or allowed by men to occur, in ignorance that it would occur, or in ignorance of its evil character. Even in respect of moral evil, the 'free will defence' will only provide justification for God allowing moral evil to occur if (9) 'Men have a free and responsible choice' and (10) 'To make it the case that men do not have free and responsible choice would eliminate a greater good than the evil it prevents'. As regards (9), that men have responsible choice is obvious—their choices can make enormous difference to whether others suffer or not. The freedom of that choice is more disputable. And (10) can be the subject of moral argument. I have suggested that it is a great good that men should have free and responsible choice of destiny. God does well to produce a universe in which this is so, even at the risk of much suffering. But the onus of argument in these matters is on the atheist. It is he who is trying to produce an argument for the non-existence of God. And it is he who is trying to show that (5) follows from (1), (2), and (3'); and to do that he needs an extra premiss (4), 'either (9) or (10) is false'. And that premiss is highly questionable. To the extent to which he cannot show (4) to be a justified belief, the atheist's argument (as stated so far) ceases to be cogent. And in so far as it is not improbable that both (9) and (10) are true, the atheist cannot even say that the existence of evil as such makes the existence of God improbable.

But, as we have noted, the free will defence in the form stated only provides justification for God allowing moral evil to occur; it does not cover natural evil. So the atheist would seem to have better prospects by reconstructing his argument, not as an argument from evil but as an argument from natural evil. (1), (2), and (3') remain as before. He then continues with (4'), 'There is no greater good served by allowing the occurrence of natural evil'. So (5'), 'If there is God, there is no natural evil', but (6'), 'There is natural evil', so (7), 'There is no God'.

The crucial premiss is now of course (4'), and this has been denied on various grounds. There is for instance the 'higher-order goods defence'—that you can't have the opportunity freely to evince various virtues without there being various evils in the face of which these virtues are to be shown. You can't, for example, show courage unless there is suffering in the face of which courage can be shown. Natural evil provides the opportunity for men to show courage. True, they might be able to show courage in the face of moral evil—you can show courage when threatened by a gunman, as well as when threatened by cancer. But just imagine all the suffering of mind and body caused by the disease, earthquake, and death unpreventable by men, removed at a stroke from our society. No sickness, no bereavement in consequence of the natural death of the aged. Many of us would then have such an easy life that we simply would not have much opportunity to show courage or indeed manifest much in the way of sanctity at all.

It needs those insidious processes of decay and dissolution which money and strength cannot ward off for long to give us the opportunities, so easy otherwise to avoid, to become heroes. True, God could compensate for the absence of natural evil by subjecting men to such temptation deliberately to cause evil to each other that there was again plenty of opportunity for courage. He could make us so naturally evil that we lacked natural affection and had inbuilt urges to torture each other, in face of which we others could show courage. But it is, I hope, in no way obvious that it would be better for God to replace disease by such an increase of inbuilt depravity (that is, a system of strong desire for what is known to be evil). Rather, I would have thought, the reverse. I am therefore inclined to think that the higher-order goods defence is an adequate defence to the argument from natural evil. Natural evils give to men the opportunity to show themselves at their best.

Courage is by no means the only virtue to which natural evil gives the opportunity of expression. Patience is another. So too is compassion. It is true that a man can show compassionate concern for the suffering which he believes another to be suffering, without that other actually suffering anything. But for God to bring it about generally that men seem to be suffering when they are not really would be to practise a large-scale deception on the human race which, plausibly, would be immoral. For a creator to deceive his creatures into supposing that they had duties to their fellows and ways of benefiting those fellows which were in fact totally non-existent where those creatures could not discover this, but were ever under the illusion, would be subjecting those creatures to a harsh moral pressure to do quite unneeded actions. I suggest as a premiss (since I shall use this point again later) (11), 'God has an obligation not to make a world in which agents are systematically deceived on important matters without their having the possibility of discovering their deception'.[3]

Given (11), the only way in which God can further the greater good of men showing compassion is by allowing others to suffer. And unless human depravity is increased considerably the opportunity for compassion can be made available to all

---

[3] This point is of course very much a Cartesian one. See R. Descartes, *Meditations* 4, 5, and 6.

on a considerable scale only by providing natural evil. It is a privilege to share, to be involved in the deepest feelings of others; and a world in which the only involvement in the life of others was an involvement in their joys would be a world in which a dimension and depth of sharing was quite lacking. A world in which a mother could not hug her child who had fallen over or a friend share the grief of one who had failed in his life's enterprise would be a shallow world of beings less deeply involved with each other.

At this point the atheist retreats further and attempts to point out kinds of natural evil for which the higher-order goods defence is inadequate. A major trouble here is that there is no known suffering to which some compassion cannot be shown. However long ago was the suffering of some child or animal, and even though no one at the time knew about it, we can later find out and be sorry. But surely compassion involves showing compassion which can be received by the sufferer? It is the better for that, but it need not involve it. The sorrow of one in a distant land who really cares for the starving in Ethiopia or the blinded in India is compassion for a fellow creature, even though he does not feel it; and the world is better for there being such concern. And that point is not affected if the suffering is past: it is good that I show sorrow at what you went through, even though I did not know about it at the time. That too is a sharing, just as men are glad to think that they will be remembered after their death, so they are glad to think that others will feel involvement and concern at their suffering. Men are glad to know that others are concerned for them, even if those others can do nothing; and if they are glad to know this, that can only be because they believe what they know is a good thing. But any past suffering of which we learn is a past suffering which we can share. If that seems fanciful, think of some of the great poems which have been written from the poet's compassion in response to a discovered corpse. On the contrary, what is to be regretted is the narrowness of human compassion. Maybe as in the future we learn more and more about the people and animals who have lived in the past (through an ability to detect more from slender remains), we shall bridge the centuries in our concern for their suffering, as well as (perhaps more important) sharing in their joys.

However, what may more plausibly be urged is that the good of the possibility of such compassion is outweighed by the suffering for which it is a necessary condition, and, more generally, that there are kinds of evil inadequately justified by any higher-order good which they make possible. Let us suppose that there are such kinds, and reconstruct the atheist's argument, understanding by 'natural evil' in (4′) 'natural evil unjustified by the higher-order goods defence'. With this understanding of (4′), in effect discounting the higher-order goods defence, is (4′) any more plausible?

Another suggested reason for the denial of (4′), of great antiquity and well enshrined in all theistic traditions including Christianity, is that physical evil can be explained as justified on the same grounds as moral evil. The suggestion is that physical evil, although not due to human agency, is due to the agency of free and responsible agents, namely Satan or many bad angels, entrusted by God with the control of the physical universe, who abuse their trust. If free and responsible agency is a good thing for men to have it is a good thing for other agents to have. The theist may not be able to prove that there are bad angels with capacities to produce disease and accident. But he claims that the mere possibility that there are casts enough doubt on (4′) to make the atheist's argument implausible.[4] Now certainly there is this logical possibility which means that (4′) could be false, but if the atheist can show that bad angels probably do not exist, he will show that (4′) is not reasonably believed on these grounds.

The 'bad angels' hypothesis would provide a satisfactory solution of the problem of evil if *either* there was quite a bit of evidence for the existence of bad angels other than the occurrence of natural evil (that is, they enabled one to explain a range of phenomena), *or* the existence of God was known with very great certainty and this was compatible with the existence of natural evil only (barring very, very improbable possibilities) given the existence of bad angels. My own judgement, which will, I believe, be shared by many theists, is that neither of these alternatives holds. If I am wrong about this, as some will certainly hold, then probably there are bad

---

[4] For this stance see Alvin Plantinga, *God, Freedom and Evil* (Allen and Unwin, London, 1975), pp. 58 f.

angels, and then we have a solution to the problem of evil. But if I am right that neither of these two alternatives do hold, then probably there are no bad angels. For in that case, in order to reconcile the existence of God and the occurrence of natural evil, we have to postulate one or more further free spiritual beings for whose existence there is not the range of evidence which there is initially for the existence of God. It is far simpler to suppose that there is just one spiritual being responsible for bringing about or (through human agents) allowing to occur the orderly occurrence of natural phenomena in the world. To add further spiritual beings is to complicate our hypothesis without adequate pay-off in the way of explanatory power. *Simplex sigillum veri*, the simple is a sign of the true.

But I now draw your attention to what I have done: I have rejected a hypothesis as improbable on the grounds of its complexity. I have assumed that there are true, culture-independent standards of probability, necessary truths about what is evidence for what, such as that the hypotheses postulating one entity are as such more likely to be true than those postulating many. I believe this; some don't.[5] But what I wish to draw attention to is that you can only knock down this countermove to the argument from evil on the assumption (12) 'There are necessary truths about what is evidence for what'. If you are not prepared to accept (12) there is no problem of evil left, for any wildly implausible account of some unobservable greater good which the evil serves will be justifiably accepted as an explanation of that evil. You can always devise some implausible Plantinga-style hypothesis of some greater good actually served by the evil. The problem remains—as long as we accept (8) and (12).

II

I now turn to what I regard as a much more satisfactory solution of the problem than the 'bad angels' hypothesis, able to explain the existence of much natural evil, including some for

---

[5] In 'The Probabilistic Argument from Evil' (*Philosophical Studies* 35 (1979), pp. 1–53), Alvin Plantinga expresses much scepticism about the existence of such standards (see p. 50).

which, others would hold, the higher-order goods defence cannot account. The solution depends crucially on (8) and (12) and won't work if these are denied. But, as we have seen, if (8) is denied the problem need not arise, and if (12) is denied the 'bad angels' hypothesis is readily available to solve it.

The solution is one for which in essence I have argued elsewhere,[6] but it has been subjected to some criticism,[7] and I seek to present it here in a tighter form. It is the solution from the need for knowledge of how to bring about good or evil if men are to have a significant choice between good and evil, and claims that that knowledge can only come from experience of good and evil. My claim is not that such knowledge from experience is necessary for free and responsible choice as such, but that it is necessary for free and responsible choice of a deeper and far more reaching kind which I call 'choice of destiny'. I must now say what that is and why it is a great good.

A free and responsible agent has a choice of destiny if among the things which he can affect by his free choice are the desire systems and knowledge systems of himself and (to a lesser extent) of his fellows. He can in part mould his own character and influence that of his fellows, affecting the sort of person he and they are. As I have said, I understand by a desire a natural inclination. An agent who has choice of destiny can over time gradually effect the sort of thing he naturally and readily seeks to attain, and he can influence his fellows too in that respect. Such an agent can also build up his knowledge of how things work in the world and of what is good and bad in it, or neglect to do so; and he can to some extent influence his fellows in this respect also. He can even allow himself and others to acquire what he initially suspects to be false views of what is right and wrong. This too surely is a great good, that a man should have the great responsiblity of

---

[6] 'Natural Evil', *American Philosophical Quarterly* 15 (1979), pp. 295–301; and developed in *The Existence of God* (Clarendon Press, Oxford, 1979), chaps. 9, 10, and 11—see especially chap. 11.

[7] David O'Connor, 'Swinburne on Natural Evil', *Religious Studies* 19 (1983), pp. 65–73; Eleonore Stump, 'Knowledge, Freedom, and the Problem of Evil', *International Journal for the Philosophy of Religion* 14 (1983), pp. 49–58; Paul K. Moser, 'Natural Evil and the Free Will Defense', *International Journal for the Philosophy of Religion* 15 (1984), pp. 49–56.

making himself a certain sort of person and influencing the formation of others. Note one aspect of it. It has the consequence, much valued by a liberal society, that men 'make up their own mind' about right and wrong. But given an objective right and wrong,[8] there can still be a situation in which men can through honest thought and hard experience come to have a deeper and deeper understanding thereof; or, through idleness and self-interest, allow themselves to have a trivial and false understanding of values, and even come to believe that there is no right and wrong. This is the good consequence rightly valued by a liberal society, which is involved in men having a choice of destiny. It is evident that men do often have such a choice of destiny. For the purposes of this paper, the most important feature of a choice of destiny is the possession of knowledge and the ability to grow in its acquisition.

If men are to have this significant choice between good and evil, they need to have open to them a range of actions with diverse natures and consequences, and to know which of those actions in virtue of their nature and consequences are good and which evil. And in order to have the choice of whether to set about acquiring such knowledge, or to neglect to do so, they need to know how to acquire the knowledge. Men need to have and to know how to acquire both practical and moral knowledge. What makes an action right or wrong is its nature, its circumstances, and above all its consequences. Saying 'I will come round to see you' is wrong if I have already promised to do something incompatible with seeing you tomorrow; and saying 'I am not married' is wrong if performed when I am married. Sticking a needle into someone will be wrong if it causes pain, unless it also forwards some greater good. In order to know whether some action is right or wrong, I need to know what morally relevant features it has (causing pain, being a lie, extending life, enriching experiences of life, etc.), and I need to know how these features add up to making it a right or wrong action. I call the latter moral knowledge (for

---

[8] In this paper I assume an objective right and wrong, the existence of moral truths, and so the possibility of moral knowledge. But nothing in the argument depends on it; the argument can be rephrased with some subjective understanding of moral judgement. For my defence of my view that there are moral truths, see my 'The Objectivity of Morality', *Philosophy* 51 (1976), pp. 5–20.

example, that causing pain is, other things being equal, wrong); and I call knowledge of which morally relevant features an action has (whether or not I know them to be morally relevant) practical knowledge.

III

The occurrence of natural processes which produce natural evil as well as much good is undoubtedly a major means by which we acquire practical and moral knowledge. Men study those natural processes and learn to control them, and through experience of their consequences learn much about which states of affairs are good and bad and so of which actions are right and wrong. I understand by a natural process one in which a cause of a given kind produces an effect of another kind in a regular way either with natural necessity or with natural probability. Natural processes are predictable processes. Observation of As being followed by Bs under various diverse conditions in the past allows us to infer that As cause Bs (that is, have caused and will cause Bs) and so gives us a recipe for bringing about a B: 'bring about an A'. If eating toadstools causes stomach pain, man can learn this by observations of past sequences. One will then have open the opportunity to cause others to suffer stomach pain (by feeding them with toadstools), to allow others (such as children) to be exposed to the risk of stomach pains (by allowing them to gather toadstools without warning them of the possible effects), or to prevent others from incurring this risk. These opportunites would not have been available without knowledge; observation of natural processes producing pain provides that knowledge.

We may not be able to produce the requisite A in its entirety at will: for example A may be an earthquake (A_1) in an inhabited region (A_2) which causes much suffering and death. Human agency can at present affect only whether an earthquake which is going to occur occurs in an inhabited region (A_2), not whether the earthquake occurs (A_1). However, if we know when A_1 will occur we can ensure that A_2 is present or ensure that it is absent (that is that the region is or is not inhabited), and thus trigger the sequence. If A_1 is produced by a natural process, even if we cannot at present discover its cause, we may be able to discover a sign of the presence of its cause and be able to predict its occurrence. Natural processes produce earthquakes, and earthquakes in an inhabited area produce great natural evil. If earthquakes occur as a result of natural processes, those processes may produce signs of whether and when earthquakes are likely, and thereby we can discover the likelihood of their occurrence at different times and places. This then gives us the opportunity to take the risk of building on areas subject to earthquake, or to make the effort to mobilize the human race to avoid in future the consequences of a major earthquake.

The existence of natural processes producing varied good and bad consequences gives to men who study them an enormous range of opportunities for moulding the future in the short or long term, by initiating or intervening in the processes. The more knowledge there is of past sequences of events at different times and places and in different circumstances, the more detailed and secure our knowledge of the natural processes will be. If our information comes only from one place or time, we may reasonably suspect that the natural process in question holds only under the circumstances prevailing at that place and time; though of course recent knowledge of how some event was produced will in general itself be more reliable, because the process of transmission of the knowledge to ourselves is shorter. All past evils of which we know provide knowledge of past events, and—more strikingly—since all natural evils occur as a result of predictable natural processes (there are no kinds of natural evil which occur in a totally random way), all such knowledge helps to build up knowledge of the natural processes which we can utilize to produce or prevent future evils. All past and present evils of which we know thus contribute to the widening of human choice.

The consequences of actions which are of by far the greatest significance for the moral status of those actions are those which consist in human experiences. Actions are good in so far as they promote pleasurable and knowledge-deepening and friendship-deepening experiences; they are evil in so far as they promote pain, ignorance, and poverty of imagination and understanding. We come to understand what those experiences are like through having them ourselves or seeing or hearing of the experiences of others with whom we can sympathize. The occurrence of natural processes provides such understanding through disease and accident which cause me and those close to me pain. Disease which causes death of loved ones teaches us what grief is. And so on. Poets and television reporters who tell me about the joys and sufferings of others in distant lands extend my understanding through extending the range of my sympathy. This understanding teaches me the effect of my own actions of killing, of allowing others to suffer, or of giving to Oxfam.

Such experiences of our own and sympathetic awareness of the experiences of others caused by natural processes is obviously also a major source of our moral knowledge. Through seeing others suffer, we learn not merely of that suffering but that it is wrong to let people suffer. And through awareness of the range and depth of kinds of possible good and evil experience, I grow in my understanding of which actions are right and wrong. Through seeing the effects of mental retardation produced by brain disease and the limitation of aesthetic and philosophical understanding which it produces, I come to learn the value of government and private spending on education for the subnormal. Much moral growth is of course produced by reflection upon our own experiences and sympathetic awareness of the experiences of others caused by the deliberate actions of others. Those with much experience of rape, abortion, and marriage breakdown come thereby to have a better understanding of the morality of actions which involve them. Nevertheless natural processes cause effects which provide much understanding of the morality of actions consisting in bringing about such effects, without humans ever needing to perform those actions.

IV

So natural processes provide us with the practical and moral knowledge which is essential if we are to have a free and responsible choice of destiny. But could not God give to men that knowledge in a different way without the heavy cost of evil which it involves? The moral knowledge could be given in a different way, but the practical knowledge could not, not without an equally heavy cost in the form of some other evil.

Recall that I understand by moral knowledge knowledge that an action of a certain type done in certain circumstances with certain consequences is good or, as may be, evil (where all the morally relevant circumstances and consequences are stated), such knowledge as that rape, or lying in order to persuade an old man to entrust his savings to you when you intend to steal them for your own enjoyment, or torturing in order to extort a confession of belief in some creed, are always wrong. Such truths are not dependent on contingent facts about the world, for I suppose any relevant such facts to be incorporated in the description of the action. They are therefore necessary truths. Whether giving someone LSD is wrong depends on the short and long-term effects of so doing, and so is a contingent matter. But whether giving someone LSD when it has exactly such and such effects is wrong is a necessary matter.

I do not know of any satisfactory proof that experience is necessary either for the acquisition of concepts or for acquisition of knowledge of necessary truths of their interconnection. Someone has a concept to the extent to which he can conceive of what it would be like for it to have application, and to the extent to which he can recognize that it does apply, and someone can see what is involved in its application (that is, know necessary truths which concern it) without ever having observed its application. A man might be born with an ability to conceive what it would be like for something to be red or green and to recognize red or green objects, even if he has never observed such; and this ability will enable him to recognize as a necessary truth that nothing can be red and green all over. The same applies to the necessary truths of morality. Someone might know what evil was when the world as yet contained none, as he might know which actions were evil and which states of affairs were bad before ever they had occurred. Our moral knowledge is not acquired in this way but there is no reason why that of some human agent should not be. God could ensure that men were given moral concepts and a deep imagination which would enable them to comprehend necessary truths about their application without their having any experience of harsh moral realities.[9]

With practical knowledge it is different, at any rate for agents, such as humans, who have a choice of destiny in that they can grow in knowledge of the nature and consequences of their actions. For them what consequences their actions will have depends not on themselves, but on something outside themselves about which they come to learn, either an unconscious process or the conscious choice of some other agent.

All knowledge of the future is knowledge of what natural processes will bring about or of what agents will bring about intentionally (or both, if intentions are moulded by natural processes; or if they mould those processes). A man may infer to a future event either by regarding what will happen as to be produced by a natural process or as to be produced intentionally. So knowledge that one's action A, which consists in bringing about some result C, will have a further consequence E, will be knowledge either that natural processes dictate that C brings about E, or knowledge that some agent on observing C will bring about E intentionally. Knowledge that putting cyanide in a man's drink will kill him is knowledge of a natural process, that cyanide kills; and knowledge that giving the order 'Fire' to a reliable subordinate in war in charge of a gun will lead to the firing of the gun is knowledge of intentional agency.

If God is to give a man a range of actions with consequences bad and good, he must ensure that human actions have these consequences, either as a result of a natural process which he implants in nature, or as a result of his direct intentional action. And if the human agent is to have knowledge of those consequences, he must learn about them either by discerning the natural process or by discovering God's intention. God could give me knowledge of the consequences of my action by telling in advance what he will bring about if I do the action. I might hear in my ear or see on the screen the English words 'If you shoot him, he will die'. But if I regard my actions as having the consequences they do in virtue of some other agent intentionally making the actions having those consequences, I

---

[9] Hence I do not find the emendation of my argument suggested by Moser (op. cit., pp. 54 ff.) satisfactory.

must regard that agent as in control of my life, and not merely my life, but since he determines the effect of my actions on others, as in control of their lives too. I must regard him as in control of the universe, at least locally. And if I use normal inductive procedures (which, I shall argue, I must do if I am to have knowledge at all) I must regard him as perfectly good, for his local freedom of operation to determine what happens is absolute, and so is his local knowledge of what will happen. Thus as the simplest hypothesis I must regard him as knowledgeable also in other fields, including morality, and free in other fields; and so as he knew the good, and was not distracted by temptation from pursuing it, as perfectly good, I would learn his intentions for the consequences of my actions by his telling me. Under those circumstances I could indeed know that certain actions would have evil consequences and certain actions would have good consequences. But I would regard my every movement as overseen by an all-knowing and perfectly good being, namely a God who would therefore wish me to be good, and value me and so preserve me, in so far as I was good. The reasons for being good would be virtually irresistible: a genuine choice of destiny would not be open to me, at least given that men are as rational as they now are.[10] If men were given a much greater inbuilt depravity than they now have their choice would still be open. By depravity I mean strong desires to do what is correctly believed to be evil. But then such extra depravity would itself be a great evil. With their present nature (involving amount of depravity), men who learnt of the consequences of their actions by understanding some sign as God telling them what the consequences were would be so suffocated by God that they had little real choice of destiny. So if God tells me 'If you fire the gun, you'll kill him' and I understand his message, it will be so obviously a good thing not to fire the gun and one which will be given its

---

[10] David O'Connor (op. cit., p. 7) argues that people may and often do perform acts when they know them to be wrong and they know that they will be punished for them—children, for example, do. This seems to me to happen only in so far as there is some doubt about the morality of the action, the certainty that the agent will be found out, or the punishment administered. In the absence of uncertainty about the latter, one's action is an action of deliberately bringing harm upon oneself, and when that action is recognized as morally bad also, it would need a person far more naturally depraved than most of us are to do it, except when we are not fully in control of ourselves and so the action is not freely chosen.

due reward, whatever that is, that I will have little temptation to fire. In order to give me the sort of choice demanded by the free will defence. God must give me some epistemic elbow-room.

This could be provided by giving me knowledge of the consequences of my actions via discovering natural processes which produce them directly (not via knowledge of God's intentions, that is while leaving open the possibility and allowing even the probability that a God produces those processes). Such knowledge, I now argue, can be obtained only from observations by the agent or others who inform him of the production of such consequences in the past.

Knowledge is justifed true belief, where the justification does not proceed through a false proposition. The point of the latter clause[11] is that if my justification for believing p is that I am justified in believing q and q entails or probabilifies p, and q is false, then even if p is true, my justified true belief that p does not amount to knowledge. It does not amount to knowledge because it proceeds via a false proposition, q.

Now could I simply find myself knowing what will be the consequence of some action of mine, without that knowledge being grounded in some other knowledge, for example of what happened in similar cases in the past? Could I just know that if I give you cyanide it will poison you? I can just know what I did yesterday. (Apparent memory needs no further justification before it is rightly taken as genuine.) Why can't I just know what will happen if I do so-and-so tomorrow? I can indeed have such a belief, but it would not amount to knowledge, because it would not be justified. A belief of mine is either a basic belief or a non-basic belief. A non-basic belief, to be justified, must be justified ultimately by a basic belief. (I understand by a basic belief simply one which is regarded by the subject as justified in part in ways other than by the rest of his system of beliefs. I do not assume that basic beliefs are infallible. Anyone who denied foundationalism in this very modest form must regard and must suppose others to regard

---

[11] The clause is of course inserted to meet 'Gettier-type' counter-examples. See Edmund L. Gettier, 'Is Justified True Belief Knowledge?', *Analysis* 23 (1963), pp. 121–3. For discussion of such counter-examples, and the need for such a clause, see Keith Lehrer, *Knowledge* (Clarendon Press, Oxford, 1974), chap. 1.

belief systems as totally self-supporting.) Given that Kant is mistaken about the possibility of knowledge of synthetic a priori truth, a contingent non-basic belief (that is a non-basic belief that some contingent proposition is true) requires for its ultimate justification at least one contingent basic belief. A contingent basic belief, to be justified, must justifiably be regarded by the subject as caused by the state of affairs believed. Our contingent basic beliefs are ones which we believe arise out of confrontation with the states of affairs believed, and so are forced upon us by them. Apparent perceptions are taken as genuine only when they are believed by the subject to be caused by what is perceived. But, given (8), it is not logically possible that any future state (let alone a possible state which may not be brought about) could cause a present experience; and so there can be no justified basic belief about the future. A belief about the future requires to be justified by some other belief, such as a belief that one has had some past experience or perceived some event in the past. And what observations of the past could give as sure knowledge of the natural processes which determine the effect of *A* as observations of past *A*s under various conditions? Sure knowledge that cyanide will poison is provided by observing cyanide poisoning under diverse conditions. And many observations at different times and places under diverse conditions provides the most sure knowledge possible. Why suppose that *A*s having been *B* in the past is what shows that a future *A* will be *B*, rather than *A*s having been not-*B* in the past? The answer is that it is simpler to suppose that *A*s will continue to be *B* rather than to suppose that at some particular moment of time *A*s all change to being not-*B* (when no new causal factor intervenes in accord with the operation of a simple law of nature). Simplicity is evidence of truth. The hypothesis which postulates one entity, one kind of entity (instead of many), mathematically simple modes of interaction (*A*s always being *B*, instead of only up to AD 2000) is for that reason more likely to be true. If there are necessary truths about what is evidence for what, these are they. They constrain us to put forward as most likely to be true the simplest extrapolation from the evidence. If (12) is correct, and so is (8), and so we cannot observe the future, the surest knowledge of the future is to be obtained by simple extrapolation from the present. And if there are no such necessary truths, if simplicity is so culture-relative a notion that it can provide no justification for inference, then (12) is false and then there is an easy solution to the problem of evil anyway. But if (12) is true the surest knowledge that much heroin will cause me an early death will be obtained from observations of such things happening to others.

The events by far the most important for the moral significance of actions which bring them about are mental events, that is experiences of sentient beings. Most sure knowledge of the experiences caused by natural processes is to be had through having experiences oneself. One's own experience is the surest source of knowledge of what it feels like to be burnt. But the public behaviour of others is very strong evidence of how those others feel. However, one can interpret the facial expressions, behaviour, and descriptions of these experiences by others only to the extent to which one is familiar with those other people and has analogous experiences oneself. Only if I normally behave in way B only when I have experienced E will I know what is the significance of behaviour B by others. Only if I normally laugh only when I am amused, and so do others, will I be able to interpret their laughter as a sign of being amused. One who has no pain will never know when it is right to ascribe it to others. (Even if some authority tells me that another is 'in pain' now, I will not understand what I am told unless I know to which mental phenomenon the word 'pain' refers. And I will not know that unless I and others manifest pain by the same characteristic behaviour.)

My knowledge of the effects of heroin could, it is true, be obtained in a somewhat more roundabout way than that described in the last paragraph but one. There could be a complicated scientific theory of which it was a remote consequence that heroin would have this effect. The theory would be confirmed by its yielding predictions of the consequences of taking other chemically similar drugs, perhaps tested sometimes on animals rather than men. The remoteness of the theory and its never having been tested with respect to heroin on men would, however, make it less reliable, and in general our knowledge of the future consequences of our actions is better justified in so far as it comes from many tests in similar circumstances (in this case with respect to heroin and men, rather than other drugs and other animals). And that some drug causes pain is hardly likely to be even remotely evidenced except via observation of other drugs causing pain (so different is pain from other things). Pain there must be to be observed if we are to have knowledge of when our actions will cause pain.

Our knowledge is less securely based if the observations which support our theory are not our own, but known only through the testimony of others; and that of course is the most usual case. My justification for believing that heroin causes death is that everyone says that anyone who takes frequent large doses of heroin dies. I am justified in believing the rumour because I believe that there are experts around who have observed these things happening in the past and would have denied the popular rumour, were it false. I believe that there are experts because I have read this; and I believe that they would have protested, were the rumour false, because I believe that in general experts pronounce on matters of public importance if false factual opinions are prevalent. Such is the net of beliefs which sustains my belief that if I take frequent large doses of heroin, I shall die. But it could be that, although my belief is true, it is on this occasion justified by a network of false beliefs—the rumour that observers have observed other heroin addicts dying therefrom (or observed things from which they could justifiably conclude that heroin poisons) might be totally false. In that case the justification for my true belief would proceed through a false proposition, and so the justified true belief would not amount to knowledge.

The argument of this section so far has been that God can give to men knowledge of the consequences of their actions only by telling men what he will intentionally bring about or by allowing them to infer what natural processes will bring about. Knowledge of the latter is to be obtained by observation of what natural processes have brought about in the past and generalizations therefrom. But if God is to give men knowledge by the latter route of which actions have bad consequences, natural processes must have operated in the past to bring about the bad consequences. But could there not be a quite different source of knowledge of the processes at work in nature other than observation of their past operation, a source of knowledge, less sure perhaps, but adequate—a knowledge machine, say, which would answer all your questions about how nature worked? You type in the words 'Will anyone suffer if I give them 10 gm. cyanide? And how will they suffer?' and it replies 'They will suffer physical pain and their spouse will suffer bereavement.' There need surely be no accidental suffering from cyanide in the past for me to know its effects in the future if there are plenty of knowledge machines around. We would know these machines to be knowledge machines by finding that they worked often. Ought not God to provide men with knowledge machines to tell them the consequences of their actions, rather than require them to infer these from observation, including observations of pain and suffering?

If there were such machines, the basic question to be asked about them would be whether they were themselves part of the natural order (that is, do they themselves work as a result of the operation of natural processes), or not. If not, if they can answer questions about the future without the ability being dependent on their detailed construction and sensitivity to facts in the present, then by previous arguments we must regard them as the mouthpiece of an all-seeing God and so regard ourselves as swamped by him. But if they are part of the natural order, operating via natural processes, there could then be an easy Darwinian explanation of the existence of such machines in terms of evolutionary advantages conferred on a race which had such machines—an explanation which would satisfy those who are easily lulled by Darwinian explanations. Yet if such machines were part of the natural order, they would be fallible, able to be misunderstood, subject to decay, and generally capable of improvement. But checking up on and improving these machines would involve getting a more direct understanding of how nature worked by observing natural processes (including their production of suffering), and using it in the reconstruction of the machines (which of course is just what physiologists do in order to improve the machines produced by natural selection, which are human bodies). The less we check up on these machines, the less sure our knowledge of the consequences of our actions. Yet if it is a good thing that we have knowledge of good and evil consequences which our actions can produce in order that thereby we may mould the world for good or ill, the surer our knowledge the better, for unsure knowledge gives us much less effective control.

Also, if the less sure source of knowledge of the consequences of our actions were in practice even fairly reliable, there would be an additional disadvantage if this source, like the knowledge machine, produced easy, automatic answers. For in that case men would not need to work (for example by doing experiments, conducting statistical studies, and founding research institutes) to learn how nature works and so what would be the consequences of their various actions. Knowledge would be available on tap. They would then have no temptation to allow themselves to remain in ignorance. Knowledge, so obviously a good thing, would be so easy to acquire that men would acquire it inevitably. Hence they would not have a choice as to whether to act in ignorance or to acquire knowledge. Only if the acquisition of knowledge is difficult is ignorance a serious option (for individuals, and for societies). Men would be saddled with knowledge; a crucial aspect of choice of destiny would be closed to them.

V

I have argued that if God is to give us knowledge of the consequences of our actions in a way that allows us to exercise a free and responsible choice of destiny, that can only come through knowledge of many and varied past evils produced by natural processes. But why is knowledge necessary? Is not belief about the consequences of our actions enough to allow us to exercise a responsible choice, whether or not such belief is true and justified with a justification which proceeds through no false proposition? And for mere belief no past experience is necessary. I could be born believing with great conviction that rabies causes a terrible disease. I need not have observed instances of such causation, nor need anyone else, in order that I should have this belief.

However, our beliefs need to be true if our choices are to be responsible, if we are to be mini-creators sharing God's responsibility for what sort of world there shall be. If I choose to allow rabies into the country in the belief that it will do no harm, I shall not have the responsibility for whether or not harm is done. We need many true beliefs in order to have significant responsibility (whether or not we have false ones as well). But why need my true beliefs be justified? Could I not just be born with them? Yes. But I couldn't take steps to acquire more true beliefs; I would be confined to my existing set. This is because in order intentionally to set about acquiring more true beliefs I have to know how to do so, and that involves knowing when a belief is justified. If I have no criteria of justification, I would not be able to choose whether to acquire more true beliefs or to neglect to do so, and that as we have seen is a significant good involved in choice of destiny. But once I have criteria of justification, I shall inevitably apply them to my existing beliefs; and if I find a belief *B* unjustified, I will believe that there is no good reason for believing that *B* corresponds to how things are in the world, and so I will cease to believe it. If an agent is to have a free and responsible choice of destiny, his beliefs must be true and justified.

But why need those true and justified beliefs amount to knowledge if an agent is to have such choice? The answer is that they need not, but that in order to bring it about that our justified true beliefs did not amount to knowledge God would need to violate (11). For it can happen only rarely that justified true belief does not amount to knowledge, unless the world is organized on a systematically deceptive basis. If our beliefs depended for their justification on false propositions it is most unlikely that they would often be other than false— barring the institution of a system designed to prevent this. For example, it is most unlikely that the false reports of observers about the past will allow us to infer to a conclusion about the future which turns out to be true, unless observers are programmed to give exactly those false reports which allow justified inference to true beliefs about the future. But suppose God to create a world in which nobody had died by taking heroin accidentally, yet to give men a justified true belief that heroin kills, he made it the case that many observers falsely report cases of taking heroin leading to death, and so on generally. This would be a world in which men were systematically deceived about the past (and so their sympathies falsely

engaged, their inferences to other matters systematically mistaken). It would be a systematically deceptive world, and so
by (11) not a world which God would make. In a world made
by God, justified true belief must in general amount to knowledge. God cannot give to men the sort of belief needed for a
free and responsible choice of destiny without producing
natural processes which bring about natural evils, and letting
men observe and experience them.

The heart of the argument of the need for knowledge set out
in the last four sections is that if man is to have a free and
responsible choice of destiny, he needs to have a range of
actions open to him, whose consequences, good and evil, he
understands, and he can only have that understanding in a
world which already has built into it many natural processes
productive of both good and evil.[12] The more and more varied
are the evils observed and experienced, the surer is the knowledge of the consequences of natural processes gained, and so
the greater is the opportunity for informed choice of action.
The more that knowledge is made available to man by any
other route than the observation of natural processes, the
more his freedom and choice of destiny is reduced.

VI

A natural reaction to this argument might be that although I
have given adequate reason why a God might bring about
some natural evil, I have not given adequate reason why a
God might bring about natural evil of the quantity and intensity which this world contains. With this reaction I have sympathy. With respect to most natural evil of recent centuries, I
think that the argument from the need for knowledge by man
provides very substantial reason why God might bring such
evil about. If you start to imagine this evil much reduced, you
find yourself imagining a world in which human opportunites
for moulding that world for good or ill are also much reduced.
On the other hand, although animal suffering (both physical
pain and such mental suffering as grief at the loss of offspring
or mate) in the long ages of pre-human evolution does provide

---

[12] For my answer to the objection that God does not have the right to impose suffering on some for their benefit or the benefit of others, see *The Existence of God*, pp. 216 ff.

men with much knowledge, there is surely too much of it to serve this purpose alone. The argument from the need for knowledge does not seem to provide an adequate reason why God might bring about that evil. With respect to animal suffering, it is however important to remember three things. First, we have no idea at what stage of evolution sentience arose. Mere avoidance of bodily damage and squirming after such damage is relatively little evidence of feeling in animals physiologically very dissimilar to ourselves. I am only at all confident that animals have sensations when we reach the level of mammals, for their patterns of behaviour are significantly similar to our own. And if (as I assume) the behaviour of other men is evident of their feelings, so too is the behaviour of animals similar to men. Secondly, however, the intensity and complexity of suffering must get less as we go down the evolutionary scale, for if at some stage there was no feeling and now with men there is much, and all the indicators of mental life show a progressive development in intelligence, belief patterns, and other aspects of mental life, we would expect a similar growth in the intensity and complexity of suffering. The lower mammals, I therefore suggest, suffer much less than humans do. On the other hand, sentience is the most primitive aspect of the mental life, and physical pain probably arrived on the evolutionary scene well before belief and desire, and so would initially be without significance for the animals who felt it: they were not sad because they had lost offspring, nor did they believe their physical pain to be inflicted by enemies. And thirdly, since suffering grows with growth of complexity of belief and desire, animals with significant suffering have themselves the capacity to show sympathy for their fellows' suffering and courage at their own, which in turn is such a good thing. The world would be poorer without the courage of the wounded deer or the grief of the bitch bereft of puppies. However, on the assumption that animals other than men do not have a free will, a full higher-order goods defence is not available here. The good of exercised virtues of courage, patience, sympathy, etc. remains; but there is no good in cowardice, impatience, and callousness unless freely chosen. However, the evil of the exercise of the latter vices provides knowledge for other observing animals of the alternative courses of action available to them, and it is good that animals should choose to exercise virtues rather than vices (albeit unfreely) in the light of rejected alternatives. It is good that animals should know what they are choosing, and that they should pursue the good in various ways open to them. Only a nature 'red in tooth and claw' would allow animals to exercise many virtues.

The 'need for knowledge' does not give a full explanation of why there is the evil there is in the world; but it does go a lot of the way towards explaining it, and there is no reason to suppose that there is just one reason why there is the evil which there is. I have earlier briefly deployed the 'higher-order goods' defence; but my concern in this paper was to show the strength of the argument from the need for knowledge.

The argument of this paper has been fairly rigorous, and anyone who writes on the problem of evil in this style must suspect that others will think him callous in the face of the suffering. Indeed, as a reader as well as the writer of this paper, I am inclined to have that thought about myself. But just as the surgeon needs to put his emotions temporarily aside in order to perform his healing operations with careful precision, so too does the philosopher in order to exercise his own careful precision to cure those who draw from the fact of suffering ill-evidenced conclusions. I hope that the perceptive reader will see that there is a positive side to the enterprise on which I have been engaged. I have been drawing attention to the fact that human (and animal) good is not just sensations of pleasure, but deeper things like the acquistion of secure knowledge of the possibilities for both good and evil in the world, involvement in and compassion for the deepest experiences of distant people and kinds, and free choice of the good in the face of temptation. The more one becomes aware of what the most important good things are, the more one comes to see that they have lesser evils as inevitable components. Those evils, as far as we know, are limited in intensity and are very limited indeed in time (to the span of earthly life). The more one reflects on this fact, the more one feels the 'argument from evil' losing its force. And that, *The Justification of Religious Belief* taught us, is grounds for supposing that the existence of evil does not count significantly against the existence of God.

10

Eternity and Omnitemporality

I. M. CROMBIE

It seems to have become received doctrine in recent years that the theist ought to say that God is an everlasting rather than an eternal being—that is to say, that God exists at every moment of time, rather than that God's existence is timeless, or 'outside time'; and that the theist ought to assert this as a deep metaphysical truth of philosophical theology. In earlier centuries the opposite doctrine has sometimes been received, for example by Aquinas.

I have no difficulty with the proposition that we have to *think of* God as a being who exists in time, and who is therefore everlasting rather than 'eternal' (in so far as this means something different). But I have grave difficulty with the view that this constraint upon us reveals a deep truth about the divine nature. The argument commonly used to support this view says that the theist needs to represent God as an agent, that actions must take place in time, and that therefore God must exist in time. There is, I think, a deeper argument which can be used to support the same view. This is that the theist wants to maintain that God is a real being, an Aristotelian first substance, a 'concrete' rather than an 'abstract' being. It is easy enough to think of entities—numbers for example—which do not exist in time, in that it makes no sense to ask when or where they are, have been, or will be. But these are abstract entities; it is a condition, the argument maintains, of the claim that something, X, is a real being, that X must have a unique spatio-temporal placing; what lacks that is an *ens rationis*, an aspect or feature, perhaps, of some thing or things which possess such a placing, and not itself, in its own right, an *ens*, something which (crudely) *has* properties, but is not itself a property. Therefore even an inert God (such, perhaps, as Aristotle's unmoved mover) must have spatio-temporal location, even if that is 'always and everywhere'. I shall have more to say of this later.

Meanwhile, Richard Swinburne in *The Coherence of Theism* makes moderate use of the argument from divine agency.[1] He says roughly this: that the theist can maintain both that God is timeless and that he is a personal agent only if he allows that the words which are involved in making this latter claim are being used in 'highly stretched senses'.[2] He further says that, whereas 'a theist would be justified on occasion in using words in an analogical sense, nevertheless too many appeals to analogical senses of words would make sentences in which the words were used empty of content'.[3] This he clearly regards as a disadvantage.

I have a special personal reason for being puzzled by this, which is that earlier in the same book[4] Swinburne says that he is in broad agreement with an account of religious language which I gave in an essay published in *Faith and Logic*.[5] But, so far as I can see, if one takes the view of religious discourse which I took in that essay, then there is an important sense in which the words used in philosophical theology *are* 'empty of content'; and the sense is such as to preclude one's arguing that, since the theist must speak of God as acting, he must conclude that it is a deep metaphysical truth that God's existence is in time, that the infinite being is a being whose existence is an endless succession of phases between which temporal relations hold.

I think I am still in broad agreement with what I wrote in that essay. But, in order to show why it seems to me that Swinburne is not, it will be convenient if I write of my views in the past tense. First, then, the position that I tried to take in that essay was in complete agreement with Swinburne's over one essential point, namely that religious statements (as made by theists) purport to be, and are to be regarded as being, true-or-false statements, as opposed to imperatives, or operatives, or whatever; and that, in so far as they refer to God, they are to be taken as being about God, and not about something else;

---

[1] Clarendon Press, Oxford, 1977, pp. 210–22.
[2] Ibid., p. 221.   [3] Ibid., p. 222.   [4] Ibid., pp. 82–4.
[5] 'The Possibility of Theological Statements' in *Faith and Logic*, ed. Basil Mitchell (Allen and Unwin, London, 1957), pp. 31–83. I also attempted to state the same position in my contribution to 'Theology and Falsification' in *New Essays in Philosophical Theology*, ed. Antony Flew and Alasdair MacIntyre (SCM, London, 1955), pp. 109–30.

and that God is to be taken as something existent which is distinct from everything in creation and which is not some aspect of the created world. My position, in other words, was meant to be just as orthodox, just as anti-Braithwaiteian, anti-Phillipsian, as Swinburne's.

But I doubt whether Swinburne is in agreement with one of the main points that I tried to make in that essay, namely that we ought not to claim that we have any understanding of the divine nature. My position, it seems to me, was much more apophatic than Swinburne's. In an important sense, according to me, the things we say about God are empty of content, in the sense, namely, that we have no positive understanding of how anything could satisfy the totality of the things that we claim to be true about God. (To be more precise, 'we' here is the ordinary theist; I allowed it to be possible that some among us, through what we might roughly call mystical experience, might acquire some insight into the divine nature; but, even in this case, 'understanding' seems to be a misnomer.) Yet we do say things about God, and believe that we are doing something serious, and something true-or-false, in doing so, and that it matters *which* things we say. It seemed (and still seems) to me that the theist must attempt to keep these two apparently inconsistent things in tension; and my essay was a, doubtless clumsy, attempt at doing this.

How is one to begin to preserve this tension? I began by trying to claim that in a negative fashion we know *which thing (quid)* we are talking about when we talk about God, even though we have no knowledge of the nature of *that thing which (id quod)* we are then speaking of. We know that we are not talking of the world of finite contingent beings, nor about any part of it. We refer what we say about God to something which *is*, but which is 'outside' that world and is in some sense its 'ground', and which is ultimate in the sense that there is nothing which stands to that being, in turn, as *its* ground—to something, therefore, which exists without limitation, not here or there, or now or then, or under certain conditions. Such a being is a being of which it is not true to say that it might not have been.

The proposition that there exists such a being is not sterile. Inferences can be drawn from it; one can say, for example, that it must be the case that that being determines the conditions under which any finite being can come to be. But, though the proposition is not sterile, it has to be allowed that no positive conception corresponds to it. I have no conception at all of how it could be true to say of any being that it stood to the world of finite beings in the relation of being their ground. Equally I have no conception at all of how it could be true of some real being that it is not the case that it might not have been. (There are of course many things—many *denotata* of grammatically substantival expressions—which are not contingent; thus it makes no sense to say of the number seven that it might not have existed. But in an intuitively clear sense the number seven is not a real being, not one of the things that there are in earth or heaven). Nor have I any conception of what it would be for some being to determine the conditions under which any finite being can come to be. We have therefore no positive conception of the divine nature. I tried to put this in the essay by saying that we know only in which direction out of the world of finite beings the things we say about God are to be referred; it is in that sense, and only in that sense, that we know which thing we are talking about, and that our credal statements are not mere predications totally unattached to any subject. The direction is indicated by (in Kantian language) an idea of reason—of a 'that than which no greater can be conceived', of a being which it is fitting to adore because it is the ground of all finite things. But, once more, if we are asked how it could hold of something that no greater than it could be conceived, or of what nature a thing must be for it to be fitting to adore that thing because it is the ground of all finite things—if we are asked this, then we have to reply '*Nescimus*—we do not know'.

The reason why the theist—or, at any rate, the Christian theist—says these things is that it seems to him that he has to in order to give expression to what he believes. His situation would be eased if he was willing to say either that God is Being (rather than *a* being), or that God is (in one natural interpretation of the phrase) the Supreme Being. It is often not too clear what is intended by those philosophical theologians who seem to favour the first fork. But one natural interpretation of such language is that to talk of God is to talk about the most general conditions under which whatever is is.

God is not that which determines finite things exist; he *is* those conditions of their existence—their finitude, their causal interaction, their spatio-temporality, and so on. To say, then, that God is, for example, loving is to say something about the most general features of the universe. *Deus* is *natura*. To take the alternative fork (as few do explicitly, but many, perhaps, in practice) is to adopt a model according to which what is ultimate is the nature of things. This is, so to speak, the backcloth. Against this backcloth far and away the most important thing that there is is God, on whom the nature of things has conferred creative power, and who has exercised this power in the bringing into being of finite things. According to this model God could have spatio-temporal location; his being could occupy all the finite or infinite space and all the infinite time that the nature of things provides. This model would therefore naturally lead (I am not, of course, saying that it is the only thing that could lead) to a preference for 'everlasting' rather than 'eternal' as the characterization of the divine duration. But to the theist, as it seems to me, neither of these two roads is open; neither does justice to how he conceives of the divine. God is not nature, nor simply supreme among the beings that nature has furnished.

The theist, then, has to allow that he can form no positive conception of how anything could satisfy the stipulations that he feels obliged to lay down with regard to the divine nature. He could make some shift to form some conception of the general conditions under which all finite things exist, or of the being of some kind of super-Zeus. But, being unwilling to take either of these roads, he has to admit to nescience. The rest, then, surely should be silence? But it is not; Christians say many things about God. Since, then, my argument continued, we claim the right to make statements about the divine, this must be because there is something within the finite world which we take to be a communication from the divine. There is of course a problem (which I did not discuss in the essay, and shall not discuss now) about how we could be justified in regarding something finite as a communication from a source about whose nature we have to confess to nescience. But there is one answer to this problem which seems quite unacceptable. When a large-scale map represents the same piece of country as a small-scale map, we can detect this because, although the former shows much more detail than the latter, we find the same general outline in each. The unacceptable account of how revelation is to be recognized says something like: we know that Jesus Christ reveals the divine nature because, though what we antecedently know about God is very schematic, we can discern in Jesus the same outlines as we have previously, through the discipline of natural theology, discerned in God. Natural theology is apophatic; it tells us nothing about the divine nature, in that it tells us nothing about how any being could meet the conditions we impose when we speak of that being as divine.

It follows that the Petrine confession—'Thou art the Christ, the son of the living God'—must stand on its own feet; at any rate, it cannot borrow from natural theology any feet to stand on. Therefore anything which is accepted as a revelation of the divine is an *arche*, a genuine starting-point. There is no going behind it and saying: 'this must be right, because this fills detail into the sketch we were already in possession of'. The Christian must, then, take the person of Christ as the source from which he derives the many things that he believes to be true about God—for example, that he forgives all sinners that repent, or that he made the world. The Christian believes these things to be true because he regards as authoritative the source from which he derives them. (Note that I am not saying that the acceptance of Christ as authoritative has to be non-rational, but only that it cannot rest on reasons derived from natural theology.[6]) But, though he believes these things to be true, he has to allow that there is a problem about the meaning that he attaches to them. There would be no problem about, for example, the meaning of the proposition that God made the world, if we were allowed to conceive of God as a finite thing causally active among other finite things in accordance with natural laws. But this is disallowed by what we say about the divine nature, and indeed, in this case, by the content of the statement itself. The 'anthropomorphic' interpretation being unavailable, what other can we fall back on in order to specify what kind of making we have in mind?

[6] An excellent account of this reasonableness is to be found in Basil Mitchell's *The Justification of Religious Belief* (Macmillan, London, 1973).

I think that Swinburne maintains that I am here stirring up a mare's nest. 'God made the world' means, I think he would say, 'God brought it about that the world exists'. Now we know what it is to bring things about. Of course when we bring things about we normally move our limbs, or at least our tongues. But it is coherent to suppose that we might bring things about without such intermediaries, and therefore coherent to suppose that God brings things about immediately. But I have grave doubts about this programme of removing 'human limitations' from concepts normally used to speak about human beings, and claiming that something remains when this is done. I sympathize with those who say that when you take away the human limitations you take away everything of which we have any conception. Thus, in the present case, I do not see how I can bring something about without its holding of me that I purposed that that thing should come about; nor how it can hold of me that I purposed something without its holding of me that some finite human thoughts were in my mind; nor, indeed, how it can hold that anything is in *my* mind unless an environment is viewed from my perspective; and I do not see how analogous things can hold of God. It does not follow that we are *wrong* to ascribe purposes to God, but only that, when we do so, we have, not a scanty and impoverished, but strictly *no* conception of the nature of what we are alleging. We cannot distil a pure essence, applicable to the infinite spirit as to human beings, from the concept of a mental act such as that of purposing. This is, of course, a very large subject, on which a great deal has been written; and I am not under the absurd delusion that I can contribute to it in half a dozen sentences. I am merely trying to indicate why I do not think that this programme of 'analogical purification' can deal with the question of our grasp of the meaning of our religious statements.

The question was: how can it be that we believe 'God made the world' to be true when we have to confess that we have no conception of the nature of the reality which, we claim, the statement truly reports? My answer was: in something a little like the way in which a man born blind can know it is true that green is a restful colour, though he has no conception of what green is, nor of what it is for one's eyes to find repose. That is, by some kind of authority. More specifically, my answer was: we have it on trustworthy authority that we shall not go religiously astray if we think of God as if he were a finite being of whom certain truths hold; we shall not go wrong in the matters with which religion deals if, with certain reservations, we put a finite being having certain properties into that gap in our understanding which constitutes the notion of the divine. I put this by saying that the things that we say about God are to be taken as parables. We have no conception of how it can be true of an infinite being that his[7] relation to finite beings can be represented by the relation of one finite being to others which were brought into existence by the agency of the former; what we have is the belief that this, though a mystery, *is* true.

There is no doubt a lot wrong with this; and certainly there is a vast deal missing from it. But it seems to me to be one way of preserving the point, which has to be preserved, that we do not in any way understand how the things we say about the infinite being can be true of any being. And it seems to me that it will be a corollary of any way of preserving this point, as it is of this way, that, when (by way of higher-level comment on various lower-level claims) we say, for example, that God acts, we shall have to concede that we are saying something which we hold to be true but must allow to be incomprehensible. But now what becomes of the argument that, since everything that we can conceive of and give the name of action to has earlier and later phases, God, since we say he is an agent, must exist in time? Surely it does not get us very far. Within the parable we must think of God as existing in time, and therefore throughout the infinity of time. But this is obvious, because 'within the parable' just means 'in so far as we are thinking of God as if he were a finite being'. The question is: does any deep metaphysical truth about the relationship between God and time follow from the legitimacy of our using such parables? In particular can we derive from it any premises which we can employ in theological reasoning about, for example, such matters as human freedom and divine foreknowledge?

In order to take this further we need to do a little sorting. So far I have spoken as if religious statements were all of a piece

---

[7] Nor have we any conception of how it can be right to use personal pronouns of the infinite being.

and could all be thought of as parables, in the sense that in making them we speak of God as if he were a finite being, predicating of him predicates which we might also use of human beings, but not intending to imply that God is such a finite being, nor that we have any grasp of what it is in the divine being which is, we believe, reliably though parabolically expressed in what we affirm. But religious statements are not all of a piece, and this notion of a parable fits some of them much more readily than others; indeed, some of them it seems to fit not at all. It fits readily enough the claim that God forgives the penitent. Here our notion of forgiving is surely the notion of human forgiving, idealized and purified, indeed, but not dehumanized; we do not suppose that we have some, even tenuous, understanding of what the mental act of forgiving amounts to in an infinite being; we believe, rather, that we are authorized to claim that the notion of human forgiving corresponds to something real but incomprehensible in the divine being. More generally, talk of parable fits well enough with those religious statements in which, as I said earlier, we predicate of God predicates which we might also use of human beings; and there are many credal statements which are of this kind. But it does not seem to fit such credal statements as that the Word was made flesh, for example, nor the doctrine of the Trinity. For obvious reasons we are certainly not claiming that we are authorized to regard ordinary three-in-oneness as a parabolic representation of something in the divine nature.[8] But there is a class of statements, to which Bishop Ian Ramsey paid attention, to which the notion of parable does apply, though indirectly. These are those theological statements in which we predicate of God predicates not used of anything else, as when we say that God is infinite, pure spirit, omniscient, omnipotent, and so on. The function of such statements (this is Ramsey's point, I believe) is to comment, and, on the whole, to comment negatively, on how other credal statements are to be taken. Thus when we say that God is omniscient we are not to be taken as saying that human omniscience is a

---

[8] There is no such thing as 'ordinary three-in-oneness'; and the things which are sometimes spoken of as symbols of the Trinity do not help. Clover leaves, for example, consist of three lobes making up one leaf. Trinitarian heresies arise from taking such symbols too seriously.

parabolic representation of something in God, so much as
that, when we think of God parabolically as a finite being, we
are not to think of him as ignorant of anything. When, likewise, we say that God is omnipotent we are saying that, when
we think of him within the parable as a finite being, we are not
to suppose that anything is beyond his power. This is a stipula-
tion we can comply with though we have no non-parabolic
conception of the power of an infinite being, nor indeed of
what it is for an infinite being to *do* anything.

I daresay there is not very much difference between, on the
one hand, treating theological statements of this kind in this
way, and, on the other, claiming that human omniscience and
omnipotence (which, of course, we never encounter, but might
suppose we can construct in the imagination by developing
erudition and competence without limit) are a parabolic
representation of something in the divine nature. But what I
certainly will not do is to suppose that we understand God's
omniscience, because we can develop erudition without
limit—and what we reach on the completion of his infinite process is exactly that which God possesses. Human knowledge is
discursive; a boundless store of it (every item of which will be
encoded in some human language) may be an adequate
parable of something in the being of God—as adequate,
perhaps, as is human forgiving of divine forgiving. But a
boundless store of items of discursive knowledge is certainly
not what God may be supposed actually to possess. What
happens, however, if somebody accepts this point but proposes to deal with it by the suggestion that we are indeed to
take human knowledge as our starting point, but that we are
to think of it not only as infinitely extended, but also as freed
from all the limitations which are due to its being the knowledge of a finite being? Will that not give us an adequate
conception of divine omniscience? The answer has to be, I
think, that if we relentlessly remove from human knowledge
the limitations which are due to human finitude, what we are
left with is, simply, nothing. The chief merit, perhaps, of
the Ramseyan treatment of such doctrines as that of God's
omniscience is that it directs our attention away from this
unpromising road.

A similar treatment is required, I think, of the doctrine that

God's being is eternal or everlasting (at this level there seems to be nothing to choose between these adjectives). What this doctrine primarily tells us is that within the parable we are not to think that there is any time at which the finite being who plays the role of God within the parable did not, or will not, exist. At this level, at any rate, the doctrine of the divine eternity regulates our parables. But it may be said that this is superficial, and that there must be some deeper level at which the doctrine is to be understood. I concede that this is so, and that in speaking of the divine eternity we are not just saying that in our talk of God we are to talk of him as if he were an everlasting human or superhuman person. We are not just outlawing such suggestions as 'Perhaps that was before God's time.' There is much to be said for the traditional view that, 'within God', God's attributes are all one; that his eternity is the same thing as his omnipotence, and both as his infinitude. To say that God is eternal, therefore, is to use one way of expressing such little understanding as we have of divinity, namely that in speaking of God we are speaking of what is ultimate and is not identical either with the whole of or with any part of finite being. But this, of course, does nothing to tell us that it is, or that it is not, a deep metaphysical truth that the divine being is temporally ordered.

Somebody might say, however, that I am ignoring an obvious point. It is surely perverse, they might argue, to hesitate over asserting that God's being is in reality omnitemporal. For, in the first place, the concept of omnitemporality is a purely formal concept, so that to predicate this property of anything is not to say anything about the *nature* of that thing, but only something about its *duration*. Such a predication therefore imposes no limitation upon its subject (in the way in which to predicate infinite erudition upon something would imply that that thing is a discursive intelligence), and there is thus no impropriety in predicating omnitemporality of God; it implies no contradiction of anything else we want to say of him (for all it could contradict is that his duration is temporally limited). And, in the second place, we understand what we are doing when we say of something that it is omnitemporal; to refuse, therefore, to accept that this is in reality a divine attribute is to generate mystery where there need be none; it may be right to say that we have no conception of the attribute for which we use the name 'omniscience', but there is no parallel case for saying that we have none of that for which we use the name 'omnitemporality'.

My response to this is to accept the first point, at any rate provisionally; it certainly seems at first sight that no harm is done by saying that God is in metaphysical reality omnitemporal. But with regard to the second point my reply would be twofold. I would say first that I do not regard as an advantage the fact that we have a clear conception of what omnitemporal existence must be (though equally no disadvantage; infinite being is a mystery, but there is no need to claim that it is totally mysterious). But I would say secondly that, while I accept that I understand what I am doing when I predicate omnitemporality of finite being, I am not sure that I understand what I would be doing if I were to predicate this attribute of God at a level deeper than that of parable. My doubts on this matter will be the theme of the rest of this essay. So far I have been trying to rebut the argument that we *must* allow that God's existence is omnitemporal, since we could not otherwise claim that he acts. My response to this is that we do indeed think of God's acting, as of that of any other agent, as taking place in time, but that this is because we have to think of God as if he were a finite being. If I am right in this, it will leave open the question whether we can say anything, and if so which of the two contending options, of the metaphysical relation between God and time. This is what we turn to now.

It is a presupposition of both the contending parties (the Boethians who say that God's existence is outside time, and those who say that on the contrary it is temporally ordered) that there are at least some propositions in the field of philosophical theology which are not, in my jargon, parabolic; and, in particular, that one or other of the two propositions about the relation between God and time is a true proposition belonging to this class. For the purposes of the following discussion I shall accept this presupposition and proceed to ask how we can understand the proposition that God's being is temporal.

That it is, if temporal, omnitemporal is not in dispute. Our concern, therefore, is with temporal duration as such. A temporally enduring substance is one whose existence is a succession of phases between which, and within each of which, temporal relations hold. This is not to say, of course, either that the existence of a temporally enduring substance is a succession of *discrete* phases (so that it would be in theory possible to count the number of phases which made up the life of something that endured for a finite time), or that it is a succession of *instantaneous* phases each containing no temporal spread. The notion of an instant is the notion of a cut in a continuum. This pen, for example, has been in existence for a number of years. To say this is not to say that it has run through an infinite series of instantaneous phases, nor that it has run through some finite number of objectively distinct phases, each having some temporal duration. We can refer to some temporal stretch of its being (for example to that which began when I last picked it up and continues till now). In doing so we are selecting an episode from the continuous life of the pen; and, obviously enough, there is no way of selecting episodes from its continuous duration which is, so to speak, metaphysically given. To speak of phases, then, is to speak of arbitrarily selected episodes. But, that having been said, a temporally enduring substance is, as we said, one whose existence consists of phases any one of which necessarily has some temporal relation with any other; the one phase must be wholly earlier than, wholly later than, wholly contemporary with, or partially overlapping the other.

This must hold of God's existence, if this is temporal. It must be in theory possible to distinguish episodes in the divine life between which temporal relations necessarily obtain (and within which this is also the case, since there is, as we said, no such thing as an episode of minimum duration). This is not to say, of course, that *we* can select such episodes or phases; but it would be quite unclear what we were saying when we said that God's existence was in time if we did not allow that this commits us to the proposition that there must *be* such phases. There must *be* moments in the divine life which *are* earlier than some other moments and later than yet others. Our problem is: what are we to make of these objective temporal relationships? In the case of finite substances temporal relationships between phases will be reflected in causal relationships. In the case of a finite substance later phases develop, we believe, out of earlier phases in accordance with the intrinsic nature of the substance and its interaction with others; and later phases are thus to be explained in terms of earlier. But one hesitates to say that this applies to the divine being. One motive no doubt which underlies the Boethian notion that God's being is *totum simul* is that development is felt to be inconsistent with infinitude; that which *is not* at some moments that which it *is* at other moments has no time at which its whole being is actualized; and this means that it at all times suffers the limitation that there is something that it might be, and is not— there is at all times unactualized potentiality. But if God is the ground of all potentiality—if he is that which determines what might be, but is not—then what grounds, so to speak, the potentiality that there is in God's being if the temporality of his being is to be understood in terms of some kind of development? Suffering this kind of hesitation, one feels impelled— perhaps wrongly—to ask: in what do the temporal relations between earlier and later phases of the divine being consist?

One might be tempted to answer this question in one or other of two ways. One of these answers (unattractive as soon as it is made explicit) is that there are two ultimate beings, God and time, and that both are infinite in duration. According to this suggestion it is logically possible—it is coherent to entertain the supposition—that there might have been times at which there was not anything else besides time; there was not yet an omniscient, omnipotent being, nor, therefore, any finite beings; and it is logically possible that there might again, one day in the future, be just time and nothing else. This suggestion is unpromising on two counts. First, inconsistently with the basic tenet of theism, it makes something exist independently of and over against God, namely time. But secondly it perplexes our understanding by inviting us to think of time as some *thing* which is such that there might, logically, be just that thing and nothing else, as if 'time' was the name of a substance. Surely this is wrong. Perhaps there is what Kant might have called a dialectical illusion which may make us momentarily readier than we should be to entertain such a notion. Suppose that there exists nothing but the world of finite beings, and that this world is of finite duration; at a certain distance backwards from now there was nothing, and at a certain distance forwards from now there will be nothing. Better, perhaps, at a certain distance backwards from now there was a state which had no predecessor, and at a certain distance forwards from now there will be a state which will have no successor. If we entertain this supposition—and it seems coherent—we may well think that the world might have gone on longer—there might have been more of it before now than there has been, and there might have been more of it after now than there will be—and that therefore there is unoccupied time (and an infinity of it, since there is no limit to how much longer the world might have lasted) at each end of the world's history. It seems, then, that, since it is logically possible that there is nothing but the finite world and that this is of finite duration, it must be logically possible that there is (that is, has been and will be) unoccupied time. Time, then, must be something that exists independently of its filling with events.

But surely we ought not to be seduced by this argument into drawing this conclusion. I do not claim to understand time, but I certainly do not think of it as something such that there might be that and nothing else. It is doubtless true that, if something is of finite duration, it might logically have lasted longer. But consider some moment of unoccupied time, and suppose we say that something might have existed *then*. How might we identify the *then* we are speaking of? Only, surely, by the last (or first) event. It is after the last (or before the first) event. But how much after (or before)? There is surely, in principle, no way of saying: it is not just that we have no means of measuring, but rather that there is nothing we would be measuring. The slipping away of moments? But surely this is nonsense (they would have to slip away in time). Surely, then, when we say of the finite-duration world we are imagining that it might, logically, have lasted longer, we mean just that—that it might logically have lasted longer. We do not mean that there are infinite stretches of unoccupied time that it might have encroached upon. To suppose otherwise is to infer a metaphysical possibility from a logical possibility. It is to infer from the premise that it is coherent to suppose a world of longer duration than the actual the conclusion that the world could actually have gone on longer, in that there once was (and will be) something that could have supported the exis-tence of events, though it did not (and one day will not). In truth, I think, if there is nothing but the finite world, and it is of finite duration, then it could not have lasted longer than its actual duration; for there is, *ex hypothesi*, nothing in which the possibility of its doing so might have been grounded. That there is nothing incoherent in the supposition of its lasting longer does nothing to contradict this.

Time, then, is not an independently existing thing, and we cannot therefore explain the omnitemporality of the divine being by saying that there is no moment in the infinite dura-tion of time which is not accompanied by a contemporary phase of God's existence. This might tempt somebody to offer the second of the two answers that we said might be given to the question what the omnitemporality of the divine being consists in. This answer would be that the finite world must be supposed to be of infinite duration, and that there never has been and never will be a phase of the finite world with which no phase of God's being is contemporary. (I suppose that this is how, on the whole, the Greeks would have thought of the eternity of the divine.) The obvious objection to this sugges-tion is that it makes the omnitemporality of the finite world a direct consequence of the omnitemporality of God; one won-ders whether those who want to insist that God is omnitem-poral intend it to be a direct consequence of this that the finite world is necessarily of infinite duration.

But there is anyhow a further problem. Both of these answers explicate the temporality of the divine being by refer-ence to something else which is allegedly of infinite duration—the infinite duration of time itself, or of the finite world—and by claiming that it is possible in principle to map the phases of God's being on to those of the other series by a one-one rela-tion. This relation is presumably that of contemporaneity. Thus the second answer maintains that for every phase of the infinite duration of the finite world there is just one phase of the divine being which is the one which is its contemporary. The temporality of the finite world is not in dispute; given, then, that we know what it is for some phase of the divine being to be contemporary with some given phase of the finite world, we establish the temporality of the divine being by the proposition that to each phase of the divine being there corresponds that phase of the finite world which is its contemporary.

But is it clear that we do know what it is for some phase of the divine being to be contemporary with (or, indeed, to stand in some determinate temporal relation with) some given phase of the finite world? It might be argued that some of God's acts consist in bringing about effects in the created world, that these effects have their temporal ordering, and that there must be a corresponding temporal ordering of the divine acts which are their causes. Thus, to take a very general case, God's sustaining of the created universe at this moment must be earlier than his sustaining of it at this, slightly subsequent, moment. Or, to take a more particular case, Abraham receives the divine injunction to take his son to the place of sacrifice, and then later receives the divine injunction not to sacrifice him. Surely we can say that we have here a divine action with earlier and later phases, in that God's bringing it about that Abraham sets out with Isaac for the mountain is the bringing about of an earlier event and his bringing it about that Abraham substitutes the ram for Isaac is the bringing about of a later event; and surely the same temporal relation must subsist between the bringings about as subsists between the events brought about. If the created world is of infinite duration, and if the whole of God's being is absorbed by his relations with his creation, then no doubt the whole of God's being could be said to be temporally ordered in this way.

But this does not seem to get us very far. It rests on the assumption that the temporal ordering of the things brought about must be matched by a corresponding temporal ordering of the divine volitions which bring those things about. But why should we make this assumption, to which everyday experience lends no support? I write to A and to B on Friday and post both letters side by side on that day: the letter to A is delivered on Monday and that to B on Tuesday. So I write to A and to B on the same day, but I get in touch with them on different days; on the side of the recipients there is a lapse of time between my communications, though on my side there is none. But, it may be said, this is because a mechanism of communication is involved in this case, whereas no mechanism (which might be swift or might be tardy) is involved in the bringing about of God's effects. The objection is fair. But it does not entirely dispose of the point, which is this. If we assume that God's volitions are instantly effective, then we can indeed order the divine volitions in the same temporal order as that of their effects. Within the parable we do indeed make this assumption (except when we suppose that God acts through intermediaries such as prophets). But to make it in the metaphysical context within which we are now groping is surely to beg the question. If God's volitions are contemporary with their effects, then it follows at once that the order of the former corresponds exactly with that of the latter. But do we know what it is for some divine volition to take place at exactly the same moment at which its effect comes about in the created world? It seems to me that I do not. I understand well enough that we can have a convention, so to speak, whereby we order divine volitions so that their temporal succession corresponds precisely with that of their effects; but that seems to me to be as far as I can go. *If* the divine acts are temporally ordered, then no doubt their ordering accords with this convention; and no doubt they are temporally ordered in the limited sense that, for those of them that have effects in creation, they are the bringing about of temporally ordered effects. But how can we get beyond this?

This second suggested answer seems, then, to go wrong on two counts. Firstly, it binds up God's being too closely with that of his creation; and secondly, in common with the first of the two suggested answers, its explication of the temporality of the divine being rests on the assumption that clear sense can be given to the notion that for each phase of some temporally ordered series—the history of time itself, or of the created universe—there exists that phase of the divine being which is the one which is its contemporary. And this surely makes plain what we have to do with the question in what the temporality of God's being consists: we have to reject the question, if it is seeking for anything more than the tautological answer that it consists in its being temporally ordered. We have to say, in other words, that it just is the case that the divine being as it is in itself is a series of phases (which of course we do not have to claim that we can discriminate), each of which stands to every other in a temporal relation. It follows, I presume, that we have to claim that God can remember earlier phases of his being and look forward to others that have not yet come to pass.

Now it is very tempting to say that this is false, or at the least incomprehensible. It is tempting to say that the notion of temporal succession is inextricably bound up with that of the development of finite substances in interaction with each other in accordance with causal laws which relate that development to the nature of the substances involved in the interaction. It is certainly very tempting to say that it is an essential part of what it is for one global state to be (say) later than another that the state we call the later is the effect of the state we call the earlier in that the later has come about by development out of the earlier through the interaction, in accordance with their nature, of the finite substances involved in the earlier. It is also very tempting to say that, even if the phases of the divine being are temporally ordered, there cannot be any *determinate* lapse of time between one phase and another, and that therefore no interval between phases of the divine being can be longer or shorter than, or just as long as, any other such interval. It is not just that we are (obviously) not in a position to measure such intervals; the doubt is whether there could be anything that could in principle be measured, even, so to speak, by God himself. But temporal duration that cannot even in principle be measured is, to say the least, very impoverished temporal duration.

But I shall resist the temptation to say that it cannot be true that the divine being constitutes a temporal series, and content myself with saying, firstly, that I have no glimmering of an idea how I could tell that it is true, and secondly, and in particular, that I have no idea of how one can avoid a radically anthropomorphic conception of the divine being as it is in itself if one insists that it is temporally ordered. My contention is that we are not in a position to decide whether the claim that God is omnitemporal rather than timeless is or is not a deep metaphysical truth.

Finally a word about the way this controversy comes up in the context of theodicy. Firstly, in denying that we can claim that God is omnitemporal I am not trying to shore up the Boethian claim that there is no problem of reconciling divine omniscience with human freedom on the ground that, since God is in his own being timeless, no knowing of his (nor any other action of his) takes place earlier or later than, or at the same time as, any event in the world of finite being, and that therefore there is no question of his *fore*knowing what I shall freely do. I am not saying that we can assert this. But equally I am not siding with those who say that we have no right, when something terrible is perpetrated by some free agent, to complain that God should have intervened earlier to prevent it. At any earlier time, T_1, they say, there is no such thing as that which a free agent A will do at T_2. It is therefore logically impossible for God to know at any earlier time what A will then do, not because of any limitation of God's knowledge, but because there is no such thing to be known until A acts. If God were timeless (they perhaps say) then, though he would not in that case *fore*know, he would in his omniscience *know* what A does at T_2; and then the question why he did not prevent it would have arisen. The doctrine that God is timeless, though it means that nothing in God takes place at any time, means also that *from our point of view* it is right to say that God knows at every moment of our time what will be done at any time— for the whole history of creation is *always* (from our temporal standpoint) open to the divine view. Therefore the doctrine of divine timelessness is inconvenient from the point of view of theodicy. But it seems to me that we cannot argue thus. Grant we cannot claim to *know* the truth of the Boethian doctrine that, from the human point of view, God knows at all times what takes place at any time; but can we, if we claim to believe in an infinite being, deny that this is *possible*? It seems to me that we have so little understanding of what we are doing when we attribute knowledge to something that is not a finite mind that we are quite incompetent to pronounce on such matters.

11

The Possibility of Incorporeal Agency

STEVEN W. HOLTZER

I

For those who stand in the Judaeo-Christian tradition, the concept of divine agency is basic. On the basis of the biblical evidence alone, there is ample support for the conception of God as an agent. In the history of Israel God is identified as the one 'who brought us out of Egypt' (Exodus 13: 14). He is also seen as the ultimate agent of creation, and the prophets see him as active in the affairs of the nations, both in Israel and in foreign nations. This view of God as agent is carried over into the gospel accounts of the teachings of Jesus as well, where the Kingdom which Jesus came to announce is seen as the coming *active* reign of God.

However, we must remember that our understanding of God as agent is based on an analogy with our understanding of ourselves as agents: yet it is this very analogy which has led some modern philosophers to reject the idea of God acting as incoherent. These thinkers argue that an essential part of our understanding of ourselves as agents is that we have bodies and it is with these very bodies that we act in the world. God, however, at least as traditionally conceived, does not have a body, and therefore it is incoherent to speak of him acting in any sense analogous to our normal understanding of what it is for a person to act. Indeed for some modern philosophers the objections to God acting not only render belief in any sort of divine activity untenable, they also render theism itself similarly untenable. In this paper I shall state some forms of this challenge as put forward by certain modern philosophers and also uncover the foundations upon which their arguments are based. I shall argue that these foundations are themselves open to serious challenge and that the theist has nothing to

fear from what at first sight may appear to be a formidable
obstacle.

II

The first case I propose to examine against incorporeal agency
comes from Kai Nielsen. Nielsen's objection is stated very
clearly in his book *Contemporary Critiques of Religion*,[1] in which
he echoes similar arguments put forward by Paul Edwards
and Antony Flew.[2] All three claim that to speak of God acting
in any way is unintelligible because God does not have a body.
However, to claim, as Christians do, that God loves mankind
entails that God can do or fail to do something, that God can
act. And to say 'that an X can act presupposes that X has a
body'.[3]

It is important to stress here that Nielsen is not claiming
that to speak of someone doing something is merely to speak of
the occurrence of certain bodily movements; he is well aware
that the concept of action is much too complex to be reduced
simply to talk of such movements. But, having said this, he
thinks that 'it would still seem to be the case that to say "X did
Y" or "X could do Y" entails "X has a body" '.[4]

Nor does Nielsen's argument require or presuppose the
empiricists' verifiability criterion, that without an observable
body claims about divine action are not empirically verifiable
and are therefore meaningless. Instead, his claim is,

that when we carefully reflect on the actual structure of our language, i.e. the depth grammar of the language, we will come to see
that 'disembodied lover' or 'bodiless action' like '3 a.m. on Mars' or
'wife without husband' is an unintelligible collocation of words. This
claim rests on no general theory of language; it is no more dependent
on neo-behaviourist or materialist conceptions than on verifi-
cationist ones. Rather, it turns on the kind of understanding we

---

[1] Kai Nielsen, *Contemporary Critiques of Religion* (Macmillan, London, 1971).

[2] Cf. Paul Edwards, 'Some Notes on Anthropomorphic Theology' in *Religion Experience and Truth*, ed. Sidney Hook (Oliver and Boyd, London, 1962), pp. 241–50; Paul
Edwards, 'Difficulties in the Idea of God' in *The Idea of God*, eds. Edward H. Madden,
Rollo Handy, and Marvin Faber (Charles Thomas, Springfield, Illinois, 1968), pp.
43–77; Antony Flew, *God and Philosophy* (Dell, New York, 1966), pp. 30–4.

[3] Nielsen, p. 119.

[4] Nielsen, p. 119.

should gain by careful attention to our actual use of words in a particular area.[5]

Thus the crux of Nielsen's claim is how our words refer in ordinary language, and in our ordinary everyday use of terms such as 'agent' or 'action' we refer to an embodied agent. The same is true for action words such as 'loving', 'giving', 'saving', 'creating', and many of the other activities which have traditionally been ascribed to God. In our ordinary discourse these terms are used in reference to embodied agents.

While Nielsen is obviously correct about the normal reference of action terms such as these in ordinary language, I do not think that this observation alone is sufficient to sustain his case against their application to an incorporeal agent. Since Nielsen is arguing as a philosopher, it seems reasonable to expect a rigorous argument for his position rather than a simple appeal to ordinary discourse. For as J. L. Austin, himself one of the founders of 'ordinary language philosophy', observed, 'The beginning of sense, not to say wisdom, is to realize that "doing an action", as used in philosophy, is a highly abstract expression.'[6] In a footnote to this statement Austin makes the point that the philosophical use of 'action' has, in Austin's words, 'little to do with the more down-to-earth occurrences of "action" in ordinary speech'.[7] Philosophers are often concerned with questions such as the role of intentions in action, how the mind and body are related in actions, whether actions are caused, etc. Everyday usage, however, does not reflect these concerns at all. Jones may see Smith walking into the library on a Saturday morning and perhaps think to himself 'Smith certainly is studying hard this term', but he would rarely ever analyse Smith's activity at a deeper, philosophical level. We simply do not do this in ordinary, everyday life. Thus for Nielsen to conclude that incorporeal agency is unintelligible solely on the basis of our more 'down-to-earth' uses of 'action' seems rather hasty.

What is required instead is an analysis of 'action' at the conceptual level rather than that of ordinary language. Here Basil

[5] Nielsen, pp. 119–20.
[6] J. L. Austin, 'A Plea for Excuses' in J. L. Austin, *Philosophical Papers* (Clarendon Press, Oxford, 1961), p. 126.
[7] Austin, p. 126 n. 1.

Mitchell surely puts the emphasis in the proper place when he states that 'the question is whether our concept of action is such as to render unintelligible all talk of incorporeal agency'.[8] By beginning his analysis at the conceptual level Mitchell can clearly see 'that the language in which we describe actions is logically distinct from that in which we describe physical movements'.[9] Rather than presupposing an embodied agent, as Nielsen claims, Mitchell correctly observes that action language merely 'presupposes a conscious agent with intentions and purposes which he attempts to realize in his environment as he sees it'.[10] Furthermore, as Mitchell points out, 'Actions may be done through the agency of others, and events which are not physical, such as concentrating and deciding, may be regarded as actions.'[11] Thus while Nielsen is undoubtedly correct about the bodily entailment inherent in most of our ordinary action discourse, Mitchell has clearly shown that at the conceptual level such an entailment does not necessarily hold. As a result, Nielsen's charge that talk of incorporeal agency is unintelligible because of certain linguistic considerations pertaining to ordinary action may be dismissed as premature.

III

However, what if the bodily entailment inherent in most of our ordinary action discourse could be shown to obtain at the conceptual level as well? In other words, what if our very concept of action necessitated embodiment? A challenge of this type, if successful, would refute Mitchell's argument, and the notion of incorporeal agency would be rendered incoherent. It is precisely this challenge which Anthony Kenny puts forward in the concluding chapter of his book *The God of the Philosophers*.[12] In the remainder of this paper I shall analyse

---

[8] Basil Mitchell, *The Justification of Religious Belief* (Macmillan, London, 1973), p. 7.
[9] Mitchell, p. 7.
[10] Mitchell, pp. 7–8.
[11] Mitchell, p. 8. It must be noted, however, that if the reductionist programme of central state materialism is correct, then talk about mental states *is* merely talk about brain states ('the mind-brain identity theory'), and therefore events such as concentrating and deciding are *physical* actions. But this theory remains unproven, and thus Mitchell's examples are still valid.
[12] Anthony Kenny, *The God of the Philosophers* (Clarendon Press, Oxford, 1979).

Kenny's claim that a body is necessary for a being to act. I shall argue that this claim is false, and that therefore the objection to incorporeal agency which is based upon it is without foundation.

In examining the concept of action Kenny places his discussion in the context of God's relation to the world. He points out that traditionally whereas the revealed word of God was conceived of as a linguistic expression of the infinite knowledge of God, 'The natural word of God was the world itself, considered as God's creation and as an expression of God's intelligence.'[13]

Now this relation between God and the world may be understood in one of two ways: the world is an expression of God's mind, either (a) in the way that our words and actions are expressions of our thoughts, or (b) in the way that a work of art is an expression of an artist's skill. Kenny rejects (a) because 'To think in that way would be to make the world God's body, which traditional theology would have regarded as objectionably pantheistic'.[14]

No doubt traditional theology would have regarded as 'objectionably pantheistic' any attempt to conceive of the world as God's body,[15] but why does (a) entail that the world must

---

[13] Kenny, pp. 125–6.

[14] Kenny, p. 126.

[15] Cf. the following statements from the First Vatican Council of 1869–70: 'The Holy Catholic, Apostolic, Roman Church believes and confesses that there is one, true and living God, Creator and Lord of heaven and earth, . . . who . . . is to be declared as really and essentially distinct from the world.' ('Dogmatic Constitution on the Catholic Faith, I: Of God the Creator of all Things' in *The Decrees of the Vatican Council*, ed. Vincent McNabb (Burns and Oates, London, 1907, pp. 18–19.) Furthermore, 'If anyone shall say that the substance and essence of God and all things is one and the same, let him be anathema. If anyone shall say that finite things, both corporeal and spiritual, or at least spiritual, have emanated from the divine substance; or that the divine essence by the manifestation and evolution of itself becomes all things; or, lastly, that God is universal or infinite being, which by determining itself constitutes the universality of things, distinct according to kinds (*genera*), species and individuals; let him be anathema. If anyone confess not that the world and all things which are contained in it, both spiritual and material, have been, in their whole substance, produced by God out of nothing; or shall say that God created, not by His will, free from all necessity, but by a necessity equal to the necessity whereby He loves Himself; or shall deny that the world was made for the glory of God; let him be anathema.' ('Canons, I: Of God the Creator of all Things' in McNabb, p. 29.)

194 *Steven W. Holtzer*

be God's body? Here Kenny follows Arthur Danto and his notion of a *basic action*:[16]

A basic action is an action which one does not by doing anything else; I may wind my watch by moving my finger and thumb, but it is not by doing something else that I move my finger and thumb. Danto suggests that a body can be defined as the locus of one's basic actions. If God can act in the world directly and without intermediary, as traditionally he has been held to, then on Danto's definition the world would be God's body.[17]

I shall return to this notion of a basic action in a moment, but first we must see what Kenny thinks of option (*b*) as a way of understanding God's relation to the world. (*b*) is actually the more traditional view of this relation, but Kenny rejects it as well. But why? Because, in Kenny's words, 'Most artists work with their hands: if the world is an artefact of God's mind, there is nothing which comes between the craftsman's mind and his work as a human craftsman's hands do'.[18] However, it seems to me that this objection is damaging only if it is a logically necessary rather than a logically contingent matter that the craftsmen and artists we know work with their hands. As with the concept of action itself, the fact that the craftsmen and artists we know work with their hands would seem to arise from the fact that we are speaking of embodied human agents, rather than from any logical requirement of the concept of a craftsman or an artist, and therefore (*b*) cannot be rejected simply on conceptual grounds.[19]

But is it adequate to defend the possibility of incorporeal action solely on the basis of logical possibility, or is something more required? I think something more is required, particu-

---

[16] Arthur C. Danto, 'Basic Actions', *American Philosophical Quarterly* 2 (April 1965), 141–8. The reference to this article in Kenny's bibliography, p. 130, mistakenly lists it as being in *The Philosophical Quarterly* (*1965*).

[17] Kenny, p. 126.

[18] Kenny, p. 126.

[19] The following statement by one of the twentieth century's leading exponents of atheism, J. L. Mackie, is also worth noting in this connection: 'Although all the persons we are acquainted with have bodies, there is no great difficulty in conceiving what it would be for there to be a person without a body: for example, one can imagine oneself surviving without a body, and while at present one can act and produce results only by using one's limbs or one's speech organs, one can *imagine* having one's intentions fulfilled directly, without such physical means. J. L. Mackie, *The Miracle of Theism* (Clarendon Press, Oxford, 1982), pp. 1–2.

larly since the heart of Kenny's argument against such action
is Danto's theory of basic actions. What more is required will
emerge as we now consider some issues in the general
philosophy of action and Danto's theory in particular.

In order to grasp the importance of Danto's theory for our
understanding of action we must refer to the work of David
Hume. Hume was greatly puzzled by the idea of causality,
particularly with respect to the origin of our idea of power or
necessary connection. And in section 7 of his *Enquiry Concerning
Human Understanding* he set out to find this origin.[20] He began
his search by looking toward the external world but concluded
that it is impossible to derive the idea of power from this
source, for when we observe external objects interacting all we
see are certain regular conjunctions of events. But we are
never able, according to Hume, 'in a single instance, to discover any power or necessary connection; any quality, which
binds the effect to the cause, and renders the one an infallible
consequence of the other'.[21]

It is not surprising that the next possible source which
Hume investigates is our experience of volition, for after all,

It may be said, that we are every moment conscious of internal
power; while we feel, that, by the simple command of our will, we
move the organs of our body, or direct the faculties of our mind . . .
Hence we acquire the idea of power or energy.[22]

Thus it would appear that here we have the source for which
Hume was searching. But Hume was not so easily satisfied,
and he set out to examine this 'pretension', as he called it.[23]

As with all natural events, for Hume the influence of volition over the organs of the body can be known only by experience,[24] and in our experience, 'The motion of our body follows
upon the command of our will. Of this we are every moment
conscious.'[25] Now, according to the 'pretension' which Hume
is here examining, the relation between the will and bodily
movement is one of cause and effect, and it is from this relation that we derive our notion of power. But, as Hume points

---

[20] David Hume, *Enquiries concerning Human Understanding and concerning the Principles
of Morals*, ed. L. A. Selby-Bigge, third edn., rev. P. H. Nidditch (Clarendon Press,
Oxford, 1975), pp. 60–79.

[21] Hume, p. 63. [22] Hume, p. 64. [23] Hume, p. 64.
[24] Hume, p. 64. [25] Hume, p. 65.

out, the means by which this union is affected is totally mysterious to us. It is not something of which we are conscious, and this raised the question of why we view the relation as one of cause and effect.

Hume's answer is quite simple. As with events involving objects in the external world, we observe the constant conjunction of As followed by Bs, but this is not because there is any necessary connection between the occurrence of an A and the subsequent occurrence of a B. It may indeed be true that, whenever someone wills to raise his arm, his arm rises in just the manner willed, with the result that we expect the same movement to follow upon a similar act of will in the future. However, because we are not conscious of any *power* in our will to bring about the intended bodily movement, Hume is convinced that none exists.[26]

As further evidence for this conclusion Hume appeals to the physiological changes which occur during a bodily movement. It is a fact that when we will to raise our arms there follow several intermediate events, such as the activation of nerves and the contraction of muscles, and in the light of this evidence Hume asks, 'Can there be a more certain proof, that the power, by which this whole operation is performed, so far

---

[26] The notion of 'power' needs further clarification here. In the context of Hume's discussion, as we have seen, he only speaks of 'power' itself, and does not distinguish between types of power. However, there are two types of power which philosophers have noted. The first type is what may be called 'transitive power', and the second is what may be called 'immanent power'. Now these two types of power are different. Some powers—the transitive—pass over into other objects, e.g. as when a saw cuts the wood. Thus the 'power' of the saw passes over into the wood and cuts the wood. This 'transitive' type of power is what Hume and I are speaking of with respect to our power to move our bodies, and we are claiming that no one is ever aware of such a power in relation to their body.

But, we are aware of exercising power when we act, though of an *immanent* type. Aquinas describes immanent and transitive power respectively as follows: 'For action and production differ, because action is an operation that remains in the agent itself, as choosing, understanding and the like . . . , whereas production is an operation that passes over into some matter in order to change it, as cutting, burning and the like' (Thomas Aquinas, *Commentary on the Metaphysics of Aristotle* (Henry Regnery, Chicago, 1961), para. 1152, cited by Roderick M. Chisholm, *Person and Object*, (George Allen & Unwin, London, 1976), p. 209 n. 42). Similarly, cf. the following comment by Reid: 'Logicians distinguish two kinds of operations of mind: the first kind produces no effect without the mind; the last does. The first they call *immanent* acts, the second *transitive*. All intellectual operations belong to the first class; they produce no effect upon any external object' (Thomas Reid, *The Works of Thomas Reid*, ed. William Hamilton, 2 vols. (Maclachlan and Stewart, Edinburgh, 1863), 1: 301).

from being directly and fully known by an inward sentiment or consciousness, is, to the last degree, mysterious and unintelligible?'[27]

Of course Hume answers his own question negatively and therefore concludes that our idea of power is not derived from any conscious awareness of power over our own bodily movements. However, for the purpose of understanding Danto's theory, the importance of Hume's conclusion lies in his acknowledged failure to discover how we bridge the gap between our volitions and our intended bodily movements.

Danto's answer, which will emerge in due course, is so simple that we may be surprised that Hume failed to see it. On the other hand, though, perhaps we should not be so surprised, for often in life where we end up is determined in large measure by where we begin. Thus in Hume's case, he begins by asking where our notion of cause comes from, and it is in the context of this question that his argument is developed.

Danto, however, sets his discussion in the context of the philosophy of action and begins by asking what kinds of actions there are. In answering his own question he concludes that there are two kinds: 'those performed by an individual M, which he may be said to have *caused* to happen; and those actions, also performed by M, which he cannot be said to have caused to happen'.[28] On this view, an example of an action which someone causes to happen is my writing this sentence. I cause the action of writing by holding the pen and moving my fingers in certain deliberate motions. These movements of my fingers are what cause the pen to move in a way which forms letters and words of the English language on this paper. The action of writing, because it is caused by another action, is what Danto labels a 'non-basic action'. But on penalty of infinite regression, not all actions can be non-basic in this sense. There must, therefore, be actions which an agent performs but which he does not cause by doing anything else first. These actions Danto labels 'basic actions'. This is not to say that basic actions are not caused at all, 'but only that a man performing one does not cause it by performing some other action that stands to it as cause to effect'.[29]

Furthermore, Danto thinks that there is a repertoire R of

[27] Hume, p. 66.   [28] Danto, pp. 141–2.   [29] Danto, p. 142.

basic actions which every normal person can perform. For example, raising an arm without causing it to rise would be included in *R*. Those people who can perform as basic actions things which most of us can only do as non-basic actions, such as dilating one's pupils 'at will', are classified as 'positively abnormal'. Those people who can only perform as non-basic actions things which the rest of us do as basic actions, such as a paralytic who cannot raise his arm without causing it to rise, are classified as 'negatively abnormal'.[30]

Finally, Danto argues, if there are any actions at all, there are basic actions, though as we have seen not all actions are basic actions. However, if something is an action performed by a person, then either it is a basic action or it is a non-basic action. If it is a non-basic action it is the terminal effect of a causal chain which began with a basic action.[31]

Danto thinks this theory of action is analogous to a certain theory of knowledge: specifically the language of action is viewed as analogous to the language of empirical knowledge.[32]

[30] Arthur Danto, 'What We Can Do', *The Journal of Philosophy* 60 (July 1963), p. 436. An interesting catalogue of activities which Danto would list as belonging to 'positively abnormal' individuals may be found in St Augustine's *City of God*: 'We do in fact find among human beings some individuals with natural abilities very different from the rest of mankind and remarkable by their very rarity. Such people can do some things with their body which are for others utterly impossible and well-nigh incredible when they are reported. Some people can even move their ears, either one at a time or both together. Others without moving the head can bring the whole scalp—all the part covered with hair—down towards the forehead and bring it back again at will. Some can swallow an incredible number of various articles and then with a slight contraction of the diaphragm, can produce, as if out of a bag, any article they please, in perfect condition. There are others who imitate the cries of birds and beasts and the voices of any other men, reproducing them so accurately as to be quite indistinguishable from the originals, unless they are seen. A number of people produce at will such musical sounds from their behind (without any stink) that they seem to be singing from that region. I know from my own experience of a man who used to sweat whenever he chose; and it is a well-known fact that some people can weep at will and shed a flood of tears' (Augustine, *Concerning THE CITY OF GOD against the Pagans*, tr. Henry Bettenson (Penguin, Harmondsworth, Middx., 1972), bk. 14, chap. 24, p. 588).

[31] Cf. Danto, 'What We Can Do', p. 436, and 'Basic Actions', p. 142.

[32] Danto expresses this relationship as follows: 'The analogy between theory of knowledge and theory of action runs very deep indeed, almost as though they were isomorphic models for some calculus. Obviously, there are things we can say about actions that do not hold for cognitions, etc., but this means very little. Suppose we have two models $M\text{-}i$ and $M\text{-}j$ for a calculus C, and suppose that "star" plays in the same role in $M\text{-}i$ that "book" plays in $M\text{-}j$. It is hardly an argument against their both being models for C that we don't print stars or that books are not centers of solar systems. I shall use theory-of-knowledge features as a guide for structuring the

In the theory of knowledge with which Danto is working it is maintained that empirical knowledge is founded on basic sentences (or basic propositions). These sentences are ones which are empirically justified but not by other empirical sentences. As Myles Brand expresses this situation,

Many epistemologists take reports of perceptual experiences, for example, 'I see a red color patch in front of me now', to be paradigmatic cases of basic sentences. Without such a stopping point for justification, it is argued, we could not know that an empirical sentence is completely justified; and since a sentence is known to be true only if it is completely justified, we could not, then, know any empirical sentence to be true. Commenting on the nature of basic sentences, Bertrand Russell says 'a basic proposition . . . must be known independently of inference from other propositions [and] . . . it should be possible so to analyse our empirical knowledge that its primitive propositions (apart from logic and generalities) should all have been . . . basic propositions'.[33]

Though Danto only sketches this analogy in a rough way, it would involve substituting 'basic sentence' for 'basic action', 'is inferred from' for 'is caused by', 'sentence' for 'action', etc.[34] Thus, just as a basic sentence is one which expresses a knowledge claim that is known directly or non-inferentially, so also a basic action is one which is performed by an agent directly. There is no 'cause' which intervenes between an agent's intention to raise his arm and the act of so raising it. The agent simply has it within his power to raise his arm directly. And if this is so then Hume's failure to find the origin of our notion of cause in our ability to move our bodies is easy to understand: there are simply no causes to be found here!

But perhaps Danto has moved too fast, for even if we have the power to move our bodies directly, how do we know that we have it? Again, the answer is simple. On Danto's view the power and the knowledge of the power come at the same time.

This seems to be one of the things a man knows directly and not, as it were, on the basis of evidence. Nor is it something I know only

theory of action. When the analogy gives way, it will be interesting to see why it does' (Danto, 'Basic Actions', p. 145 n. 2).

[33] Myles Brand, 'The Logic of Action' in *The Nature of Human Action*, ed. Myles Brand (Scott, Foresman and Co. Glenview, Illinois, 1970), p. 224.

[34] Danto, 'What We Can Do', p. 436.

because I notice it happening. That is, had I not noticed it (or had it brought to my attention because someone else noticed it and told me), I might not otherwise have known. If one day I should notice that my arm was rising and lowering, and then realize that, if I had not noticed, I would not have known it was doing this, this would be for me a terrifying experience, a sign that I had lost contact with part of myself, that my arm had become an alien entity.[35]

With this passage from Danto we may now move to an evaluation of his theory in order to see if it supports Kenny's argument.

It should surely be clear why Kenny thinks Danto's theory is so damaging to any notion of incorporeal agency. By definition, an agent, whether divine or human, is someone who acts, and on Danto's theory a person must perform a basic action at some point in order to act at all. But *a body is necessary* for the performance of any basic action, so it is incoherent to speak of an incorporeal agent. The situation is made even more difficult for the theist when we remember that traditionally God has been held to act directly in the world without intermediary,[36] and therefore any act of God in the world would be a basic action.

Of course the theist may once again reply that a body is not a *logical* necessity entailed by the concept of action, but merely a requirement which arises from our human embodiment. But, while this reply was effective against Nielsen's linguistic argument, I do not think it is effective against Kenny and Danto. For, if Danto is right, our very conception of action involves having a body. It does not do much good to say that we must understand divine action as analogous to human action and then to say that the analogy holds except at the point of embodiment if, as in Danto's theory, without a body our whole concept of action disappears.

But the theist can surely appeal to the conceivability of an incorporeal mind, and then, even if Danto's theory is correct, the theist can simply say that how God acts is a total mystery. After all, there are other mysteries in theism, so why not here? I fully agree that there are mysteries in theism, but if we hold that God acts in the world directly, that is all his actions are

[35] Danto, 'What We Can Do', pp. 440–1.
[36] Cf. e.g. Aquinas, *Summa Theologiae*, vol. 2, Ia, 8, 3.

basic actions, an appeal to mystery will not help us escape the force of Kenny's challenge. For, as Terence Penelhum points out,

if I agree to say that raising a table could be a basic action for a spirit, then I shall feel strongly tempted to say that the table, at least at the time when it is raised, becomes temporarily the body of the spirit. For in order to say the raising of the table is a basic action one has to say that . . . there is nothing the spirit has to do in order to raise the table. But then the analogy with the physical movements of the embodied person's body is as close as it can be, and why not draw the conclusion?[37]

The situation is parallel to that described by Flew, namely that we must link

the question of the essentially incorporeal nature of persons with the question of the existence of a God defined as both incorporeal and in some sense personal. If it makes no sense to speak of incorporeal persons, then it can scarcely make sense to speak of such a God.[38]

Paraphrasing Flew, we can see that if it makes no sense to speak of incorporeal agents, then it can scarcely make sense to speak of such a God!

Thus, if Danto's theory is correct, the theist would appear to have only two options open to him: he may give up his theism altogether in favour of atheism or agnosticism, or he may opt for a form of pantheism or panentheism. But these alternatives are only forced upon the theist *if* Danto's theory is correct, and I am not persuaded that it is correct. Indeed, as I shall show in what follows, it is flawed at the very points which are absolutely crucial if Kenny's challenge is to succeed.

The first flaw in Danto's theory is one which Hume would quickly point out, and that is Danto's claim that in any basic action we are directly conscious of the power by which we move our bodies. Hume failed to find any knowledge of such a power, much less the direct knowledge which Danto claims,

---

[37] Terence Penelhum, *Survival and Disembodied Existence* (Routledge & Kegan Paul, London, 1970), p. 42. Cf. Danto: 'If someone could raise a hat as one of his basic actions, the hat would be his in a philosophical, rather than a legal sense: it would be part of him' ('What We Can Do', p. 445).

[38] Antony Flew, 'Survival', in Hywel D. Lewis, *Persons and Life After Death: Essays by Hywel D. Lewis and some of his critics* (Macmillan, London, 1978), p. 95.

and this failure contributed to his overall scepticism about necessary causal connections. Nevertheless, as we shall see, in the case before us at present I think that Hume's scepticism is justified and Danto's claim to have direct knowledge of the power to move his body is false.

Humean scepticism aside, there are simply too many physiological facts which cannot be gainsaid. Thus when I intend to move my arm, this intention is not followed immediately by my arm moving but rather by changes in my brain and nervous system which in turn activate contractions and/or relaxations in certain of my muscles. Provided these processes function normally and there is nothing restraining my arm, my arm will move in the manner I intend. But even if my arm moves in accordance with my intention, I am not aware of the operation of any transitive power to move my arm, and even if I had the knowledge which Danto claims I have, it could not be immediate knowledge because of all the physiological processes which intervene between my intention and my arm moving. At best this knowledge is mediated or indirect, but I would claim with Hume that we do not even have knowledge of any power to move our bodies:

Here the mind wills a certain event: Immediately another event, unknown to ourselves, and totally different from the one intended, is produced: This event produces another, equally unknown: Till at last, through a long succession, the desired event is produced. But if the original power were felt, it must be known: Were it known, its effect must also be known; since all power is relative to its effect. And *vice versa*, if the effect be not known, the power cannot be known nor felt. How indeed can we be conscious of a power to move our limbs, when we have no such power; but only that to move certain animal spirits, which, though they produce at last the motion of our limbs, yet operate in such a manner as is wholly beyond our comprehension?[39]

Nor is this all, for Danto's claim regarding the power by which we move our bodies carries with it a corollary which must also be analysed. For the sake of argument let us agree with Danto that we do indeed possess not only the power to move our bodies but also a direct knowledge of this power.

[39] Hume, pp. 66–7.

Now if we do possess such direct knowledge, this entails that we must be conscious of *all* our bodily actions in this same direct way; what Elizabeth Anscombe speaks of as 'knowledge without observation'.[40] There is no need for evidence because we simply cannot act without knowing that we are so acting. I *know directly* that my arm is moving and I have no need of evidence because there is no room for error on my part. This claim to possess such 'knowledge without observation' entails that I cannot claim to be performing a basic action, such as moving my arm, with my usual assurance, and yet be mistaken. In other words, if I claim 'I know that I move my body', then it is true that I move my body.

However, there is a major difficulty with this aspect of Danto's theory as well, namely that there is too much phenomenological evidence against it. I am referring here to the so-called 'phantom phenomenon', probably the best-known form of which is a case in which someone feels pain in a limb he has lost, say his right arm. Though he no longer has a right arm, he claims to experience pain in this 'phantom limb' just as if he still had a perfectly normal right arm. But if this phenomenon can occur with respect to pain, could it not also occur with respect to our basic actions? As the following situation illustrates, could not someone be deceived in his belief that he is performing a basic action with a part of his body which he no longer has?

Someone may, unknown to him, have had his legs amputated. Some time after the operation he says, 'I am wiggling my toes'. His intention and his sincerity are evident, but his toes are in another room and he is not wiggling them. The surgeon and nurses will not be persuaded by his making the claim, to think that he is wiggling his toes. But they *will* be persuaded by his making the claim, to think that the local anaesthetic *must* have worn off. The patient will not be persuaded that it does not feel as if his toes were moving.[41]

Nor are the implications of such a possibility lost on Danto, for he realizes that if we can indeed be deceived in this way, 'then might not this be our situation at any minute? One discerns here the first crack which can widen into a skeptical

[40] G. E. M. Anscombe, *Intention* (Basil Blackwell, Oxford, 1957), pp. 13–14.
[41] C. B. Martin, 'Knowledge without Observation', *Canadian Journal of philosophy* 1 (September 1971), p. 17.

abyss'.[42] However, the major implication for Danto lies elsewhere, as he himself states:

but I am less troubled by this [skeptical abyss] than I am by the fact that my own position is threatened if not destroyed. For I have said that when one moves one's arm, one knows this, knows the thing itself, and not on the basis of some kind of evidence. But if illusions are possible, there must be space for them to enter, and if there *is* the required space, where, and between what, can it, on my account, be located? But if there is no room for a gap on my account, how can I be right?[43]

Thus in the example of the amputee wiggling toes he no longer has we must ask why he thought he was wiggling his toes even though he no longer had any toes. He is *as certain* of his claim in this case as he was the week before when he wiggled toes he still had, so the question arises as to what his latter, incorrect, claim is based upon. Whatever it is based upon, it cannot be based upon something different from his identical, albeit correct, claim one week earlier when he still had toes. Danto himself is insistent upon this. Speaking of arm movement rather than toe-wiggling he states that, 'The two cases cannot differ except for the moving of the arm in the one case and its not moving in the other.'[44]

Now of course Danto is completely correct at this point. For if the basis of the man's claim were different in the two cases, he could tell on the basis of the difference whether or not his toes were wiggling. But the *only difference* in the cases is movement of the toes in the first and lack of movement in the second.[45] As mentioned in the illustration, the patient will not be persuaded that it does not *feel* as if his toes were moving. But is this feeling that he is moving his toes the basis for the claim of movement in both cases? Danto considers this possibility:

This invariant factor, let us suppose, is a kinesthetic sensation, a

---

[42] Danto, 'What We Can Do', p. 442.

[43] 'What We Can Do', p. 442.

[44] 'What We Can Do', p. 442.

[45] I have spoken of the movements of the toes as the 'only difference' in the two cases because this is the way Danto phrases the distinction. However, strictly speaking there may be other differences in the two cases, e.g. physiological changes due to the amputation of the man's legs. Therefore, the technically correct way to phrase the difference in the two cases is that 'there is no difference in the two cases *with respect to the awarness of the man*'.

feeling, perhaps, that one is moving one's arm. Call this K. Then the account—which I shall term the Inductivist Account—runs this way. A man associates K, over time, with the moving of his arm. At some time this noticed correlation becomes for him a habit of expectation. So whenever he has K he expects that his arm is moving, and commonly he is right, since his arm moves. But we all know how it is with inductions. It is possible at any point that K will fail to precede the arm motion it is taken to herald, it being only our man's great luck that it never actualizes. But we are thinking now of a case where it does become actual. By contrast, the normal case is this: (a) the man has K; (b) the man expects his arm to move; (c) the man's arm moves.[46]

Danto, however, cannot accept this Inductivist Account of how we know we move our arms, for he can imagine a case where (a), (b), and (c) are all true but the man does not move his arm. The two events, (a) and (c), may be situated in parallel causal chains, just as if on a ship the connections between the pilot room and rest of the ship had been severed and reattached elsewhere. The pilot would continue to steer the ship and the ship would proceed in accordance with his steering, though the pilot was not in fact steering the ship. As Danto describes the situation, 'The pilot rests complacent in a sense of efficiency when credit ought properly to go to a pre-established harmony between pilot-moves and ship-moves'.[47] And according to Danto the Inductivist Account cannot escape this type of error unless it adds a fourth truth condition: (d) the man moves his arm. But of course (d) cannot be added if (a)–(c) is an exhaustive analysis of how we know we move our bodies.

Danto's rejection of the Inductivist Account of how we know we move our bodies seems to me to be correct. Without the added truth condition (d), (a)–(c) could all be true and yet, as we have seen, the man's claim to move his arm would be false. But then how do we know that we move our bodies? Danto's solution, which is entailed by his theory of basic actions, is to say,

that there is no connection between me and my body to be cut. There is that much point to the negative metaphor that I am not in my body the way a pilot is in a ship. There is no empty space

---

[46] 'What Can We Do', p. 443.   [47] 'What Can We Do', p. 443.

between me and parts of me for a cartesian spirit to haunt. Which
does not mean that the self, as I have characterized it, cannot admit
of temporary or permanent diminutions, but only that it should
know when this happens (barring the final diminution to zero).[48]

There are two essential features of Danto's theory to notice in
this passage. First of all, on Danto's theory of basic actions the
type of error to which the Inductivist Account is liable simply
cannot occur. Thus my earlier hypothetical illustration of an
amputee mistakenly claiming to wiggle his toes he no longer
has *is merely hypothetical*; it could never actually happen. As
Danto concludes,

My arm can move without my knowing it, but I cannot be moving it
without knowing it. My arm can fail to move when I would have
thought it was moving, but I cannot fail to move my arm without
knowing that I have failed; and so I cannot be in a position to say
that I am moving my arm and then find out, through noticing that
my arm is not moving, that I was wrong.[49]

Secondly, we can now see a further reason why Danto's
theory is so damaging to any belief in incorporeal agency, and
thus so important to Kenny's case against such agency. For if
our theory of action cannot allow for an 'empty space between
me and parts of me for a cartesian spirit to haunt'—and on
Danto's theory there simply is no such space—then it follows
that there is no need to postulate the existence of such a spirit.
We can explain selfhood in thoroughly material terms,[50] and
the direct, infallible knowledge which Descartes claimed only
for one's mental states can now be extended to our bodies as
well. Thus this appeal to Danto's theory of basic actions is the
key to Kenny's case.

But is Danto's theory correct? I have already said that I do
not think it is, and now I shall show why. The reason is that
there is simply too much phenomenological evidence against
the theory. I referred above to a hypothetical example of an
amputee claiming to wiggle his toes even though he no longer
had any toes to wiggle. This example was merely hypotheti-

---

[48] 'What Can We Do', p. 443.
[49] 'What Can We Do', pp. 443–4.
[50] Cf. 'What Can We Do', p. 439: 'I should in fact like to adopt as a *criterion* for
something being a part of a man's self that he should be able to perform basic actions
with it.'

cal, but Danto realizes that if such a situation actually occurred it would mean the end of his theory. Naturally Danto chose to reject the possibility of our being deceived in this way and instead endorsed his theory as correct.

However, the so-called 'phantom phenomenon' will not go away as easily as Danto and his followers might have hoped, for this phenomenon is not merely an obscure philosophical conundrum to be conveniently used as a 'trump card' in discussions of epistemology and action. Rather, it is a universal phenomenon which is experienced in some form by about 98 per cent of all amputees,[51] occurring even in cases of congenital amputation.[52] It has a medical and literary history which extends back in time at least 425 years, and has fascinated such great literary figures as Herman Melville in *Moby Dick* and Erich Maria Remarque in *All Quiet on the Western Front*.[53] That it is a conundrum no one can deny, for despite the fact that its medical and literary history is replete with attempts to explain the mechanism of its occurrence, this mechanism remains a mystery.[54]

Even though the reason for the occurrence of phantom limbs remains a mystery, what is crucial for my purposes here is that this phenomenon does in fact occur. But how precise are the descriptions of phantom phenomena by those who experience them? After all, we cannot overturn a theory of action simply by pointing to several cases of vague sensations of, e.g. pain. Unfortunately for Danto's theory however, these sensations of pain are not vague. On the contrary they are very distinct to those who experience them.

> The pain is felt in definite parts of the phantom limb. A common complaint, for example, is that the phantom hand is clenched, fingers bent over the thumb and digging into the palm, so that the whole hand is tired and painful.[55]

But phantom pain, even if the sensations can be felt and

---

[51] Marianne L. Simmel, 'On Phantom Limbs', *A. M. A. Archives of Neurology and Psychiatry 75* (June 1956), p. 637.

[52] Arthur S. Abramson and Arie Feibel, 'The Phantom Phenomenon: Its Use and Disuse', *Bulletin of the New York Academy of Medicine 57* (March 1981), p. 99.

[53] Abramson and Feibel, p. 110.

[54] Ronald Melzack, 'Phantom Limb Pain: Implications for Treatment of Pathologic Pain', *Anesthesiology 35* (October 1971), p. 409.   [55] Melzack, p. 410.

described this distinctly, is not enough to overturn the theory, that is to prove it false. What we need to know is whether someone can be convinced with his usual certainty that he is performing a basic action with his missing limb, for this is something which, on Danto's theory, simply cannot happen.

Once again however, the medical evidence is against Danto. As one medical report states, the missing limb 'is as "real" to the patient as an intact limb with normal sensory and motor functions; it occupies a definite position in space, [and] *is capable of spontaneous and voluntary movements*'.[56] Indeed the missing limb is so 'real' to the amputee that 'at first the patient may have the impression that the expected amputation has not been done until he discovers that the part, which can be felt so vividly, is absent'.[57] And, as these comments already suggest, the 'reality' of the phantom limb extends to what would normally be basic actions.

It is quite natural that . . . the missing part should seek to take its place along with other limbs *in the performance of more or less automatic everyday actions*, as in dressing, using the hand to pick up objects or catch a ball, stepping out of bed on the missing foot, crossing the knees with a thigh stump, or while in bed, moving the stump if anyone is about to sit where the foot appears to be.[58]

Furthermore, in the light of my earlier—and at the time merely hypothetical—toe-wiggling example, it is worth documenting that an amputee 'feels that *he can wiggle his fingers or toes* and flex or extend the wrist or ankle and that he can perform these movements more or less at will'.[59]

As we have already seen, Danto himself realizes that if such phenomena actually occurred, his theory would be destroyed. Given the irrefragable medical evidence that these phenomena do occur, what are we to conclude but that Danto's theory of basic actions is wrong? Of course there may yet be those who are not convinced of this conclusion, but

[56] R. Melzack and P. R. Bromage, 'Experimental Phantom Limbs', *Experimental Neurology 39* (1973), p. 261. Italics mine.

[57] W. R. Henderson and G. E. Smyth, 'Phantom Limbs', *Journal of Neurology, Neurosurgery and Psychiatry*, NS 11 (May 1948), p. 92. Cf. Simmel, p. 641: 'The foot of the amputated leg may tingle and itch, and, as the patient reaches down to scratch it, he reaches for an empty space. He may feel the bedsheets on the arm or leg.'

[58] Henderson and Smyth, p. 97. Italics mine.

[59] Simmel, p. 641. Italics mine.

Danto at least is not one of them: in the twenty years since he proposed his theory he has also come to reject it as wrong, and the abundant counter-evidence of phantom phenomena apparently played a role in persuading him of the incorrectness of his theory.[60] As I stated earlier, there is simply too much phenomenological evidence against the theory, and this counter-evidence cannot be gainsaid. That it often has been is aptly expressed by Danto himself: 'It is perhaps impossible to overemphasize (*mea culpa*) the degree to which a certain physiological recklessness has dominated the philosophy of action in recent times.'[61]

But the answer to 'physiological recklessness' is surely to pay careful attention to the facts of physiology in constructing a theory of action. I have attempted to do just that in analysing Danto's theory and have found it untenable. Since it is this theory which forms the basis of Kenny's claim that a body is necessary for a being to act, that claim may also now be dismissed as vacuous.[62] Thus we have returned to the point made by Mitchell against Nielsen, namely that there is nothing in the *concept* of action which requires that an agent be embodied.[63]

---

[60] Arthur C. Danto, 'Action, Knowledge, and Representation' in *Action Theory*, ed. Myles Brand and Douglas Walton (D. Reidel, Dordrecht, 1976), p. 19.

The fact that Danto himself no longer believes that his theory of basic actions is tenable may give rise to the question of why I wrote this essay. This is a legitimate question; however, it also has a legitimate answer.

To begin with, the fact that Danto no longer accepts his own theory does not necessarily mean that the theory is false. Danto's current belief could be false while the theory remains true. Secondly, Danto's original formulation of the theory is still accepted by some philosophers, e.g. Kenny. Thus it needs to be re-examined in the light of the challenges it may still pose to a belief in incorporeal agency. Thirdly, though the counter-evidence from phantom phenomena apparently played some role in Danto's rejection of his theory, his own reasons for rejection were based mainly on other evidence. Thus, the argument here is different and is not merely a repetition of Danto's own reasoning. Fourthly, and most importantly for my purposes, Danto does not consider the implications for incorporeal agency of the demise of his theory.

[61] Arthur C. Danto, 'Basic Actions and Basic Concepts', *The Review of Metaphysics* 32 (March 1979), p. 474.

[62] In the light of the preceding discussion, the following comment by Irving Thalberg is worth noting: 'we might ask why so many philosophers take it for granted that actions and bodily movements are identical. I have run across few explicit rationales for this assumption' (Irving Thalberg, *Perception, Emotion and Action: A Component Approach* (Basil Blackwell, Oxford, 1977), p. 54).

[63] I would like to thank David Charles and Stewart Goetz for their helpful comments on earlier versions of this essay.

12

'Necessary' and 'Fitting' Reasons in Christian Theology

DAVID BROWN

A major contribution of Basil Mitchell to the philosophy of religion has been the direction he has given it towards considering non-deductive forms of justification for religious belief.[1] In pursuing this path he chose to do so exclusively with reference to the initial postulate of belief in God. However, it seems to me a point of wider applicability, as relevant to arguments within Christian theology as to any preparatory justification of it. What, therefore, I want to do in this paper, to illustrate how this might be so, is to take the most famous deductive argument within the Christian theological tradition, and see what emerges from an examination of it.

This undoubtedly occurs in Anselm's *Cur Deus Homo*, in which Anselm attempts to argue for the necessity of the Incarnation without reference to revelation. My discussion proceeds by four stages. First, I offer an analysis of Anselm's argument. Next, I examine in some detail what he means by what he calls 'fitting' as distinct from 'necessary' reasons. Then, I note some of the decisive objections to his argument. Finally, I return to the notion of 'fitting' reasons and argue that this can be developed in such a way as to provide a satisfactory alternative to Anselm's deductive approach.

Most students of theology probably only know his argument in something like the following simple form:[2]

(*a*)   It is man who owes satisfaction to God for sin.

---

[1] Basil Mitchell, *The Justification of Religious Belief* (Macmillan, London, 1973), *passim*.

[2] A misapprenhension helped by Anselm's own expression in II, vi, popularized for example by J. Hopkins as 'Only man ought to; only God can; therefore, necessarily a God-man', cf. J. Hopkins, *A Companion to the Study of St. Anselm* (University of Minnesota Press, Minneapolis, 1972), p. 195.

(*b*) But only God is able, in the sense of has the power, to make such satisfaction.

(*c*) Therefore, if satisfaction is to be made, it must be made by someone who is both God and man.

But such a simple form belies the subtlety of Anselm's argument and the care with which he anticipates objections. A more plausible reading of the text is the more complex argument given below. (It should be noted that where no explanation is given for the introduction of new premises, their justification is in fact discussed later in the paper.)

(1) All men have sinned: *passim.*

(2) Eternal salvation, viz. human happiness, is impossible without freedom from sin and its effects: I, x.

(3) These effects cannot be eliminated by an act of divine forgiveness: I, xi (cf. also I, xv; I, xxiv; II, v).

(4) Therefore, either punishment must follow, or compensation must be paid: I, xiii.

(5) But God must wish some men to be saved: I, xvi–xviii.

(6) Therefore, compensation must have been the chosen alternative.

(7) But 'to sin is nothing else than not to render God his due':[3] I, xi.

(8) Therefore, compensation must consist in giving to God what is not his due. ('We must observe that when anyone pays for what he has unjustly taken away, he ought to give something which could not have been demanded of him.'); I, xi. (The point here is simply that, unless more is returned than what is owed, it can hardly by claimed that any compensation has been paid for the wrong inflicted.)

(9) But, 'if in justice I owe God myself and all my powers, even when I do not sin, I have nothing left to render to him for my sin': I, xx.

(10) Therefore, compensation must be paid by an act, not owed to God, performed by a person other than one of whom (9) is true.

---

[3] Though I have occasionally given my own translation, I have mostly followed that of S. N. Deane in *Saint Anselm's Basic Writings* (Open Court, La Salle, Illinois, 1979), 2nd edn.

(11) But, given what we owe to God, any sin is of infinite extent: I, xxi. ('Let us inquire whether they can satisfy for a look so small as one look contrary to the will of God . . . Not to delay too long; what if it were necessary either that the whole universe, except God himself, should perish and fall back into nothingness, or else that you should do so small a thing against God? When I consider the action itself, it appears very slight; but when I view it as contrary to the will of God, I know of nothing so grievous, and of no loss that will compare with it.')

(12) Therefore, compensation 'cannot be effected, except the price paid to God for the sin of man be something greater than all the universe beside God . . . Therefore none but God can make this satisfaction': II, vi.

(13) But it is necessary that the person paying the compensation be also a man: II, viii. ('For, as it is right for man to make atonement for the sin of man, it is also necessary that he who makes the atonement should be the very being who has sinned, or else one of the same race. Otherwise, neither Adam nor his race would make satisfaction for themselves. Therefore, as through Adam and Eve sin was propagated among all men, so none but themselves, or one born of them ought to make atonement for the sin of men. And, since they cannot, one born of them must fulfil this work.')

(14) 'If it be necessary, therefore, as it appears, that the heavenly kingdom be made up of men, and this cannot be effected unless the aforesaid satisfaction be made, which none but God can make and none but man ought to make, it is necessary for the God-man to make it': II, vi. ('Si . . . necesse est ut de hominibus perficiatur illa superna civitas, nec hoc esse valet, nisi praedicta satisfactio, quam nec potest facere nisi Deus nec debet nisi homo: necesse est ut faciat Deus-homo.')

(15) But it is impossible for the Father or the Holy Spirit to be incarnated; II, ix.

(16) Therefore, the requisite compensation must be

achieved by the incarnation of God the Son, and, from (8), such compensation will involve that 'he somehow gives up himself, or something of his, to the honour of God, which he does not owe as a debtor': II, xi.

(17) But 'every reasonable being owes his obedience to God': II, xi. Cf. (9).

(18) 'Therefore, must it be in some other way that he gives himself, or something belonging to him, to God': II, xi.

(19) But mortality is not an essential attribute of human nature 'since, had man never sinned, and had his immortality been unchangeably confirmed, he would have been as really man': II, xi.

(20) 'Therefore, he who wishes to make atonement for man's sin should be one who can die if he chooses': II, xi.

(21) Therefore, compensation/satisfaction/atonement will be made by the innocent death of God the Son.

That the argument was intended as a strictly deductive argument without an appeal to scriptural premisses, there can be no doubt. Thus in his preface he explicitly asserts that his object has been to 'prove by necessary reasons' that, even if we had known nothing of Christ, salvation would still only have been possible through him ('Remoto Christo, quasi numquam aliquid fuerit de illo, probat rationibus necessariis esse impossibile ullum hominem salvari sine illo'). Indeed, on one occasion he even apologizes for the digressionary character of an allusion to the facts of Christ's life: 'Let us now return to our investigation of him, as if he did not exist, just as we began.'[4] But this does not mean that reason is being accorded higher authority than revelation. On the contrary, he tells us[5] that even when something seems proved by reason (*ratione probare*), it should still only be held provisionally (*interim*) until confirmed by the higher authority of Scripture. Even so, what is intriguing about his argument is how much he claims to be able to prove—not just the need for atonement but all the details of traditional atonement theology as well. So all five elements in his conclusion (cf. 21) are held to be established

---

[4] *Cur Deus Homo*, II, x.
[5] Ibid., I, ii.

by reason as essential, namely compensation, innocence, death, God, and the Son.

But 'essential' disguises the fact that not all the elements are seen as having the same kind of probative force. For, though Anselm seems to have spoken of proof (*probatio* and *probare*) in a very wide range of contexts[6] and not just with respect to formal deduction, in general he does appear to have drawn a distinction between two types of reason, necessary (cf. *necessarius*), which are conclusive, and the fitting or appropriate (*conveniens*).[7] Hopkins suggests that Anselm took a demonstration of unfittingness in respect of God to establish that something is necessarily not the case. He offers in support a passage from *Cur Deus Homo* in which Anselm moves from certain things being unfitting (*inconvenientia*) to 'ergo necesse est'.[8] Confirmation could have been obtained from what he says elsewhere about not even the smallest inappropriateness being tolerated in God: 'Quoniam ergo quam-libet parvum inconveniens in deo est impossibile'.[9] But Hopkins is less persuasive about its positive meaning: 'He aspires to demonstrate in some minimal sense of "reasonable" that it is not *un*reasonable (his italics) to subscribe to these teachings in the absence of stricter argumentation.'[10]

It is possible, I think, to probe more deeply by looking at some of the supporting reasons he gives for some of the premisses in the argument outlined above. So, for example, in support of (15) the argument for the inappropriateness of the Father or the Spirit being incarnated is along the following lines:

If the Father becomes incarnate, there will be two grandsons in the Trinity; for the Father, by assuming humanity, will be the grandson of the parents of the virgin, and the Word, though having nothing to

---

[6] F. S. Schmitt's Index Generalis, s.v. *probare*; *probatio*, reveals a wide range of uses including appeals to authority and the use of analogy as well as more formal proofs. Cf. F. S. Schmitt (ed.), *Anselmi Opera Omnia* (Nelson, Edinburgh, 1938–68), vol. 6, p. 289.

[7] So, for example, in I, iv the demonstration of *necessitas* is seen as more fundamental than the exposition of *convenientiae*, while in II, xvi a conclusive proof is described as 'non solum conveniens sed etiam necessarium'.

[8] Op. cit., p. 51. The passage is in *Cur Deus Homo*, II, viii.

[9] F. S. Schmitt (ed.), op. cit., vol. 2, p. 26, 1.3–4 (*Epistola de Incarnatione Verbi*, 10).

[10] Hopkins, p. 52.

do with man, will yet be the the grandson of the virgin, since he will be the son of her son.[11]

Here, when such things are called *inconvenientia*, it is hard to see what more is meant than 'messy' or 'untidy' (a messiness that could only be avoided by taking the view that the persons of the Trinity gain their names from their role in the revelatory process rather than antecedently).[12]

That *conveniens* has something to do with tidiness and elegance of arrangement is further strengthened by the argument he offers in favour of (5), that God must wish some men to be saved. It may be set out as follows:

(*a*) 'There is no question that intelligent nature, which finds its happiness, both now and forever, in the contemplation of God, was foreseen by him in a certain and reasonable and complete number, so that there would be an unfitness in its being either less or greater': I, xvi.

(*b*) But some angels have fallen and cannot be restored to their original state without unfairness to those who have been preserved 'without even witnessing the punishment of sin': I, xvii.

(*c*) Therefore it has been 'proved that the evil angels must be replaced by members of the human race': I, xvii.

(*d*) But it would be wrong for the elect to 'rejoice as much over the fall of angels as over their own exaltation, because the one can never take place without the other': I, xviii.

(*e*) Therefore, the total number of the elect must be greater than the total number of angels: I, xviii.

The fact that in this case not even the number of the saved is allowed by Anselm to remain undetermined by reason, makes one wonder whether in his view for a perfectly rational being like God nothing whatsoever can be a matter of indifference. However that may be, in this particular instance the intended claim is even stronger. It is not just that it is 'more fitting' (*decentiorem*) that God chose one number rather than another, but he even talks about 'the perfect number', such that, when the

[11] *Cur Deus Homo*, II, ix.

[12] That is, through holding that whichever person becomes incarnate leads the life of a Son and therefore most appropriately should bear that name.

later stages of the argument cause him to increase the number of men saved above the number of angels fallen, he then transfers that unknown perfect number to the combined totals of saved men and angels. All this surely suggests a very high degree of concern with order and arrangement, as though perhaps the principal objective behind 'fitting' reasons was the creation of a whole or system in which each element could find its appropriate place and interlocking part.

This suspicion finds confirmation in one of the four variants of the reason offered in support of (3), that the effects of sin cannot be eliminated by an act of divine forgiveness. Two variants appear to give it in the form of a necessary reason. So at one point (I, xxiv) we are told that 'such compassion on the part of God is wholly contrary (*contraria*) to the divine justice' and so 'impossible', while at another (I, xii) we are given what is presumably simply a necessary reason put negatively (with 'unbecoming' implying 'necessarily not'): 'with God there will be no difference between the guilty and the not guilty; and this is unbecoming to God'. A third version also moves quickly from *inconvenientia* to *impossibilia* to *necesse est*. But what is particularly interesting about this version is the way in which Anselm uses 'beauty of arrangement' as a test of what is fitting. Thus forgiveness is ruled out on the grounds that 'there would be, in the very universe which God ought to control, an unseemliness (*deformitas*) springing from the violation of the beauty of arrangement (*ordinis pulchritudo*), and God would appear to be deficient in his management'. (I, xv.)

It is in fact an appeal that had already made its appearance in his introductory chapters. So in I, iii, he mentions how fittingly (*convenienter*) the balance between fall and salvation was achieved:

(*a*) 'sicut per hominis inoebedientiam mors ... ita per hominis oebedientiam vita' (as through one man's disobedience death, so through a man's obedience life).

(*b*) 'causa nostrae damnationis ... a femina, sic nostrae justitiae et salutis auctor ... de femina' (as the cause of our damnation was from a woman, so the author of our justification and salvation was also from a woman).

(*c*) 'Et ut diabolus, qui per gustum ligni ... hominem vicerat,

per passionem ligni . . . ab homine vinceretur' (that the
devil, who had conquered man through the taste of a tree,
should himself be conquered by a man through his passion on a tree).

The beauty of the chiastic structure of the Latin reinforces the
point he then goes on to make about the nature of the contrast,
that such proportion shows 'the indescribable beauty' (*inenar-
rabilem . . . pulchritudinem*) of the way in which our redemption
was procured. In the following chapter Boso then objects that
unless such 'paintings' (*picturae*) are to appear to have as their
canvas nothing more substantial than a cloud, they will need
as a support 'the rational solidity of truth'. The rest of *Cur
Deus Homo* is concerned to provide just such a support, but
intriguingly the image of reason as an artist is not one which
he abandons in what follows. Indeed, when those very same
contrasts occur later in his argument (II, viii), they are introduced by the same image of the artist, painting on the 'solid
foundation of the truth' ('Pinge igitur . . . super solidam
veritatem').

Given the influence of the Augustinian and Pseudo-Diony-
sian tradition of equating truth, goodness, and beauty,[13] it is
perhaps not surprising that Anselm should use beauty as a
guide to truth. Our own age is much less confident that such
concepts are commensurable. An illustration of the difficulty
might be the rape scene in Stanley Kubrick's film *A Clockwork
Orange*: morally, it is unqualifiedly evil, but aesthetically its
form as ballet turns it into a work of art and beauty. But even
a cursory glance at his discussion of the nature of truth in his
De Veritate reveals that such an admission would be for Anselm
inconceivable. For, while his starting point is an Aristotelian
correspondence theory of truth, with him declaring in chapter
2 that 'vera propositio significat esse quod est', this is quickly
developed into a Platonic participatory view of truth, according to which *rectitudo* in actions, thoughts, perceptions, and so
forth, as well as in propositions, is always measured in terms
of their participation in, or correspondence with, the Supreme

---

[13] For God as Beauty cf. e.g. Pseudo-Denys, *De divinis nominibus*, IV, vii, and for the
continuing influence in the Middle Ages of his equation of truth, beauty, and goodness cf. R. Assunto, *Die Theorie des Schönen im Mittelalter* (DuMont Buchverlag, Köln,
1982).

Truth who is God. Significantly, his last chapter is entitled 'That the truth in all things is one truth'. During its course we are warned that 'the mere fact that there are many things in which there is rightness does not mean that there is a plurality of rightnesses', and his final sentence is: 'So, too, Supreme Truth, subsisting in and of itself, is not the truth of any particular thing; but when some thing is in accordance with Supreme Truth, then we speak of the truth, or rightness, of that thing.' *Rectitudo* and *ordo* are of course allied terms and it is therefore particularly intriguing to observe that Anselm's final view of truth is of the coherence of all types of order in the single, unifying Whole that is the Divine Mind.

This 'coming together' (cf. the root meaning of *conveniens*) into a unified whole is still sometimes used as a guide to truth even today. A contemporary example in the philosophy of religion would be Keith Ward's *The Concept of God*. He divides human beings into two categories, those who 'tend to view reality, from the first, as a whole' and those who view it 'as a wholly contingent collocation of diverse and essentially unrelated elements', with the former characterized as those likely to use God to give that overall unity through God as 'the ground of the meaning and value in reality, called one because apprehended under a unitary integrating image'.[14] But even the theist must entertain serious reservations about pursuing such fitting or integrating reasons too far. In the first place, they could mislead more than they inform. So, for example, have we any reason to think that the search for the 'perfect number' of the elect would be anything other than misguided? Or again, will not the search for balance and counterbalance in the Fall and Redemption, as with the role of the tree ('per gustum ligni . . . per passionem ligni'), not lead to the imposition of artificially imposed patterns, as in this case? In the second place and more worryingly perhaps for this approach, what reason have we to think that divine motivation is a unified whole? For instance, why should the world not have

---

[14] K. Ward, *The Concept of God* (Fount Paperback, 1977), pp. 53, 117. W. Pannenberg adopts a similar approach in *Theology and the Philosophy of Science* (Darton, Longman & Todd, London, 1976), e.g. pp. 303–7. For a related aesthetic criterion one might compare Swinburne's use of simplicity in *The Existence of God* (Oxford University Press, Oxford, 1979), pp. 56 ff., 145 ff.

been created with man as but one of the motives, with delight
in variety or creativity for its own sake as an independent,
uncoordinated motive? Nor need this indicate any
failure of rationality. It would only seem to do so if the two
reasons running independently but parallel with one another
were also somehow in conflict, for then there would have been
a failure to anticipate that the satisfaction of both motivations
could not be jointly realized.

In making these criticisms of Anselm's concept of fitting
reasons, I should not be taken as discounting their use
altogether. Far from it. In a moment I shall endeavour to
defend a new role for them in atonement theology. But, as this
is contingent on the abandonment of Anselm's claim to necessary reasons for the Incarnation, it will be useful to observe
first why this approach of his has generally been abandoned.
The most commonly quoted modern objection is the extent to
which his exposition is tied to medieval feudal notions of
honour, with Jesus seen as rendering satisfaction for offended
honour in the manner of a vassal to his feudal overlord.[15] Most
of what Anselm says, however, can be disentangled from this
analogy. As I shall argue shortly, 'satisfaction' can be given a
less culturally bound sense. But it remains true that there is
one aspect that is only really readily intelligible against its
medieval context, and that is the support he offers for (13).
We are simply told that 'it is necessary that he who makes the
atonement should be the very being who has sinned, or else
one of the same race' ('necesse est, ut satisfaciens idem sit qui
peccator aut ejusdem generis'), but no further justification of
this principle is offered. The likely explanation is that, just as
on the medieval theory another member of one's family could
make satisfaction, so here that principle is being extended to
the whole human race. Presumably the idea is not too dissimilar to the modern acceptance of someone's fine being paid by
another, though with the difference that on the medieval view
satisfaction seems to have required some connection between
the two parties through the notion of corporate responsibility
(one shares in responsibility for what those connected with
one do). But while we still have some overlap with the

[15] For example, F. W. Dillistone, *The Christian Understanding of Atonement* (James
Nisbet, London, 1968), pp. 190–4.

medieval view to the extent that we think it intelligible that someone voluntarily undertake responsibility for the actions of other members of his family, strong resistance is likely to be encountered if the claim is made that such responsibility is necessarily entailed (except in the case of minors), and complete incomprehension if the range is extended to the whole human race. To this it may be objected that such resistance is mistaken, that we do share in responsibility for what others do. But that would seem to depend on whether we could reasonably have expected to do something to prevent the conduct in question, and certainly in the case of the human race as a whole it is hard to see what sense could be given to a claim that one was ashamed to be a human being, simply in virtue of what someone else had done.

As a matter of fact the first major challenge to Anselm's argument was on quite other grounds, and ironically it was to some degree anticipated by Anselm himself in the only remaining variant of the four which he gave as a reason in support of (3) that has hitherto not been mentioned. In support of the view that the effects of sin cannot be eliminated by an act of divine forgiveness, he comments: 'God does this from the necessity of maintaining his honour; which necessity is after all no more than this viz. the immutability of his honour, which belongs to him in himself, and is not derived from another; and it is therefore not properly called necessity,' (II, v.) Anselm's hesitation as to whether or not God is being bound by necessity is precisely the point at which Aquinas and later, and more thoroughly, Duns Scotus were to challenge his argument.

One of the major themes which is to be found in the latter's writing is that of the divine freedom, and so he insists that divine decision for an Incarnation must have been independent of what human beings might decide to do, and equally that, sin having entered the picture, what might constitute its satisfaction was an entirely free divine decision. So in his *Opus Oxoniense* he tells us, applying a general principle, that 'just as everything . . . is good because wished by God and not conversely, so that merit was good in so far as it was accepted; and thus it was a merit because it was accepted and was not, conversely, accepted because it was a merit and good'. Then a little later in the same *quaestio* he draws the more specific implication that the infinite value assigned to Christ's death must simply be the result of divine decision: 'Deus . . . potest ratione . . . *personae patientis acceptare bonum velle Christi, et ejus passionem pro infinitis, quia tantum et pro tot valet, quantum et pro quot acceptatur a Deo*'[16] (God can by reason of the person suffering accept that good will of Christ and his passion as infinite, because the degree and extent of its worth is determined by the degree and extent of its acceptance by God).

Not only that, he challenges Anselm's claim that satisfaction has to be greater than anything a creature could offer by maintaining that, 'saving his reverence' (*salva reverentia sua*), 'it would have sufficed to have offered a good greater than was the evil of the man who sins', and for that 'one or many acts of loving God for his own sake' would have sufficed.[17] This could lend itself to rather crude calculations, but that does not seem to have been Scotus' intention, and in any case he has still retained the most fundamental principle of Anselm's analysis, that for something to count logically as satisfaction or compensation it must do more than merely restore the status quo—the good must be greater than the evil.

Anselm's argument in (7)–(9) seems to have gone wrong through a failure to distinguish between different sorts of debt or obligation. From the fact that I am under a debt of gratitude to God as my creator it by no means follows that all I can ever return to him is what I owe to him as a duty. It may well be that all morality can be subsumed under duties to God, but this cannot be established by the logic of gratitude. For, if I receive something as a gift, while I am 'indebted' to that person, that does not mean that the donor has thereby put me under an obligation to do something for him in return, still less something of equivalent value. I may choose to express my gratitude, but I cannot be required to do so by him. Otherwise, the initial bequest, even when it is the gift of life itself, could not count as pure gift. So, from the mere fact that from gratitude 'I owe God myself and all my powers', it

---

[16] The work is also known as the *Ordinatio* and the *Commentary on the Sentences*. Both passages come from *In Sent.* III, d. XIX, q. unic. (n. 7 & n. 14)—*Opera Omnia* (Vivès Edition, Farnborough, 1969), vol. 14, pp. 718, 726.

[17] Ibid., III, d. XX, q. unic., n. 8. (Vivès Edition, vol. 14, p. 736).

by no means follows that therefore anything I do with them can only be classed as the return of a duty. Thus, just as there are many things which we can do for our fellow men which we are under no obligation or duty to perform for them, so likewise must it be in the case of God, at least as far as any argument from gratitude is concerned. To this it may be objected that from the recipient's perspective there would seem something morally improper in him failing to express his gratitude, his indebtedness, in some tangible way. That seems right, but it remains true that, to the degree that the original bequest was a gift, this cannot be required of him by the donor, and in any case, and more importantly, nothing follows about such expressions of gratitude having to be on the same scale as the original gift, as this would once again call into question its status as a gift.

Apart from removing the necessity of the Atonement, one other reason why this analysis is often rejected is that it is thought to go to the other extreme, as it were, and impose obligations on God, in virtue of the good done that cannot be classified as duty. But this is again to confuse obligations of duty and gratitude, though in God's case 'gratitude' does not seem quite the right word. For it is not that he has benefited by our actions as in the human case, but rather that he has reason to be pleased by the extent to which they have transcended the basic requirements of morality. In such circumstances, as with gratitude, some response might be appropriate, but it is hardly required or necessary.

With the use of those terms we at last reach the possibility of an alternative to Anselm's use of 'appropriate' and 'necessary' reasons in atonement theology. Scotus can only help us to a very limited extent. For, though Bertoni talks of the '*sublime beauté de la thèse scotiste*',[18] Seeberg legitimately complains of Scotus' failure to give a proper sketch of his positive alternative to Anselm's position: '*Duns hat sich leider nur sehr kurz (sowohl im Opus Oxon. als in den Report. Paris.) über die positive Gestaltung der Lehre ausgesprochen.*'[19] A number of motives for the Incarnation are in fact mentioned by Scotus, but intriguingly the one Seeberg chooses to emphasize is *die Offenbarung der*

[18] R. P. A. Bertoni, *Jean Duns Scot* (Levanto, 1917), p. 319.
[19] R. Seeberg, *Die Theologie des Johannes Duns Scotus* (Leipzig, 1900), p. 287.

Liebe Gottes, which will then induce a 'thankful devotion' in us, and he stresses that that sense of gratitude for this demonstration of divine love can only be increased by the realization that the act was not strictly necessary: '*Diese Dankespflict wird nur gesteigert durch die Erwägung, dass nicht notwendig gerade auf diese und keine andere Weise erlöst werden mussten'*.[20] Though Scotus does not seem to have pursued the logic of gratitude in terms of 'fitting' reasons, it is worth pursuing the question of whether Anselm's basic insight of the need for satisfaction or compensation cannot be better expressed in these terms.

For both Anselm and Scotus satisfaction clearly involves restitution plus something more, and, if we think of satisfaction in terms of compensation, that is clearly right. One can hardly claim to have offered compensation to someone for a wrong done unless not only is the wrong righted but something also built in to compensate for the inconvenience or worse caused in the process. But it is doubtful whether the issue is always best approached in this quasi-legal way. Indeed, even in the case of those who wrong us whom we do not know, we do not always regard it as appropriate to view the situation in this light, and certainly in the case of those close to us, family or friends, it would seldom be so. In the case of the latter we frequently waive our rights to restitution, while even with strangers we often do likewise, at least if the harm or inconvenience caused to us is small.

What, however, we do seem much less prepared to do is waive what might in some sense still be seen as satisfaction, and that is the making of amends. Unlike compensation, this is not quantifiable. It is simply the requirement that for the situation to be restored there must be some expression of regret for what has happened. What this amounts to will vary considerably from case to case. Sometimes a verbal apology will suffice. Sometimes a bunch of roses or bringing one's partner a cup of tea in bed is regarded as a more appropriate way of saying sorry. Sometimes only something on a much grander scale will do. If in a fit of temper I break a friend's favourite ornament, the purchase of some article which I believe will come to have a similar place in his affections may be the only

[20] Ibid., pp. 286, 287.

appropriate course of action. Again, if my nation is responsible for terrible outrages to another country, the only fitting response may thought to be to help build that nation's shattered ruins, in much the same way as the German youth helped to rebuild Coventry Cathedral. But even in these cases, it is important to observe that there is no quantitative trade-off. The vital issue is the expression of sorrow, the making of concrete amends, not that any sense of equivalence should be reached.

Thus, the area towards which such an analysis seems to be pulling us is at a considerable distance from Anselm's necessary reasons. Not only is compensation not required, but not even restitution, if we take seriously our intuitions about personal as distinct from legal relations. Intriguingly, according to E. P. Sanders' recent book *Jesus and Judaism*, this was one of the main sources of dispute between Jesus and the Judaism of his day, namely his insistence on offering forgiveness without any prior conditions of restitution or compensation.[21] Whether true or not, preference for this interpretation does indicate how deep our assumption is that care for the individual person is incompatible with any formal calculating of a compensating balance.

Against this some may argue that, unless we are let off, restitution is in fact required, if it can be made, even among family and friends, especially where the amounts involved are not small. Certainly, one might well expect to pay for damage to a friend's car, but this may be more a matter of the way in which the bill can readily be ascertained than anything to do with a requirement for exact restitution. One might contrast that situation with the breaking of an antique ornament, where among friends or family I do not think that any attempt would be made to fix retrospectively an exact value for a corresponding restitution payment. Even in the car case, the picking up of the bill is usually thought unnecessary in particularly close relationships, as between husband and wife, and, if our starting point is God as a God of love, it is hard to see why the legal parallel should be preferred to the marital one.

[21] E. P. Sanders, *Jesus and Judaism* (SCM, London, 1985), pp. 204–8.

But to this it may be objected, why not go one stage further and also dismiss the need for even the making of amends? I have already conceded that for restoration of the relationship such action is only fitting, not strictly necessary. But why should we even say that it is 'fitting'? The answer has, I think, something to do with the fact that we are embodied beings, for from this flows the need to express ourselves in tangible ways. A parallel may be drawn with the circumstances under which we are prepared to say that someone is a loving person. A necessary condition is that the person perform loving acts, actions having good consequences of the kind that a loving person might be expected to perform, help to those in need, and so forth. But of itself this is not sufficient. For if the actions are done in a cold way, without a smile, without signs of gentleness, we hesitate to move beyond the description of such a man as 'good' to talk of him as 'loving' or 'compassionate'. So similarly, while sometimes it is sufficient to say 'I forgive you' for the relationship to be restored, normally we expect some expression of the appropriation of that forgiveness before we are prepared to talk of the relationship as fully restored. The offer has, as it were, been made but not received, until physically appropriated in some way, and of course this appropriation may precede or follow the expression of forgiveness. Expressions of sorrow sometimes lead into declarations of forgiveness, and sometimes they follow them. Perhaps the point can be put best by saying that, since we communicate physically not just through our voices but through our facial expressions and actions, the making of amends is appropriate because without it there would be no proper confirmation that the relationship has in fact been restored.

But, that conceded, is there any sense in which the manner of Christ's life and death could be seen as fitting or appropriate? Could it be seen as the making of amends, and if so, by whom? One possible answer is that the relationship between God and man is restored through man identifying with that perfect life of Christ as his means of saying sorry. Certainly, the New Testament sometimes seems to view the matter this way.[22] But it is surely not hard to find secular parallels.

[22] E.g. Colossians 1: 18–23.

Imagine the case of a gang of hooligans who wreck an old-age pensioner's garden. Suppose one of them who has done nothing comes back to restore the damage, and the others are then persuaded into identifying with this form of saying sorry by also lending a hand or offering to do some errands on behalf of the pensioner. In some ways they are clearly making amends in their own right, but it is also true that the decisive act was the first act of the innocent hooligan. Even if one wanted to place almost exclusive emphasis on the act of the innocent man, the analogy would not need much alteration in order to bring this out. So we might instead think of the youth repairing all the damage himself but the others saying sorry by identifying with his act through, for example, saying to the old-age pensioner, 'I'm sorry for what happened, and I'm glad that "Bob" came back to repair the damage.'

But so far this analysis in terms of what is 'fitting' or 'appropriate' lacks any reference to what Anselm would have regarded as the most important element in his account, the fact that it had to be God who became incarnate. It is at this point that Duns Scotus' remarks on gratitude begin to have some relevance. Let us adapt our illustration yet again. Suppose this time that instead of an innocent hooligan we have the old-age pensioner himself taking the initiative. He begins to repair the damage, but, when the vandals join in, he continues to help, working alongside them. Clearly this will produce a very different attitude in them, than had he chosen to stand by and watch them at work. Such aloofness could only increase their sense of guilt, and perhaps even provoke fresh rebellion, whereas working alongside them is likely to invoke both gratitude and something more: gratitude at the way in which the expression of their contrition is made easier, and something more in that from that gratitude there is likely to emerge enthusiasm for what they are doing, instead of grudging effort. The 'fitting' element in the response in the theological case then would be the way in which the concrete expression of gratitude becomes more appropriate, the more it is realized that it is God as not only the innocent but also the offended party who is initiating the means of reconciliation.

But if that can provide a fitting reason for response on our part, we are still left without any reason either necessary or fitting as to why God should become incarnate in the first place. One could of course respond that it was in order to evoke this response of gratitude. But it seems hardly either necessary or fitting that God should intend to evoke such an attitude, any more than that should be the intention of the old-age pensioner working alongside the vandals. Gratitude is at most a foreseen consequence of an intention to help make the task easier for them. In fact, it looks as though there is no way available of defending the necessity of the incarnation for atonement, other means of encouraging the making of amends always having been possible. But this is not to exclude necessary reasons altogether. For example, if God wished to have direct experience of what it means to suffer, then he could only do so by becoming incarnate, by becoming a man or some other creature.

But more relevant to our immediate concerns is the identification of a fitting reason. Here Scotus is rather disappointing. In response to the question, 'An Verbum incarnatum fuisset si Adam non peccasset' (whether the Word would have become incarnate, if Adam had not sinned), his reply is an emphatic affirmative. Bertoni summarizes it in this way: 'L'Homme-Dieu apparaît au faîte du grand édifice mondiale. Jésus-Christ prédestiné avant la chute d'Adam, voilà l'ordre établi par Dieu. Que si notre premier parent n'eût pas péché, le Christ serait venu, non comme saveur et rédempteur, main comme glorificateur de son divin Père.'[23] But, while this synopsis certainly offers the possibility of developing a fitting reason, unfortunately Bertoni seems to have misrepresented where the real thrust of Scotus' position lies. For his point was not so much that there was a fitting reason why God the Son should become incarnate whether or not man had sinned, as that it detracts from the freedom and dignity of God to suggest that the predestining of human nature to the glory of union with the divine nature of the Son was merely contingent upon the achievement of some lesser good such as correction of the results of the Fall. As he puts it at one point: 'Nec est verisimile tam summum bonum in entibus, esse tantum occasionatum, scilicet propter minus bonum.'[24]

[23] Op. cit., p. 319.
[24] *In Sent.* III, d. vii, q. 3, n. 3. (Vivès Edition, vol. 14, p. 355).

Perhaps the fitting character of the Incarnation could be brought out in this way. It was fitting that God as Creator himself perfectly express man as he intended man to be, and, even if man had not fallen, this would still have been appropriate because of the way in which such perfect expression would explicitly relate each man as fellow-son to Christ as their Head as First Son of the Father. This is of course to conceive of salvation in essentially mystical terms, as divinization, as ultimately involving incorporation into the very life of the Godhead. There is not the space here to pursue the issue of how this might be rendered intelligible. All one can note is that it does represent a long-established possible perspective within Christianity. Indeed, it seems to lie behind a much earlier insistence on the fittingness of the Incarnation even without the Fall, namely in the writings of St Irenaeus,[25] though a more pessimistic view eventually prevailed in the Western tradition.

In short, then, my suggestion in this paper has been that as in the philosophy of religion so in theology itself the collapse of formal deductive arguments which helped to produce a closely integrated system need not be seen as a cause for despair. As this case of the Atonement illustrates, 'fitting' reasons can take the place of necessary ones, and, though their strength may be hard to estimate, they do offer an explanation both of why it might be appropriate for God to become incarnate and why likewise it might be appropriate for us to respond when that life takes a particular form.

But, it may be said, is the character of such reasons not alarmingly imprecise by contrast with the clarity of Anselm's approach? To answer that objection, let me end by relating their role specifically to Anselm's original project. For him the need for atonement necessitates an incarnation. My suggestion is the admittedly much weaker one that all we can say from an analysis of the morality of atonement is that, if the incarnation happened, it is appropriate that it happened. It cannot of itself justify a belief in an incarnation, as Anselm had hoped. For that one must rely on rather complex

[25] Irenaeus does not use the language of fitting reasons, but it is not hard to see how passages like *Demonstratio* 6 and 12 and *Adversus Haereses V*, 1 might be developed along these lines.

historical arguments.[26] But this is not to say that such fitting reasons then only have a role in making sense of what one already knows to have happened. For the very appropriateness of the act will strengthen one's belief that it did happen, giving as it does a plausible motive why God might choose to act in this way.[27]

[26] Complex not just historically but also because of the philosophical and conceptual issues involved. Cf. my *The Divine Trinity* (Duckworth, London; Open Court, La Salle, Illinois, 1985).

[27] For comments on an earlier draft I am indebted to my colleague at Oriel, Richard Swinburne, and to members of the Philosophy Department at the University of York, especially Martin Bell, Christopher Megone, and Susan Mendus.

13

The Intelligibility of Eucharistic Doctrine

MICHAEL DUMMETT

I

The distinction that we are accustomed to draw between theology and philosophy is, I believe, peculiar to the Christian tradition. Theology attempts to capture in words the thought-content of religion, to use the terminology of Frege: that understanding, in large part only implicit, of God, of ourselves, of the world, and of God's dealings with the world and with us that informs our practice of our religion and our conduct of our lives in the light of it, in so far as we do conduct our lives in the light of it. It thus constitutes crystallization, not interpretation. It supplies the formulations of dogma, but, even in the one church that continues, though rarely, to formulate dogma, it goes far beyond this. What any religious association, even the most dogmatic, chooses to demand as the minimum body of propositions to be assented to as a condition for membership must fall far short of what any one individual believer could regard as encapsulating his religious faith, as he lives by it and as it governs his attitude to events in his life and in the world; and so theology must offer far more than any theologian would dream of proposing as indispensable doctrine.

It is to philosophy that the task of interpretation falls. Theologians, and preachers who would not claim that status, are fond of remarking that, while we must cleave to Christian doctrines as true, we cannot properly understand what they mean. As a beginner in philosophy, I used to regard this remark with contempt: how can you believe anything if you do not know what it means? You can, it seems, do no more than believe that a certain *sentence* expresses a true proposition, without knowing which proposition that is: but you cannot believe the proposition without knowing what it is. But now I think that the mistake that such theologians and preachers make is to regard their observation as applying peculiarly to religious truths. Whatever arouses philosophical perplexity is in like case. In our everyday thought and speech, as well as in highly theoretical disciplines, above all in physics, we know, or at least are fairly confident, what to affirm; but we do not properly understand it. Our language and our thought are so complex that we fail, in Wittgenstein's phrase, to command a clear view of them: we have grasped enough to know how to operate with our concepts in the contexts in which we find ourselves, in those interchanges of discourse in which we regularly engage; but, like troops in a battle, we are unable to grasp what exactly it is that we are doing when we operate with them. Philosophers seek primarily to understand the world (and only secondarily, if at all, to change it), and their only means of doing so is to try to gain an understanding of what we say about the world, that is, to attain that clear view of our language and our thought which, immersed in activity, even if only verbal activity, we ordinarily lack. If their success is exceedingly partial, that is because the task is immensely difficult. What the theologians deliver, the philosopher must attempt to interpret, in precisely the same spirit as that in which he tries to interpret our everyday utterances or those of the physicist or psychologist. It is not for him to judge, among theological statements, which are true and which false, save for those of which he concludes that they cannot possibly be true, because they are conceptually incoherent.

Theology has many sources on which to draw: scripture and the teachings of the Church, past and present, naturally; what we know of the world, by observation and by scientific and historical investigation; and religious practice. Between practice and theory there is an interplay. Theology attempts, among other things, to articulate the understanding which underlies liturgical and devotional practice; but this practice may in turn, though more rarely, be influenced by theology. A good example of this is the whole practice of devotion to Christ in the consecrated species, whether during the celebration of the Eucharist or outside it. According to Gregory Dix, there is no trace of gestures of reverence to the consecrated

sacrament until the early fourth century, or of words of devotion addressed to Christ in the sacrament until a century and
a half later, in both cases from Syria in the first instance. As
for devotion to the reserved sacrament, while reservation itself
appears to have been the usual practice from the earliest centuries, prayer before it, expositions of it, and processions with
it do not appear to have occurred during the first Christian
millennium. The Palm Sunday procession with the sacrament, later transferred to the feast of Corpus Christi after it
was instituted, seems to have originated in Canterbury in the
late eleventh century; exposition in the monstrance began in
Germany only in the late middle ages. In all these instances
Rome itself manifested the greatest reserve in accepting the
new practices; in the East, they never arose at all, although of
course the sacrament has always been reserved.

I do not mean to suggest that these expressions of devotion
to Christ in the consecrated species were promoted by theologians. Quite the opposite: it is part of my point that they were
not promoted by theologians or by ecclesiastical authorities.
They arose, in the main, as manifestations of popular piety, in
which church authorities eventually acquiesced. But they
arose, or at least spread and intensified, *after*, and not before,
the formulations of doctrine by which they could be justified.
The formulations were not designed as interpretations of these
practices: rather, the practices arose in response to the belief
in the doctrine. The definition of transubstantiation by the
fourth Lateran Council in 1215 was not accompanied by any
advocacy of eucharistic devotions, within the celebration of
the Eucharist or outside it: on the contrary, it was accompanied by an attempt to suppress the custom of reservation
within a hanging pyx, as demanded by the Devonshire rebels
in 1549 ('We will have the sacrament to hang over the high
altar and there to be worshipped, as it was wont to be'), in
favour of the use of an inconspicuous aumbry.

For this reason, these practices cannot be regarded as
supplying grounds for eucharistic doctrine, being, rather,
consequences of it. This is the less usual order, however. More
frequently, doctrine follows practice, as a means of precipi-
tating in propositional form the rationale of that practice. Of
which established practices, then, must we see the doctrine of

transubstantiation as formulating the rationale? I propose to understand the doctrine as requiring no more than that the correct and unqualified answer to the question, 'What is it?', asked of either of the consecrated elements, is 'The Body of Christ' or 'The Blood of Christ': that is, to assume that the use of the term 'substance' carries with it no commitment to any specific philosophical thesis. So understood, the doctrine is obviously intended, in the first place, to enshrine the most direct and, in itself, natural manner of construing both the words of scripture and the language in common use concerning the Eucharist in the early Church.

Now, plainly, the most direct manner of construing the words of our Lord or of the authors of the New Testament writings cannot always be the correct one. No one has ever supposed that, because Christ spoke of himself as the true vine, we are required to conceive him to be in any direct sense a vine: we have here an obvious metaphor. To come closer to our subject, the same has traditionally been taken to be the correct attitude to St Paul's teaching that the Church, the body of the faithful, is the Body of Christ. He was teaching that the activity of Christians is, in some important sense, a continuation of that of Christ while on earth, and that, by membership of the Church, we in some manner participate in the life of Christ: but not that what is referred to by speaking of Christ's resurrected Body is simply the totality of the Christian people, bound together by a common belief and a common worship. Quite recently, theologians who consider themselves advanced have proposed precisely the latter view, explicitly accepting the consequence that the story of the empty tomb is purely symbolic, and that nothing in fact left the tomb, so that our Lord's bones presumably lie to this day somewhere in the modern city of Jerusalem; this, naturally, has consequences for our understanding, not only of the Resurrection, but of the Eucharist. But, however strongly proponents of this view insist that the community of Christians is *literally* the Body of Christ, they have no way of giving substance to this 'literally'. They cannot succeed in making the Pauline teaching into more than a metaphor, since they do not wish to assert that Christians are not what they seem, namely human beings, but really cells (or larger constituents) of another human body;

and so their effect is not to impose any new interpretation on St Paul's doctrine, but merely to interpret the Resurrection itself as a metaphor.

Since there can be no demand that the most direct way of construing hallowed and accepted language be always adopted, the doctrine of transubstantiation requires more grounding than just the language of the New Testament and of the early Church concerning the Eucharist. That further grounding must lie in practice. Notoriously, article XXVIII of the Church of England accuses the doctrine of overthrowing the nature of a sacrament; it is difficult to see this otherwise than as reversing the true order of analysis. The concept of a sacrament was no ingredient of the original Christian teaching: it was elaborated later, as a theoretical aid to understanding Christian religious practice. According to traditional belief, the individual sacraments were given to the apostles by the Lord: but it is no part of that belief that he also classified them as sacraments, or laid down any features they must be regarded as having in common. It is only the theologians who have attempted to do that; and if their attempted classification should fail to fit the practices they are trying to classify, then it is evidently the classification, and not the practices, that must give way. In point of fact, the seven rites recognized as sacraments both in Latin and in Eastern churches differ very markedly from one another, and can only with much difficulty be forced into a common mould, as the scholastic theologians attempted to do. It is a merit, not a defect, of theology concerning the Eucharist if it simply looks at eucharistic practice as it exists, with a view to crystallizing out our understanding of what that practice signifies, rather than starting from some antecedent conception of the nature of sacraments in general.

The practice of which the doctrine of transubstantiation most evidently provides the rationale is, of course, that of reserving the consecrated sacrament, a practice solidly attested to, from early times, both for the purpose of sending the *fermentum* from the bishop's Eucharist to dependent congregations, and for that of enabling individuals to communicate themselves in times of persecution, in the intervals between eucharistic celebrations. It appears to me, however, that there is another salient feature of traditional Christian worship to which it is also a response. For the reason given above, we are setting aside all the manifestations of devotion to the reserved sacrament that have grown up in the Roman church, for the most part only since the late Middle Ages: processions with the sacrament, exposition of the sacrament, benediction with the sacrament, prayers before the reserved sacrament. These set aside, the practice of reservation still, of course, touches the lives of lay Christians, but only in particular circumstances: at the liturgy of the presanctified, observed in the West only on Good Friday, but, in the Byzantine rite, on every Wednesday and Friday of Lent; when they receive the viaticum; or when, like Mary, Queen of Scots, like one of the early hermits, or like almost everyone in the times of the early persecutions, they are permitted to communicate themselves in the absence of a priest. But the feature I have in mind affects the entire pattern of communal worship, and it surprises me that it is so little discussed. The Reformation effected one enormous change in that pattern, namely to replace the Eucharist, as the eminent and normal act of worship, by some service of prayers, hymns, and psalms, whether modelled on the daily hours or not. Among all Orthodox and Catholics, including Anglo-Catholics, 'going to church' means, primarily, attending the celebration of the Eucharist, with or without receiving communion; among all Protestants, including moderate Anglicans, it means taking part in some non-sacramental service.

This difference appears to me of profound importance. Differences of practice are of two kinds: those that (after the initial surprise) we can accommodate as mere divergences of custom or of culture, and those that strike us as reflecting differences of principle. The distinction is *prior* to the formulation of the underlying principle. We apprehend a divergence of practice from our own either as merely a different way of practising the same religion, even if not to our own taste, or else as signalling that the religion of those who observe the divergent practice is not quite the same as our own: and, in the latter case, we ordinarily recognize the divergence as being of the second kind before we can put into words the difference of principle that we feel to exist. If you do this, or if you do not do that, we want to say, you must understand what you are doing in an essentially different way from that in which we understand it; recognizing this to be so does not require that we have any means at hand to formulate that difference of understanding. It is in this that we see most clearly reflected the priority of practice over doctrine that usually prevails: the doctrine attempts to give verbal expression to a significance that is apprehended in advance of that expression. That is why differences of practice, when they are of the second kind, are of greater importance than differences of formulated doctrine. We know that differences of formulation are treacherous: radically different beliefs may be expressed in the same words, while different words may express what, upon close analysis, amounts to just the same. In any case, genuine differences of belief that affect nothing in our religious lives— in the way we pray in private or practise our religion in common, in our attitudes to others or in our moral princi- ples—strike us as essentially unimportant, however great a weight bishops and theologians may attach to them.

That is why I find it perplexing that so little is made of the difference I have indicated. We must, of course, all long for the reunion of the Christian churches. For this reason, we shall all be profoundly grateful if it proves that the differences in eucharistic doctrine that once appeared so profound have diminished to little or nothing. If reunion is to occur, great variations in practice will have to be accommodated, perhaps greater than now exist between the various ancient rites. Within a single church, there would surely be room both for those in whose religious practice extra-liturgical eucharistic devotion played an important role and those who neglected it altogether. But I find it hard to conceive of a universal church containing both those for whom the eucharistic liturgy was the principal communal act of worship and those for whom it was a mere communion service, attendance at which was pointless for those not intending to receive the sacrament.

For each of the sacraments it is laid down who may validly administer it. Anyone may administer baptism, save the reci- pient: one cannot baptize oneself. The ministers of the sacra- ment of marriage are the bride and groom, who administer the sacrament to each other; for all the other sacraments, a priest or bishop is needed. But here the great difference appears between the Eucharist and all the rest: what essentially matters is not who gives communion to whom. Reservation is not, in itself, the critical feature. Chrism, after all, is said to be consecrated, rather than merely blessed, and regulations concerning the safe keeping of the holy oils were as strict as, and indeed conjoined with, those governing the safekeeping of the reserved eucharistic sacrament. On the contrary, if the Reformers had truly wished to make the Eucharist analogous to the other sacraments, they would have encouraged reservation, while making the consecration an occasional act, to be performed only as often as necessary to ensure a supply of the consecrated elements, attendance at which was as inessential to intending communicants as it is inessential for confirmands to have attended the consecration of the chrism to be used on them.

In any case, to make the present point, we do not need to advert to communion from the reserved sacrament. I am afraid that I do not know what the practice is in Nonconformist or Lutheran churches; but in the traditional Christian churches, if I may so term them, it has always been the custom to permit deacons to distribute communion, and, in special cases, those in lower orders, lay people, or even the communicants themselves. It is, above all, the practice of self-communication that makes it plain that the 'minister' of this sacrament is not the one who gives the consecrated elements to the communicant; for how is it possible for anyone to administer a sacrament to himself? We do not, of course, require attestation of the practice of self-communication, since it is universal for the celebrant to communicate himself; but attestation, from the earliest times onwards, is plentiful. The contrast is clear. The chrism is consecrated on Maundy Thursday, and then kept under lock and key: but no one can, in virtue of its prior consecration, administer to himself the sacrament of confirmation. A priest is needed for the *celebration* of the Eucharist, but not for the giving of communion; and this bespeaks a way of regarding the consecrated eucharistic elements wholly different from that in which even the chrism is regarded. In some manner, which is expressed in the language whereby they are referred to as the Body and Blood of Christ, and which it is the business of the theologian to

articulate, the entire sacramental virtue resides in the consecrated Host and Chalice, and not in the giving of them. In the
receiving of them, indeed, since, obviously, one who does not
receive them has not received the sacrament: but it must be
they which he receives. I presume, though I confess I do not
know, that in cases of emergency any of the sacraments
requiring anointing with oil may be administered with any
vegetable oil available: at least, it seems natural to assume
that this would not invalidate the sacrament. But, from the
point of view of the Eucharist which Christians have always
taken, it would be senseless to suppose that, in an emergency,
one could receive communion by consuming any bread and
wine that happened to be at hand: that would be to miss the
entire point.

In these respects, I have dwelt not upon the practice of
reservation, which was so unfortunately made a matter of
controversy, but upon aspects of our practice universal among
Christians of every denomination. I am not, of course, arguing
that only the doctrine of transubstantiation can make sense of
that practice: merely that the practice, in regard to the
Eucharist, differs radically from that governing all other
sacraments, and that it is that for which the doctrine seeks to
supply a rationale, or perhaps better, to articulate an existing
set of attitudes. Reservation, in itself, would have attracted no
objections, were it not that what I have vaguely called the
sacramental virtue lies in the consecrated elements. The
blessing or consecration of water or oil to be used in the
administration of a sacrament, however solemn, can only be
thought of as a preparation for its administration: who, then,
could find anything to object to in performing such a blessing
in advance, and keeping the water or oil so blessed until the
time came to use it? The two distinctive features of the
Eucharist go together. In all other sacraments, the central
liturgical action is the reception of the sacrament, which, from
the other side, is its administration. Those other than the
recipient and the minister who are present at a baptism,
confirmation, wedding or ordination are there essentially as
witnesses, though no doubt in some sense participating, as
members of the Church, in the Church's action in conferring
the sacrament. It is precisely because, in the Eucharist, the

central liturgical action is *not* the giving of communion that, according to the traditional practice, abandoned by the Reformers, non-communicants are present as much more than witnesses. In the Eucharist, the essential function of the priest consists in his performance of the great prayer—the canon or anaphora—that effects the consecration of the bread and wine: this consecration is not, therefore, a preparation for the central liturgical action, but is that action. Since it does not itself take the form of an administration of the sacrament, but is that which implants within the elements the sacramental virtue, this sacramental virtue is naturally seen as consisting in the actual presence of Christ under the sacramental forms. There is, indeed, no other natural way to explain the matter. The action of all the other sacraments upon the recipient is held to be the action of Christ: if, in the Eucharist, the central action is not that of administering the sacrament, but that which sanctifies the material elements, that can only be because it effects something greater than the action of Christ upon the soul; and that something greater can hardly be anything but his very presence.

Of course, although it is difficult to think how otherwise to construe our practice in the Eucharist, differing so greatly from that in any other sacrament, we should not presume to draw such a conclusion from it if we did not have the record of our Lord's words of institution. Or, rather, this is stated in reverse: our practice, descending to us from the earliest Christians, would never have been as it is if it were not for those words and, from the outset, such an understanding of them. Now my aim in what I have said so far has not been to argue for the Catholic, as against the Protestant, doctrine. It has been only to elicit, as far as possible from universal features of Christian eucharistic practice, and at any rate from features traditional from the earliest times until the Reformation, what it is of which Catholic doctrine is an attempted verbal crystallization. It may be that an account of these features is to be given in some different way: but we need to bear clearly in mind which features are to be accounted for before we can understand the motivation behind any account. Philosophy cannot, of course, judge on religious grounds between alternative accounts: all it can do is attempt to test their coherence and to clarify their content. It is with a strictly philosophical examination of transubstantiation, understood, as I have said, as unburdened with metaphysical baggage, that I shall be concerned in the rest of this essay.

II

Wherein lies the problem of making sense of the doctrine of transubstantiation, from the standpoint of contemporary philosophy? One part of the problem is independent of standpoint or of philosophical framework, namely that of determining precisely what it is that the doctrine requires us to say. We have before us, in the consecrated elements, what look like bread and wine. According to the doctrine of transubstantiation, they are not bread and wine, but the Body and Blood of Christ. The doctrine instructs us, then, how we are to answer the question, 'What is it that is there?': but does it tell us how to answer other questions concerning what is done to what is there? If so, how should we answer them? How are we to think and speak of such actions? Various things are done to the sacramental elements: they are moved from place to place, put into or taken out of one vessel or another, made visible or concealed, taken into the mouth and swallowed. Are we to say that these things are done to Christ's Body or to his Blood? If not, to what are we to say that they are done?

These questions and similar ones concern the content of the doctrine; and any account of that doctrine must indicate how they are to be answered. But, while it may or may not require the assistance of philosophy to answer them, they are not, as they stand, philosophical questions: they are questions that anyone might ask when first acquainted with the doctrine. The primary philosophical question is, rather, how it is possible to deny propositions that pass all the normal tests for truth, namely that this is bread and that wine, and affirm in their place propositions that pass none of those tests. Or, at least, this is what strikes *us* as the primary philosophical question. It did not so strike scholastic writers on the subject; but, withered as the positivist conception that there could be a test of meaningfulness may now be, the positivist critique has at least, and very properly, made us more chary of assuming that we may indulge in mystery to an unlimited degree without incurring the penalty of altogether depriving our statements of sense. And so the first and most pressing question is whether the doctrine of transubstantiation is so much as intelligible.

Before we attempt to answer this question, we must first refine it. There is, of course, no difficulty merely in the denial of what appears to have very strong evidence in its favour on the part of one who believes himself to have counter-evidence that will overthrow it, or who merely has a hunch that such counter-evidence is to be found or will come to light. Strong evidence is not the same as *conclusive* evidence: to say that evidence is not conclusive is just to say that its existence does not preclude the existence of stronger evidence the other way. Of course, what is called conclusive evidence is usually not strictly conclusive, but only evidence requiring very strong grounds indeed to overthrow. The evidence of our senses is usually of this kind. It can certainly be overthrown in any case in which we can be shown to have been the victims of an illusion; and precisely this was the account of transubstantiation given by followers of Descartes. According to them, God systematically induces sensory illusions in us after the consecration. If he did not, we should perceive upon the altar a human body and human blood: they really are there, but God causes them to appear to us exactly as did the bread and wine that were formerly there.

This account is repugnant and certainly to be rejected: but its rejection is just what poses our problem. Our question is not just how we can claim that what look like bread and wine, satisfy all normal observational criteria for being bread and wine, and will pass any ordinary test for being bread and wine, are nevertheless not bread and wine, but how we can so much as intelligibly make this claim simultaneously with the assertion that we are suffering from no illusion.

Is not to say that what looks and tastes to us like wine is not wine but blood simply to say that we are under an illusion of sense? How could there *not* be an illusion in such a case? A degenerate use of the notion of substance attempts to answer this question by denying, in effect, that anything is, in the strict sense, a *criterion* for answering the question, 'What is there?'. On this view, all we ever truly know are appearances:

whenever we judge, on the basis of what we see or hear or feel, that an object of any given kind is present, we are making an act of faith, essentially in the mercy of God: for, save for our trust in that mercy, we should never have any reason for inferring, from the fact that something gives rise to those appearances that we associate with, say, tables, that it is not, for instance, a hippopotamus. This idea should be dismissed out of hand, and certainly does not represent the purpose for which the scholastics invoked the Aristotelian notion of substance in this connection. The idea of (first) substance was introduced as that of the prototypical subject of predication: it is that of which we say that it is round or square, white or brown, and so on; it is that which *has* properties. By a singular process of philosophical decay, involving the metaphors of inherence and underlying, it becomes that which has no properties, and whose presence can therefore not be certified, or even (save for the mercy of God) made in the least more probable, by the presence of anything displaying these or those properties. The conclusion exactly contradicts the premiss: so the process leading from one to the other must be invalid, unless the notion of substance is trivially self-contradictory, which it plainly is not.

A genuine scholastic doctrine, that of the persistence of the accidents of bread and wine, may, however, be seen as a partial attempt to answer our question, and, at the same time, to the other questions with which we started, concerning the subject of actions upon the consecrated elements. The word *'species'* used by the Council of Trent in place of 'accident', presumably in order to avoid a commitment to a metaphysics of substance and accident, is ambiguous: it may mean merely that there *appears* to be something white, say, or round; that is indeed evident, but does not serve to rule out the neo-Cartesian theory, or, indeed, any other philosophical account; to avoid doing so was presumably the purpose of the formulation. But the corresponding accidents do not consist in *appearing* white and round, but in *being* white and round, and *these* persist, according to the scholastic theory: the ambiguity is here resolved. It is because the accidents of whiteness and roundness are really still present that our senses ought not to be said to deceive us: they bear true witness. An illusion, on such an account, consists in something's appearing to have some quality which it does not have: its giving the appearance of being a different object, or an object of a different kind, from that which it really is, is not, on this account, to be reckoned as an illusion.

This solution provides an answer to our question; but it is an answer purchased at great cost. Not only does it propose that, to vary the instance, redness and a sweet taste are truly present without there being anything that can properly be said to be red or to have a sweet taste, but it requires a belief in that curious category of entities, introduced into philosophy by Aristotle, particularized qualities. If some particular wine is red, the wine obviously exists, and the colour exists. The colour, in this sense, may be called a universal, in the sense that other things may have the same colour. We may indeed speak of the particular colour of the wine, meaning thereby the precise shade. This, too, is a universal: there may not happen to be anything else of just that shade, but there could be. There is neither need for nor sense in the supposition that, besides the universal quality, there is a particular one, the colour-of-the-wine, understood as something which could not be possessed by anything other than this very wine. Of course, the existence of the wine and of the colour red do not together amount to the wine's being red. But that is properly expressed only by the *sentence*, 'The wine is red': the existence of no additional entity can either replace or be equated with the truth of the sentence, and, if it could, it would be the fact that the wine is red, and no more a particularized quality than a universalized object.

Even particularized qualities, if there were such entities, would have to be qualities *of* something. Aquinas is highly conscious of this, and proposes the extraordinary theory that, among the persisting particularized qualities of the bread and wine that were formerly present, one of them, their dimension, as it were acts as a subject for the rest. Aquinas intends us to distinguish the dimensions of an object—its size and shape—from the region of space that it occupies. We must of course do so, in so far as, if rigid, it may, without changing size or shape, be moved from one place to another. But there is no reason why we should not identify its dimensions with the region of space that it occupies at any given moment. We speak of the axis of the earth, for example, as a determinate line; so considered, it is a line that moves in orbit round the sun as the earth moves round the sun, rather than a line in the sense in which it makes no sense to speak of a line's changing position. In the same sense, we may conceive of the size and shape of an object as the space it constantly occupies, however much it may move: a region of space that moves as it moves, and alters shape and size as it does. So expressed, Aquinas's theory involves that, after the consecration, the space formerly occupied by bread and wine now not only has a certain shape and size—a proposition with which we cannot quarrel—but also has a certain colour, a certain taste, a certain mass, and so forth; or, at least, that it as it were has them.

This, however, nullifies the entire theory. For, if it makes sense at all to ascribe such qualities—whether particularized or universal—to a region of space, then the same ascription must surely be made to the space occupied by the bread and wine before the consecration. To be sure, the scholastic's reply will be that *then* the subject of the qualities is the bread or the wine. Indeed; but he can have no objection to its being said that, in another sense, the regions of space that the bread and wine occupy have those qualities: just that sense, namely, in which those regions of space are said to have the same qualities (and at that stage to be the sole subjects of those qualities) after the consecration. And now the thesis may be advanced that the presence in a given location of an object characterized by certain qualities simply amounts to the possession of those qualities, in the appropriate sense of 'possession', by the relevant region of space. This thesis is only a version of the contention with which we are centrally concerned, that it is unintelligible to deny that bread and wine are present when all the ordinary criteria for their being so are satisfied. We have taken it as the most crucial problem to find a retort to this contention; but the thomistic theory, in the form in which we are now considering it, no longer looks like providing a solution to this problem. It has provided an answer for the first range of questions, which asked what is the object of the actions performed upon the consecrated elements. It has done so by giving an answer to the question, what is the subject of the persistent particularized qualities: their subject may then be taken as also the object of those actions. But the cost of providing that answer has been to lose all appearance of resolving our second, and more crucial, question.

This is not to maintain that an adherent of the thomistic theory can give no retort to the thesis. He can say that what constitutes the presence of an object in a given location is not simply the possession by a suitable region of space of the qualities proper to the object: what is required, in addition, is that the object should occupy that region of space. But, in saying this, he is coming perilously close to adopting the degenerate conception of substance which we rejected above; for he has no account to offer of what it is for this additional requirement to be satisfied. And, in approaching so nearly that merely mystificatory use of the notion of substance, he has forfeited all claim to answering our crucial question.

Furthermore, the theory has now rendered the connection between the consecrated elements and Christ's Body and Blood exceedingly tenuous. Aquinas is extremely cautious in treating the question of whether the Body of Christ is in the place in which the consecrated Host is located. He does not wish to deny outright that it is in that place, for to do so would be to reject any belief in the real presence of Christ in the Eucharist; but he is equally chary of affirming it outright. Christ's Body may be said to be there, but it is not there after the manner of a body which occupies a space in virtue of its proper dimensions. Now anyone who adopts a 'realistic' interpretation of the Eucharist must tread warily in answering this particular question: but Aquinas is especially constricted by the theory he has propounded. According to that theory, the accidents of the bread and wine persist, and attach to certain regions of space, in the sense explained, as their quasi-subjects. And, as a quite separate fact, the Body and Blood of Christ are in some special sense present, though not exactly as occupying those regions of space. On this account, there is no connection between the two. The consecrated elements are, as it were, merely the discarded husk of the bread and wine earlier present, and have no more intimate connection with the Body and Blood of Christ than that. It is as if the bread

and wine have stepped aside to make room for Christ's Body
and Blood, which could not otherwise be present, and, in so
stepping aside, have, so to speak, left their mortal remains
behind. Aquinas's words read very impressively; but, as soon
as we pause to reflect upon the theory he is actually advancing, we cannot but conclude that the conception it embodies
must have gone astray.

III

The neo-Cartesian theory makes the mistake of supposing the
change effected by the consecration to be a physical one. The
mistake, though crude, is a natural one, in that the change is
described as consisting in the replacement of one material
body by a quite different one: nevertheless, it is not conceived
of as a *physical* event. It is not that no difference is to be perceived by ordinary macroscopic observation: no difference is
to be expected at the microscopic or submicroscopic level,
either. Nothing that could, even in principle, be observed by
instruments, or inferred, on the basis of physical theory, from
what could be observed by instruments, if those instruments
were functioning correctly and we were perceiving them correctly, is to be supposed to have altered. Hence there is no
difference in the molecules, in the atoms composing the
molecules, in the electrons and nucleons composing the atoms,
or in any yet more basic particles that may compose them.
For, if there were any such difference, it could not constitute
the presence of the Body and Blood of Christ: and hence there
is no point in supposing that there is such a difference.

Where the neo-Cartesian theory assumes a physical
change, the substance-and-accident theory assumes a
metaphysical one. *Its* mistake is to conceive of metaphysical
reality after the model of physical reality, underlying it and
differing principally only in its inaccessibility to sensory observation. I remember watching a television programme about
some religious festival, in which the interviewer asked a priest
about the holy water that was used in the ceremony: did he
think that the blessing made any difference to the water? The
priest, not unnaturally, was perplexed to answer; those who
assume that religion is superstition would interpret this

hesitation as reluctance to acknowledge its superstitious nature. But suppose that a man treasures a ring that his father used to wear in his lifetime, and is very distressed to lose it. If a friend offered to obtain, or make, an indistinguishable ring to replace it, he would be utterly missing the point; and he would put his misunderstanding on display if he were to ask, 'But do you suppose that your father's having worn the ring you have lost made any difference to it?' It did not *make* a difference, either physical or metaphysical, that subsequently persisted: it *is* the difference. In the physical realm, a property conferred on an object by a past event must consist in some feature of its present constitution: but to suppose that a non-physical property, one relating to the object's significance for us, must likewise consist in some feature of its present constitution, even though at a level inaccessible to observation, is philosophical superstition.

These reflections lead naturally to consideration of the relatively recent theory of the Eucharist known as 'transignification'. I am afraid that I know this theory only in the version expounded at one time by Charles Davis, and cannot be sure that this is representative. In this version, at least, the fundamental idea, said to be derived from Heidegger, is that the character of an object depends upon our attitude towards it and the use we make of it: since we *treat* the consecrated elements as being the Body and Blood of Christ, that is what they *are*. This account seems to me to come near to being correct, but, as stated, to fall short of the truth of the matter through generalizing without warrant a principle that has only limited application. There are indeed kinds of object of which the principle holds: for a given object to be of such a kind requires that we treat it in a particular way. An obvious example is a coin. For something to be a coin, it has to be of metal and roughly in the shape of a disc, but these properties are plainly not sufficient: it must be or have been treated as a token of monetary exchange in some society having the institution of money. The principle also applies to kinds of object less directly dependent upon convention than coins. I have in my college room a Pyrex dish, intended by the manufacturers for use in cooking, which I bought to use as an ashtray, because it was far cheaper than anything of the size advertised as an

ashtray. It *is* an ashtray, not merely because it can be so used,
but because I use it as such and permit those who call on me
to do so: if I did not smoke, it would still be an ashtray if I
allowed others to use it for that purpose, but would not be
merely because some did so use it without my permission. But
the principle does not apply indiscriminately: it applies only
to kinds of object characterized in large part by their use. A
dog is a sheepdog, whatever its breed, if it has been trained to
act as a sheepdog and does so act; but whether an animal is a
dog or not does not depend in any way upon how it is or can
be used or on how it is treated. The concepts of bread and
wine, and of a human body and human blood, are of this latter
kind, and not like those of a coin and of an ashtray: whether
something falls under the concept of bread or of a human body
does not normally in any way depend upon our attitude
towards it or how we treat it. It is true that the concept of food
does so depend: nothing can be food unless we, or perhaps
some other creatures, treat it as such. It is part of the concept
of bread that it is a substance ordinarily used as food; but this
is a partial characterization of the meaning of the word 'bread'
as a mass-term, not of the conditions of its application to any
particular piece of matter. In the same way, it is a part of the
concept of gold that it is regarded as a precious metal, used in
an honorific way, as in wedding rings and royal crowns; but it
is not a condition for any particular item, say one employed in
a laboratory experiment, to be recognized as being made of
gold that *it* be so used or regarded. The point therefore does
not imply that what is not used as food, or not to be so used, is
thereby deprived of the character of bread. The bread left by
diners on their plates may be destined to be thrown away, but
it remains bread; and if it were the custom to burn that left by
a king lest it be retrieved from the dustbin and consumed by a
beggar, it would still be bread until relegated to the flames.

The version of the transignification theory which we are
considering commits an error similar to that committed by
those who employ the degenerate notion of substance: namely,
they both ignore the order of dependence between items of the
Christian faith. It would not be possible for someone who did
not believe in God to believe in the Incarnation, since the
latter belief would have no content. It ought likewise to

be impossible to believe in the real presence of Christ in the Eucharist without believing in his divinity: but both the degenerate notion of substance—to which, as we saw, the thomistic account is driven uncomfortably close—and the transignification theory, in the form under consideration, make such a belief perfectly intelligible, if unreasonable. According to the degenerate conception of substance, it would always be intelligible to suppose that any range of accidents inhered in any substance whatever, of however disparate a nature, or, presumably, that the accidents persisted without a subject, in the concomitant presence of any substance whatever: and so it would be possible to suppose that the accidents of bread and wine persisted without a genuine subject, in the concomitant presence of the Body and Blood of Christ, without believing even in the existence of God, let alone in the Incarnation, provided that one believed Christ's Body and Blood were still in existence. Against this, the transignification theory has at least the merit that it does not allow the possibility that Christ's Body and Blood should be present, in place of bread and wine, quite unknown to us, whereas even this is conceivable according to the degenerate conception of substance: on that conception, the possibility could be ruled out only by appeal to the improbability that God would permit us to be so woefully deceived. But the transignification theory *would* allow a non-Christian, or even an atheist, to acknowledge the truth of the doctrine of the real presence: indeed, he would, on that theory, be committing a conceptual mistake if he failed to acknowledge it, since the mere fact that, in Christian churches untouched by the Reformation, the consecrated elements are treated as being the Body and Blood of Christ would render it the case that that is what they are.

This by itself is surely enough to indicate that something is amiss with these two theories: any belief in the Eucharist must be as dependent on a prior belief in the Incarnation as the latter belief is dependent on belief in God. An improvement upon the transignification theory is obtained if we appeal to the concept of *deeming* something to be so: not as in the case of deeming a candidate to have passed an examination, but, say, in that of deeming a boy or man to be another man's son. The former case is not an instance of deeming, in the proper sense, but of judging, since there is normally no other criterion for whether a candidate has passed an examination than whether he has been assessed as passing. The appropriateness of the concept of deeming for our purpose lies in the fact that it is not integral to the concepts which may be deemed to apply. It is integral to the concept of a coin that it has that status, or is an object of that kind, only if it is accepted as capable of being used in a specific conventional role. It is, equally, integral to the concept of a chair that it is both capable of being used to sit on, and in fact is or has been intended by its owner to be so used; and similarly with the concept of an ashtray and of any other utensil, tool, article of furniture, or the like. Likewise, it is integral to the concept of an examination that there are examiners, and to that of passing an examination that this depends upon their declaring themselves satisfied, which is why their declaration is not an expression of their deeming the successful candidates to have passed, in the proper sense of the word 'deem'. But it is not integral to the concept of a son that someone may be deemed to be someone else's son, even though he did not in fact engender him. We cannot say that it is, on pain of having to say that the concept of deeming is integral to virtually every concept save logical and mathematical ones: for there is no way of circumscribing the range of facts that may be deemed to obtain. There are, indeed, certain constraints. One is that only a present or past state of affairs can be deemed to obtain or to have obtained: there is no such thing as deeming that some state of affairs will obtain in the future. Another is that nothing can be deemed to be so which would render someone morally culpable, if he would not have been so otherwise. Yet another is that what is deemed to be the case cannot be a quite general proposition: it must be a particular one, relating to specific individuals, or, at worst, must have a direct particular application. Within these constraints, however, there is no restriction of the power of deeming something to be so in virtue of the character of the concepts involved.

It would indeed be unintelligible to deem something to be so unless its being so or not being so had some significance for us, in the sense of having moral, social, legal, or religious consequences, but the state of affairs deemed to obtain need not be one which is in itself of a conventional or instrumental character. That is not, of course, to say that we are free at any time, within these few constraints, to deem anything we please to be the the case, provided that it has the right degree of significance in our lives. Only one who undertakes the obligations created by a given state of affairs, or who has the right to impose or rescind such obligations, is in a position to declare that that state of affairs is to be deemed to obtain; and the declaration is unlikely to be accepted if it is made frivolously and without serious reason.

Appeal to the concept of deeming avoids the weakness of the transignification theory, that it grossly misclassifies the concepts of bread and wine, and still more those of a human body and of human blood, as depending upon convention or instrumentality for their correct application. The Last Supper is not the only passage in the New Testament for whose interpretation the notion of deeming appears in place. St John the Baptist remarked, 'God is able from these stones to raise up children of Abraham': and we may well wonder how he could have thought even God capable of that. No doubt God could raise up men and women from those stones: but how could they have been *children of Abraham*? To be a child of Abraham is to have a certain origin, which men raised from stones simply would not have. But, after all, elsewhere in the New Testament baptized Christians are assured that they, too, are children of Abraham, so we cannot dismiss the Baptist's words as rhetorical exaggeration. The people raised from stones would have counted as children of Abraham in God's sight: and who can be more a child of Abraham than that?

In ordinary instances in which something is deemed to be so, the normal application of the concept is not lost. If someone is deemed to be the son of another, there is no sense in which it would be true to say, 'He is not his son': but there remains a sense in which it is true to say, 'He is not *really* his son', a sense which we capture by qualifications such as 'He is not his son by blood', or, in the modern style, 'in the biological sense'. This hangs together, but should not be identified, with a further feature: we do not suppose that, by deeming something to be so, we alter anything other than the state of affairs deemed to obtain, together with its consequences, and that correlatively deemed not to obtain. If someone is deemed to be another's son, he thereby acquires the rights and obligations of that relationship; but the circumstances of his birth and upbringing, let alone his appearance, are not regarded as in any way other than what they formerly were.

In the special case of the Eucharist, the two features come apart. We *deem* the bread and wine to be changed, by the consecration, into the Body and Blood of Christ: but it is not problematic that this has no effect upon the physical circumstances, in that sense of 'physical' specified above, and we need no apparatus of substance and accident to explain this. That is not to say that we do not need to take pains to answer the first range of questions, concerning the subject of actions performed upon the consecrated elements, with care; simply that the general form of response to the objection that it does not appear that the bread and wine have undergone any change is determined by appeal to the concept of deeming something to be so. But that is not to say that we ought to admit some sense in which, although the consecrated elements are properly said to be the Body and Blood of Christ, they are not *really* that. We must avoid the mistake made by the transignification theory, of making it in principle possible to believe in the real presence of Christ without believing him to be God, or believing in him at all. That theory justified our identifying the consecrated elements with the Body and Blood of Christ on the ground of our treating them as being that: and that made the transformation the effect of human power, after the manner in which we have the power to make something a medium of monetary exchange simply by treating it as one. It then followed that the transformation was one that could in principle be effected whether we had any warrant for our practice or not: and that is patently an error. When we appeal, instead, to the concept of deeming, we must not repeat that error.

When, for example, a marriage is annulled, it is deemed never to have taken place; and those who respect the authority of the court that granted the annulment will so deem it. We need, therefore, to distinguish between deeming something to be so, and declaring that it is to be deemed to be so. According to the case in question, only particular individuals or bodies may issue such a declaration, and no one is in a position to deem the given state of affairs to obtain unless that declaration has been made by competent persons; but, when it has been made, it would be wrong to say that only those who made it deem that state of affairs to obtain: *everyone* is required to do so. It was therefore no error to say that *we* deem the consecrated elements to be Christ's Body and Blood: but the authority which licenses us to do so is not our own. The authority, or so we believe, is Christ himself; and even he could not be recognized as having such authority if he were not God made man. That is why this account does not render it even in principle possible to believe in the real presence of Christ in the Eucharist without believing in the Incarnation.

The belief that the consecration effects a change of substance rests upon what is taken to be divine authority. When someone stands proxy at a baptism for a godmother who is unable to be present, she is deemed, during the ceremony, to be the person who is to become godmother; and when, at the baptism of an infant, the godparents make the baptismal vows in the child's name, the child is deemed to be undertaking them: that is what it means to speak in the name of another. But, because these things are done by merely human authority, there remains a sense in which the proxy was not *really* the godmother, and the child did not *really* undertake the vows. When something is deemed to be so on divine authority, the matter stands differently: there can be no sense in which it is not really so. We have, of course, to recognize that the consecrated elements are Christ's Body and Blood in virtue of being deemed to be so, rather than naturally; for, if we did not recognize this, we should be back with the neo-Cartesian theory that God subjects us to mass illusion. But we take ourselves to have divine authority for their being Christ's Body and Blood in God's sight: and it would be presumptuous, if not blasphemous, to say that, all the same, they were not *really* so. Indeed, it would be unintelligible. We are impelled by a drive to discover how things really are in themselves, that is to say, independently of the way they present themselves to us, with our particular sensory and intellectual faculties and our particular spatial and temporal perspective. I doubt whether it is possible to represent this notion of reality as it is in itself as even coherent, save by equating how things are in themselves

with how they are apprehended by God: without that identification, there is only the description of the world as it appears
to us and as how we may usefully represent it to ourselves for
the purpose of rendering its workings and regularities survey-
able. However this may be, anyone who believes in God must
equate the two things: there can be no gap between how God
sees something and how it really is in itself. There is, of course,
dispute among Christians over how our Lord's words at the
Last Supper are to be understood; and I have not intended, in
this essay, to engage in that dispute. My concern has been
only to explore the intelligibility of the Catholic (and, I think,
the Orthodox) doctrine in this matter. From the standpoint of
that doctrine, we have been told, by Christ our God, that his
Body and Blood are present. Supposing that to be so, we have
no room within which to ask whether or not they are really
there. *Nil hoc verbo veritatis verius*: Truth himself speaks truly, or
there's nothing true.

We began with the question of how we can intelligibly deny
that bread and wine are present, when all the ordinary criteria
for their being there are satisfied, and assert that the Body and
Blood of Christ are present, when none of the ordinary criteria
for *their* presence is satisfied, at least without maintaining that
we are subject to an illusion: this was presented as what is,
from a modern standpoint, the most critical philosophical
question. The answer appeals to two distinct features of the
case. First, we have (or take ourselves to have) divine authority for saying that what is there is Christ's Body and Blood.
Law and social convention have only limited control over
relationships: so there are respects, relevant to parenthood, in
which an adopted son differs from a natural son: he may not
look like his parents, for example. It is this which gives the
sense to saying 'he is not *really* their son'. Over some things,
such as property, the law has complete power: something is
my property only if the law would recognize it as such. Now
God has complete power over everything, not just in the sense
that he is able to bring it about that something is so by the
ordinary criteria for its being so, but also in the same sense as
that in which the law has power over whether something is
someone's property. This is not a point over which an atheist
need differ from a believer: he too should allow that, if there

were a God, then the fact that he had declared something to be so would be an unchallengeable ground for considering it as so, overriding every other ground.

This consideration does not stand alone: if it did, it would merely authorize us to use a form of words devoid of content. We are required to deem the consecrated elements to be the Body and Blood of Christ: and our doing so involves our treating them as such. There is such a thing as mistaking tea for coffee, and there is also such a thing as pretending that tea is coffee: but there is no such thing as deeming tea to be coffee, since there is no such way of behaving as acting on the statement, 'That was tea, and continues to look and taste like tea, but is now coffee'. It would therefore be not merely ludicrous but senseless for someone to profess to believe such a statement on divine authority. But, conversely, the fact that we treated what appeared as bread and wine as Christ's Body and Blood would not, of itself, make them so. If (as is utterly unlikely) the Eucharist were a ceremony invented, and known to have been invented, by the Church, we should have no cause to treat the sacramental elements as more than the *symbols* of Christ's Body and Blood, at the very most. We should, no doubt, be capable of treating them as actually being his Body and Blood; but we should have no warrant for doing so, and we should not, thereby, make them to be his Body and Blood, but should merely commit idolatry, since something is rendered so by being deemed to be so only when the pronouncement that it is to be so deemed has been made by those having the required authority.

IV

In what, then, does our treating the consecrated elements as the Body and Blood of Christ consist? It is important here that the appearance of bread and wine is an *objective* one, not an illusion: our sensations neither lack the customary physical stimuli, nor are misinterpreted, as with an optical illusion. If an appearance is known to be illusory, the right course is to ignore that appearance in our actions; but, since this appearance is not illusory, the appropriate behaviour, capable of expressing our belief that the Body and Blood of Christ are present under the forms of bread and wine, is to behave towards them as to the Body and Blood of Christ in those respects in which the appearance is not relevant, but as to bread and wine in those respects in which it is. We may say that an adoptive father shows that he considers a boy to be his son by treating him as his son. This does not mean 'treating him as if he believed that he was his natural son': it means treating him as he would treat a natural son save in those respects which his recognition that he is not his natural son demands. Similarly, treating the sacraments as the Body and Blood of Christ under the objective appearance of bread and wine means treating them as we should treat the Body and Blood of Christ save in so far as our recognition that the appearance is objective demands. Of course, the proviso is very extensive; it remains that only those parts of our liturgical and devotional practice which involve behaving towards the sacraments as to Christ's Body and Blood can be an expression of our belief that this is what they are.

Which parts of that practice are these? Certainly not our eating and drinking the consecrated elements. Those actions are proper to bread and wine, and not at all to their being human flesh and blood: eating something is in no way an expression of taking it to be a living human body. On the contrary: if we did not have our Lord's express command to consume them, our doing so would express our taking them to be bread and wine and *not* his Body and Blood. Of course, we understand Communion in the light of our belief in the Real Presence; but that does not make it an expression of that belief.

In St Paul's time, the Eucharist seems not yet to have been dissociated from the agape. The consecration and reception of the bread was thus separated from that of the wine by an intervening meal, as at the Last Supper. He could therefore not have taken the expression of belief that the one was, after consecration, the Body of the Lord, and the other his Blood, as consisting in eating and drinking them, since this was also done to the other constituents of the agape-meal. Rather, the way in which this belief was expressed must have lain in what marked the difference between the way the consecrated elements and the other elements of the meal were treated.

This, it seems to me, can only be that we make of the

Eucharist a commemoration, an anamnesis, of Christ's passion. In the Catholic tradition, it may be spoken of as a sacrifice, and the Roman liturgy is full of expressions of the offering of a sacrifice. Now, of course, although the words of administration used by our Lord at the Last Supper are strongly sacrificial in character, the Eucharist was instituted by him with the external form of a meal, not of a sacrifice. In the context of the Temple sacrifices, the latter form could have led only to misunderstanding from the start, since the Eucharist is a sacrifice only in being Christ's sacrifice, and it is only in virtue of our incorporation into Christ that we are said to offer it. The realization that the Eucharist can be regarded as an oblation which we offer dates back to very early times, but only rather gradually won general acceptance: while some early writers speak of it as an oblation or sacrifice, or apply the prophecy of Malachi, others say that Christians have no sacrifice save prayer and the service of God. That is not surprising, in view of the sharp contrast between the Eucharist and the sacrifices of the old law and of the pagan religions; in a similar spirit, early Christians often denied that Christians had priests or temples. But, from the very outset, the connection between the Eucharist and our Lord's sacrifice offered on Calvary was made, and was prominent in Christian consciousness; and it must from the start have been expressed within the celebration of the Eucharist, just as it is in the earliest liturgical records. Whether the word 'sacrifice' is used or shunned, this, rather than its character as a sacred meal, is that feature of the Eucharist that makes it an act of worship as well as the administration of a sacrament; and it is this that constitutes our treating the sacramental elements as Christ's Body and Blood. Among the Reformers, Luther wished to retain the doctrine of the Real Presence, but to jettison the conception of the Eucharist as a sacrifice. But the position proved an unstable one, and the foregoing discussion makes it possible to see why: for, by jettisoning the one, he deprived the other of its content.

V

I have no space to deal with the questions concerning the subject of predications like 'appears round', 'is carried to the hospital', etc., more than cursorily, and will content myself with discussing some issues underlying the search for answers to them. On the one hand, these questions appear as demanding no more than the selection of a suitable terminology: on the other, they are of considerable difficulty, and a failure to answer them would leave it in doubt whether the doctrine of the Real Presence was coherent. Aquinas believed that, after the consecration, two *particulars*, though not of course two *substances*, were present, where a particular is a subject of predication: the Body of Christ, say, and the 'dimensions' (*quantitas dimensiva*) of the bread. This makes it possible for him to hold that certain predications have the latter rather than the former as their subject. It is on this basis that he denies that the Body of the Lord can be said to be broken or moved about, and allows that it is only 'sacramentally' eaten: as he expressed it in his celebrated hymn, *Lauda, Sion,* 'Nulla rei fit scissura, Signi tantum fit fractura, Qua nec status nec statura Signati minuitur'. Now if the scholastic theory that the accidents of the bread and wine persist after the substance is no longer present be rejected, it would appear that this solution is no longer available: there is only one particular in each of the relevant places. If so, only it can be the subject of the relevant predicates. We need not say, indeed, that when the Host is broken, Christ's Body is broken: it only *appears* to be broken, whereas nothing is *really* broken. But it jars even to say that it appears to be broken, since it does not appear that Christ's Body is broken: what appears to happen is that some bread is broken. We might explain this by the following analogy. If Charles, disguised as Henry, does some conjuring tricks, it looks to the audience as if Henry turns a handkerchief into a rabbit: but it is *Charles*, and not Henry, who looks as though he has turned a handkerchief into a rabbit.

But does the account I have sketched entail that there is only one particular? I allowed that no physical change occurs at the consecration: does this not imply that the *matter* remains? When a man goes bald, the man is the subject of the change; it is the same man who once had hair and now has none. When substantial change occurs, the matter is the subject of the change: the matter that was once wood is now ashes. Transubstantiation is therefore surely not a change in this strict sense, at least as interpreted by the thomistic theory, since there will be no subject of the change. Aquinas, however, thinks it important that it be acknowledged as an instance of change. I have suggested that his theory severs the connection between the Body and Blood of Christ and the persisting accidents, but he thinks that the connection can be maintained provided that transubstantiation is taken to be change: it would be severed if the bread and wine were regarded as merely being annihilated. He therefore insists that, in the Eucharist, the matter of which the bread is composed is converted into the matter of which Christ's Body is composed: his ground is that, if the matter remained, we should have mere substantial change. But this would follow only if the matter which formerly composed the bread and wine now composed Christ's Body and Blood. Aquinas is of course operating with Aristotle's distinction of matter and form. That distinction was, indeed, applied at different levels, but, in the present connection, it was assumed that there is a fundamental level wholly devoid of structure. This is surely a mistake. Not only do we know that structure appears at a great many different levels, making a simple differentiation between matter and substance grossly inadequate, but identifiability depends on structure: a subject of change cannot be identified save by its persisting structure. We do not need to descend to a very deep level, that of subatomic particles, to see that we are compelled to say that the matter persists. The individual molecules composing the bread and wine do not become the Body and Blood of Christ, because neither bread nor wine is a chemically pure substance; they must therefore remain unchanged. But there is no ground for supposing that the matter which composed the bread and wine comes to compose the Body and Blood: Christ's Body remains where it is. To avoid problems about its present location, we may consider the Last Supper. There was Jesus, among his disciples. When he handed them the bread, with the words, 'This is my Body', his weight did not suddenly increase because the matter composing the bread had thereupon become part of his Body: his Body remained where it was, in view of them all, unchanged. We should do better to say that, without ceasing to be where it was, each place where the Bread was located—each place where his

Body was sacramentally present—became also the place where his Body was physically present, as if space were folded like a surface on to itself. This is only a picture; but it is one that may help us from falling into perplexity, and guard us from supposing that the doctrine of the Real Presence leads inescapably into contradiction.

B. G. Mitchell's Principal Writings

BOOKS

1957   *Faith and Logic* (editor), George Allen and Unwin. Introduction, pp. 1–8; 'The Grace of God', pp. 149–75.

1967   *Law, Morality, and Religion in a Secular Society*, Oxford University Press.

1971   *The Philosophy of Religion* (editor), Oxford Readings in Philosophy, Oxford University Press. Introduction, pp. 1–12; 'Theology and Falsification', pp. 18–20.

1973   *The Justification of Religious Belief*, Macmillan.

1980   *Morality: Religious and Secular*, Oxford University Press.

CONTRIBUTIONS TO COLLECTIONS

1955   'Theology and Falsification' in *New Essays in Philosophical Theology*, ed. Antony Flew and Alasdair MacIntyre, SCM pp. 103–5.

1968   'Ideals, Roles and Rules' in *Norm and Context in Christian Ethics*, ed. Gene H. Outka and Paul Ramsey, Scribner's, pp. 351–65.

1969   'The Historical Approach to Ethics, especially those of Christianity' in *Biology and Ethics*, ed. F. J. Ebeling, Academic Press.

1970   'Austin Marsden Farrer' in *A Celebration of Faith*, Sermons by Austin Farrer, ed. Leslie Houlden, Hodder and Stoughton, pp. 13–16.

'Indoctrination', appendix B in *The Fourth R*, Report of the Commission on Religious Education in Schools, ed. I. T. Ramsey, SPCK, pp. 353–8.

'Law and the Protection of Institutions' in *The Proper Study*, Royal Institute of Philosophy Lectures 1969/70, Macmillan, pp. 204–19.

1971   'Some Philosophical Comments: Man's Citadel and Man's Interests', a dialogue with R. M. Hare in *Personality and Science*, ed. I. T. Ramsey and Ruth Porter, Churchill Livingstone, pp. 93–101.

1977   'Remarks on the Groundlessness of Belief' in *Reason and Religion*, ed. Stuart C. Brown, Cornell University Press, pp. 181–5.

1981   'A Summing Up of the Colloquy: Myth of God Debate' in *Incarnation and Myth*, ed. Michael Goulder, SCM, pp. 231–40.

'I Believe: We Believe' in *Believing in the Church*, Report of the Doctrine Commission of the Church of England, SPCK., pp. 9–24.

1983 'Two Approaches to the Philosophy of Religion' in *For God and Clarity*, New Essays in Honor of Austin Farrer, ed. Jeffrey C. Eaton and Ann Loades, Pickwick Publications, pp. 177–90.

'The Church and the Bomb' in *Unholy Warfare*, ed. David Martin and Peter Mullen, Basil Blackwell, pp. 172–9.

1985 'The Role of Theology in Bioethics' in *Theology and Bioethics*, ed. Earl E. Shelp, Reidel, pp. 65–78.

LECTURES AND ARTICLES

1957 'Varieties of Imperative', *Proceedings of the Aristotelian Society*, supplementary volume 31, pp. 175–90.

1961 'The Justification of Religious Belief', *Philosophical Quarterly*, vol. 2; reprinted in *New Essays on Religious Language*, ed. Dallas M. High, Oxford University Press, New York, 1979, pp. 178–97.

1964 'Theology and Metaphysics', *Union Seminary Quarterly Review*, vol. 20, no. 1, pp. 9–19.

1968 *Neutrality and Commitment*, Inaugural Lecture, Oxford University Press.

1976 'Reason and Commitment in the Academic Vocation', *Oxford Review of Education*, vol. 2, no. 2, pp. 101–9.

1977 'Authority in Belief', *New Fire*, vol. 5, no. 3, pp. 260–3.

1979 'Religion and Truth', *New Universities Quarterly*, Autumn 1979, pp. 459–71.

'Traditionaliste Malgré Lui', A Note on Maurice Wiles, *Theology*, pp. 31–8.

1980 '"Does Christianity Need a Revelation?", a Discussion with Maurice Wiles', *Theology*, pp. 103–14.

'The Homosexuality Report', *Theology*, pp. 184–90.

'Faith and Reason: A False Antithesis?', *Religious Studies*, vol 16, pp. 131–44.

'Religious Education', *Oxford Review of Education*, vol. 6, no. 2, pp. 133–9.

1983 'Austin Farrer the Philosopher', *New Fire*, vol. 7, no. 57, pp. 452–6.

1984 'How is the Concept of Sin related to the Concept of Moral Wrongdoing?', *Religious Studies*, vol. 20, pp. 165–73.

1985 'Review article: Warnock', *The Modern Churchman*, vol. 27, no. 3, pp. 43–9.

Index